**ENFANT TERRIBLE!**

EDITED BY MURRAY POMERANCE

# ENFANT TERRIBLE!

*Jerry Lewis in American Film*

**New York University Press** • *New York and London*

**NEW YORK UNIVERSITY PRESS**
New York and London

© 2002 by New York University

Library of Congress Cataloging-in-Publication Data
Enfant terrible! : Jerry Lewis in American film /
edited by Murray Pomerance
p. cm.
Includes bibliographical references and index.
ISBN 0–8147–6705–2 (cloth : alk. paper) —
ISBN 0–8147–6706–0 (paper : alk. paper)
1. Lewis, Jerry, 1926—Criticism and interpretation.
I. Pomerance, Murray, 1946–
PN2287.L435  E54  2002
791.43'028'092—dc21           2002007532

New York University Press books are printed on acid-free paper,
and their binding materials are chosen for strength and durability.

Manufactured in the United States of America

10  9  8  7  6  5  4  3  2  1

*for Eva in memory*

The impression of the comic will be produced . . . when we are shown the soul *tantalised* by the needs of the body.

—Henri Bergson

# Contents

# Acknowledgments

This book was conceived as a response to a response. In the spring of 2000, I organized a panel for the Society for Cinema Studies titled "Jerry Lewis: Paragon of American Masculinity," imagining that a small number of scholars might be interested in giving limited consideration to some of what Jerry Lewis manages to accomplish onscreen. I was startled to see that the response was more far-reaching and deeper than I had expected, and this project took shape shortly thereafter. It could never have been imagined without the stalwart encouragement of David Desser and Frances Gateward, whose breadth of knowledge and friendship have constituted a beacon. Also, without the persistent encyclopedic knowledge of Chuck Hsuen, Toronto and Halifax, morning, afternoon, and late night for many years, I could never have managed this. I am grateful as well to Keith Alnwick, Toronto; Michael DeAngelis, Chicago; Joe Di Cesare Jr., Newburgh, New York; Wheeler Winston Dixon, Lincoln, Nebraska; Kristen Erickson, Toronto; Krin Gabbard, New York; John Hajdu, Toronto; Andrew Hunter, Toronto; Scuppy Kaplan, Brooklyn; Elizabeth Kerr, London; Barbara Klinger, Bloomington, Indiana; Bob Kolker, Atlanta; Jerzy Kowal, Toronto; Karal Ann Marling, Minneapolis; Melanie Panitch, Toronto; Eric Smoodin, Berkeley; Vivian Sobchack, Los Angeles; Lesley Stern, San Diego; and Joyce Troy, Buffalo.

My colleagues at Ryerson University have been extremely supportive, often by displaying very precise curiosity. I have received support from the Office of Research Services at Ryerson, especially Robert Dirstein and Rose Jackson.

I have had the pleasure of working with my collaborators at New York University Press, as kind as they are perceptive. I am particularly grateful to Despina Papazoglou Gimbel, Maya Hamilton, Andrew Katz, Joanna Mullins, Edith Alston, Emily Park, and Eric Zinner for helping to make this book.

Curtis Maloley has seen this book through with me almost from its beginning, with an exceptionally sharp eye and a prodigious affability. He is a voracious researcher whose camaraderie and insight helped at every step of the project. Barry Keith Grant's generous wisdom has been balm for my editorial aches, and his wit has helped illuminate my pleasures. To my loyal friend and teacher Leslie Fiedler and to Sally Fiedler, my thanks for allowing themselves to be moved by my pleas and provocations and for their excellent hospitality and trust.

My closest collaborators are Nellie Perret and Ariel Pomerance, film lovers and writers whose patience with my obsessions is greater than I deserve.

# ENFANT TERRIBLE!

Onscreen he seems an animal out of its cage. Jerry Lewis (r.) with Dorothy Malone (l.) in *Artists and Models* (Frank Tashlin, Paramount, 1955). Frame enlargement.

# Introduction

Murray Pomerance

Speak what we feel, not what we ought to say.
—*King Lear* 5.3.390

ONE THING EVERYBODY knows about Jerry Lewis is that he is beloved by the French, those incomprehensible hedonistic strangers in that Brigitte-Bardot-and-Jean-Paul-Sartre fantasyland across the sea. Those French, yes, *understand* him, while over here—where the buffalo roam and John Wayne walks softly and carries a big stick—he is at best a riddle, an invasive particle, *not one of us*. More, he is someone we take profound pleasure in excluding. As Frank Krutnik put it in his book *Inventing Jerry Lewis*, a recent critical analysis of the artist's persona and production, "American film and television reviewers routinely vilified his work before he even directed his first film" (2000, 15–16)—a reception reserved for few, if any, American filmmakers of the twentieth century. There is indeed a smorgasbord of vilification laid out for Mr. Jerry Lewis, notwithstanding an important fact that Jean-Pierre Coursodon once emphasized:

> Lewis was the only Hollywood comedian to rise from mere performer to (in his own, quite accurate phrase) "total filmmaker" during the sound era. The uniqueness of this achievement alone deserved sympathetic attention rather than the hostility or indifference it met with. (1975, 15)

Indeed, the "indifference" and "hostility" were still alive and well on February 19, 2000, when Michael Posner suggested in the *Globe and Mail* that Lewis might well be "what various journalists and chroniclers of his life . . . have painted him as through the years: an egomaniacal, completely narcissistic, narrow-minded, arrogant, mean-spirited, temperamental, socially antiquated, boor."

It is the aim of this book to transcend this kind of denigration. Interestingly, many who focus only on his performances complain that they do not find Jerry Lewis funny, or observe with Andrew Sarris (1968, 244) that he is possessed of an "embarrassingly tinny" and self-righteous sentimentality, or note with Krutnik (1994, 16) that his "reactions are often so overextended that they outstrip the motivating context of the gag," and use this as an excuse for rejecting him. But when I watch Jerry Lewis onscreen I am often stunned to reflection and meditation. Moved to laugh or not, I see something startling and suggestive, even profound. For example, the idea conveyed by the central transformation in *The Nutty Professor* (1963) (the most widely recognized and remembered moment in all Lewis's film work) that a hypernerd like Julius Kelp might actually metamorphose into a maestro of suaveness like Buddy Love is hardly in itself a yuk. Robert Leslie Liebman sees here, indeed—meandering quite a long way from laughter, I would say—a case of a "hormonally active Jewish youth [indulging] in a Supergoy fantasy not as a luxury but to vicariously compensate for biological deficiencies"; in short, Jewish self-hatred (1984, 197). But whatever theoretical boxcar one chooses for storing it, the transformation itself represents a highly charged invocation of identity and masquerade, a query about masculinity and power and social relations, and also a play about film, at the same time being both patently preposterous and also completely true: What timid bookworm is not quietly humming "That Old Black Magic" in his heart of hearts and wishing to be a movie star? What lounge lizard is not inwardly a cowering dreamer? Lewis's filmic work—his own features and his performances in those of Norman Taurog, Frank Tashlin, and others—is full of such inspiring moments, which only the most nervous and self-conscious viewer is compelled to call laughable. If Lewis is importantly a comedian, he is more importantly a filmmaker.

As this is written, Jerry Lewis is approaching his seventy-sixth birthday and living in apparent retirement from screen performance. While he is perhaps the most versatile of modern-day entertainers—he is a veteran of virtually every form of show business, from vaudeville to *tummling* in the Catskills; stage singing routines; radio; the celebrated cabaret, stage, and television comedy performances with Dean Martin that lasted exactly ten years, from July 25, 1946, until July 25, 1956; many appearances on television, on the legitimate stage, on casino stages, and on the lecture circuit; and his continuing presence at the helm of the annual Muscular Dystrophy Association Telethon—it is principally in his career in motion pictures that attention is paid to him in these pages. That he is a paragon of stand-up comedy, a conductor, a composer, a writer, a singer, and a serious actor of notable talent—as well as the inventor of the video assist,[1] now a commonplace in the strategy of studio and location shooting—may deflect attention from the sheer volume and fascination of his screen work: appearances in sixteen films, from 1949 through 1956, in partnership with Martin, and in more than thirty others since (as well as dramatic television appearances), many of which he directed or wrote and directed as well. *The Nutty Professor* and *The Ladies Man* (1961), both by Lewis, and *The King of Comedy* (1983) by Martin Scorsese have become widely recognized, while far too much of Lewis's screen accomplishment has been taken completely for granted not only by the public but also by an aggressively hostile critical establishment.

I think there are three genuine roadblocks to serious consideration of Jerry Lewis. First, the screen "Jerry" frequently seems intemperate and therefore asocial, even mortifying. He is strident, brash, dysfunctional, uncoordinated, immature, inarticulate, imposing, hyperactive (while at the same time, as Scott Bukatman has noted [1991], being paralyzed), irritating (even debilitating), rude, untutored, uncivilized, inconsiderate, and often ugly—note the dental closeups in that Kelp-to-Love transmutation—all this, and to an extreme degree. Further, when he whines and wheedles, screeches and drones, the amplitude of his vocalization, as recorded, exaggerates volume and pitch so that his expression is an acoustic weapon, what conventional listeners would call unmusical. When, in his walk or posture, he configures himself asymmetrically—Jerry getting a massage in *Artists and Models* (1955), Jerry in the steamer trunk in *Scared Stiff* (1953), Jerry in the foldaway bed in *The Delicate Delinquent* (1957), Jerry running away from Sandra Bernhard in *The King of Comedy*—he seems without grace, therefore unblessed, even morally twisted. The syntax of his speech is likely to be warped, his social response apparently miscalculated, his needs uncivilized. Jerry doesn't know how to behave. "The Kid," he calls himself, and I say, "*L'enfant terrible.*"

What is the importance and meaning of this *fortissimo* that Lewis persistently produces? While many whom he makes uncomfortable want to know "Why can't he clean up his act?" I think a more useful question is "Precisely why is this activity bothersome, and to whom?" The conventional regard—frequently disregard—for Jerry Lewis places him against an implied ideal of sedate, tranquil, utterly bourgeois, suburban, restrained (even repressed), modest, obedient tameness. Onscreen, then, he seems an animal out of its cage—a monkey, some have said, and as he bombards Fred Clark and Janet Leigh with light bulbs from high up in a chandelier in *Living It Up* (1954), the epithet seems to fit. But Jerry is, to our great (and often inadmissible) delight, much more than a monkey. The apparent extremity of a performance specifically references the stance from which it is measured as such, in this case the unexpressive meter of bourgeois life. Lewis is a primitive and therefore also a modernist. In his apparently unathletic movement (which demands meticulous coordination, balance, and timing) he may make us wonder at our adoration for the proportionate, domesticated, and subjugated etiolations against which we measure him. (In the Martin and Lewis vehicles, domestication was blatantly present in the figure of the "cool" Dean Martin.) If Jerry Lewis onscreen frightens many viewers because he is so out of control, we must ask who demands this control, for whose ends it is so precious that pleasure must never be derived from threatening it.

Jerry Lewis's screen intemperateness raises the issue of social order and the lengths to which we are willing to go to create and enforce it. Steven Shaviro sees Lewis's comedy intrinsically linked to the social: he suggests, indeed, that it "seems oddly based on an exaggerated respect for social values and norms, rather than on a gleeful defiance of them" (1993, 109) and highlights our moral dependence on propriety and appearance, noting that "when Lewis's characters turn into performers, they transmute, but they do not escape, their humiliating dependency upon others' judgmental regards" (113). With social order and idealizing "others' judgmental regards" comes the brutality necessary to prevent disorder. Lewis's performances have no such brutality, only expression. In that, they derive in part from Buster Keaton but go further, since they relinquish Keaton's hold on the cultured and approved, his perfect poise (for more about which, see Cavell 1988, 176). When Jerry loses vocal poise and yawns, whines, warbles, or shrieks, he draws attention to the expressive range of the human voice.[2] We are in a position to see discipline as a feature of social organization and therefore, ultimately, of the control of the powerless by the powerful. In Lewis's work, discipline has no *inherent* value: it again and again reveals subjugation, since it is learned with the end of serving power in sight. Other deficiencies of discipline that are far from accidental include the bubblegum explosion in the cramped elevator in *The Errand Boy* (1961); the extension and duration of the gurney escapade in the finale of *The Disorderly Orderly* (1964); the extent of Buddy Love's manipulation and of Julius Kelp's introversion in *The Nutty Professor*; the zany unboundedness of Eugene Fullstack's adoration for comic books in *Artists and Models*; Kreton's cloying earnestness in *Visit to a Small Planet* (1960).

A second obstruction to watching Lewis carefully derives from what I would call "backstaging," the viewer's tendency to read screen performances in terms of information or theory about the extradiegetic career of the performer animating the exegesis—to read a character as a direct emanation from an actor always persisting behind or underneath it. Erving Goffman refers to this as the "Doctrine of Natural Expression" (1979, 7). In many ways Jerry Lewis can be taken as a paradigm. For example, Jerry is host of a telethon that has raised a huge amount of money for the benefit of children whose movements are hampered; when, therefore, he moves onscreen in a hampered way (something he was doing long before being involved with the Muscular Dystrophy Association), he is read as "imitating" or "mocking" those children and undermining his sincerity as the telethon's host. We persist in viewing the Lewis character onscreen as being played by an *actual* Lewis who is truly, deeply, originally, fundamentally, and personally as out of control as his character is, if not physically then at least in personality. Who, indeed, but a man completely out of control could so believably portray a man completely out of control? Appearing belligerent, impolite, or hostile in a particular social context—during an interview, say—he is readable onscreen as a man closeting deep hostilities under the questionable and vulnerable fabric of a shabby comedy. Although all screen performers have an extradiegetic career, and although the history of Hollywood has been fraught with performances by people whose behavior offscreen may have given reason for querying those performances, Jerry Lewis seems exceptionally prone to such (mis)reading. Yet we have no agency for experiencing Lewis offscreen except "Jerry," another character. If one implication of this relentless mediation is that we are doomed never to meet the man, another is that the screen image of Jerry can make sense entirely *without* our invoking the kind of person "Jerry Lewis" must be in real life. The strange expressions we see need not be generated directly from a hidden (and equally strange) source to seem what they seem, and we need not pursue that "source."

If, too, Jerry were only "being himself" onscreen, only manifesting what some backstage *actual* Jerry *really, irrevocably, truly was*, then the fact of his diegetic presence—that he is up there for all us lurkers in the dark theater to see—would owe entirely to the cult of personality, not to any skills or knowledge he had employed, any social position he had exploited, any act of performance on his part at all. To give him only a backstage reading, then, is to discredit his professionalism, while a respectful approach to Jerry Lewis's work as professional would consider the work on its own merits. The essays in this book attempt to show exactly how calculated, how artful, and how skillful Jerry Lewis's screen work is.

The third blockage is in some ways the most troubling, perhaps because it is the hardest to dissipate, at least for the youngest readers of this book and viewers of these films. Jerry's work (in which I hesitate to include the *Nutty Professor* remakes with Eddie Murphy, although he was involved in producing them) is not of our time, in the particular sense that its aesthetic, often its dialogue, is innocent of so much that young contemporary viewers take as a requirement for the diegetic authenticity that alone seems to merit their full engagement. To appreciate Lewis one must go back in time, bringing a certain curiosity and perhaps nostalgia. One quick example: In the 1950s and early 1960s, when the bulk of his films appeared, the popular critical consciousness that could point to social structure as patriarchal had not yet been fostered. Society was patriarchal, to be sure, but to say so was a radical act. We might now look back, say, at *Hollywood or Bust*, marveling at how it fails to escape a patriarchalism that was everywhere and hence all but invisible; few popular viewers would have taken the trouble to notice it, and Hollywood filmmakers breathed it like country air. Also displaced historically, many young viewers who see *The Nutty Professor* or *The Bellboy* today perk up with the comment that Lewis reminds them of Jim Carrey, while at best this is a reversal of historical syntax (for a revealing discussion of Carrey, see Sobchack 2001).

Why should anyone be thinking about Jerry Lewis at just this time? Because he artfully contrives onscreen to reflect to us the militant, judgmental, sadistic, even cupidinous face of our most tyrannical selves, our drive for domination and control; because his work is quintessentially cinematic; because the work contains much interesting social critique; and because, as these essays show, Lewis in fresh ways gives us so much to consider about the human condition. What should seem salient now is that earlier critical attention so frequently managed not to see this. Measured by the contemporary cultural standards that esteem muscle, Machiavellianism, and mystification, Jerry's is entirely the wrong kind of manliness, entirely the wrong kind of expressivity, entirely the wrong kind of bodily discipline, entirely the wrong kind of economy. He does not save enough, or destroy enough; he does not attack (he expresses complexly—and is thus easily labeled as attacking) but is relentlessly made vulnerable. He is lonely, not gregarious (he is no Tom Hanks); he is the wrong kind of model for an urban gentleman or a hip global traveler or a slick thug (he is no Ralph Fiennes), neither heteronormative enough nor genteel nor gentile enough to please the fundamentalists (he is no Robert Redford); and not articulate and circumlocutive enough to please the pretensions of the academy (he is no Hugh Grant or Matt Damon). His energies are expended willy-nilly, which is to say without a view to relentless profit, and in an economic logic that is generous to a fault and too agitated to be calculating. Onscreen he was totally uncool—even when being hypercool—in an age when coolness was everything. We still live in such an age, though coolness has less to do now with personality. To look at Lewis carefully is to see one's own investment in arrogance, bullishness, sanctioned brutality; one's fetishizing of the mechanical; one's fear of spirit.

But there is one more reason for considering Lewis now, and that is that, at least in the way he is treated in this book, he has not been considered yet. Have we been unready, as a culture, to see what he was doing? As Lewis put it himself, "When the masses loved Laurel and Hardy nobody ever proclaimed them of any worth . . . when the masses chose to grow and get on to other things to love, the critics silently at night snuck in and discovered what the masses had already abandoned" (Wilde 2001). No collection of essays from a varied group of highly sensitive and perceptive scholars has been devoted to this prodigy's contribution to American cinema. As a performer, as a director, as an inventor of technology, as a musician, as a writer, indeed, as one of the paramount *students of film* in the twentieth century, Jerry Lewis has simply failed to exist for the critical community as he does in these pages. Some recent monographs have treated the man and his work—Shawn Levy's *King of Comedy: The Life and Art of Jerry Lewis* and Frank Krutnik's *Inventing Jerry Lewis* (both referred to substantially by authors in this book)—and some examinations appeared in book form several years ago, including Robert Benayoun's *Bonjour Monsieur Lewis;* Jerry Lewis's autobiographical *Jerry Lewis in Person*, with Herb Gluck; and Lewis's own manifesto, *The Total Film-Maker*. These and a number of published articles and journalistic accounts, listed fulsomely by Krutnik, have persisted in giving one critic's view more or less in isolation, sometimes abbreviated and sometimes expanded, and virtually always with a single bias. In Lewis's own books he has been a raconteur, not an analyst, as might be expected. The time was ripe—with the *Nutty Professor* remakes, with plans for remakes of other Lewis films, with Lewis's successful tour and Broadway run in "Damn Yankees," with the prominent feature about him in the *New Yorker* (Kaplan 2000) and two others in the *New York Times* (Wolff 2001; Bogdanovich 2002); with his disastrous appearance shortly after a bout of pneumonia on the 2001 telethon, only days before the World Trade Center catastrophe—for him to emerge as the subject of a serious and multivocal consideration. It has become vital and necessary, from a sociological posture, a psychoanalytic posture, a postmodern posture, an ideological posture, even from just an informed cocoon of enjoyment, to look at this fascinating body of film—the choreographic body of Jerry Lewis that, as Charles Tesson suggests, went beyond Chaplin (2001, 37).

None of these essays has appeared in print before, although it is true of many of these authors that they have written elsewhere—and with repute—about Jerry Lewis; or else, as in the case of Leslie Fiedler, that they have written about virtually everybody else. The book is divided into four parts, of which the first, "Jerry and Me," treats Jerry Lewis, on- and offscreen, as a principal player in the author's biographical experience. For Fiedler, and for Lewis's biographer, Shawn Levy, Jerry as a person and as a maker of and performer in film has, first and foremost, a personal significance. Since, for many in his audience and many who will read these pages, Jerry is similarly personal before he is a subject of analysis, intimate before he is a phenomenon to study at scholarly remove, it seems appropriate to begin with these particular reflections. In

"Whatever Happened to Jerry Lewis? 'That's *Amore* . . . ,'" Leslie Fiedler addresses a theme he has wanted to write about for a very long time— since growing up, like Jerry Lewis, in Newark—but until now has never had the opportunity to shape. In it, Lewis's screen self is shown to be a personification that is purely American and purely of the twentieth century, a figure touching on the deepest roots of the contemporary personality—the shifting population, urban angst, the heroically multiracial. As he has done in a long and esteemed career, Fiedler here once again takes on received wisdom, this time what is for him the politically too-correct view that Lewis's comedy is to be questioned for "making fun" of cripples. This essay, meticulously considering Jerry's work in the context of various historical conventions for representing the disabled, links Lewis to minstrelsy and suggests that his films cannot easily be categorized as either tragedies or melodramas; that Jerry's protagonists find themselves in a world in which "politics and religion play no important role" and in which "state houses and churches seem to be permanently closed."

Shawn Levy's "Being Rupert Pupkin" is a bittersweet reflection on his own experience writing *King of Comedy*. Jerry Lewis, it would seem, is a figure who has haunted this author, not only because of the well-documented falling-out that took place on Jerry's yacht while Levy was finishing the biography but also because Lewis persisted in being, even for a biographer studying him at the closest range, a figure of inestimable proportions. The book manuscript, for instance, came in at almost three times the contracted length, as though the subject had somehow begun to swell as he was studied. Further, although he felt wounded, Levy believed in the biographer's need to maintain objectivity: "Given the frame of mind in which I lived those months," he says, "the responsibility to present something like a blank face to the world was a tremendous challenge." But most intriguingly, Levy presents himself as a writer who had spent innumerable hours researching Lewis in every conceivable direction, a person who had amassed a tremendous amount of information about his subject, and who still, in the end, was left with the feeling that "I still really can't say who I was dealing with or if it was even a single human being. The scrim of individual identity, even more than that of fame, keeps the essential Jerry— if there is such a critter—at an impassable distance."

Part 2, "Jerry Lewis, Faces Off," is devoted to considerations of the screen personality of Jerry Lewis as a masquerade. Considered here are

not only the variations of his screen personae and some of their implications but also the significance of Jerry's multifaceted diegetic presence. In many ways the most accessible and celebrated view of Lewis's
screen work consists of an acknowledgment of his frenetic posturing,
his wildly changing presentation of self. Andrew Horton's opening discussion, "Dreaming of Jerry Lewis's Arizona Dream," offers one of the
few discussions in print of Lewis's deeply confrontational performance
in Emir Kusturica's bizarre and intoxicating *Arizona Dream* (1993). Horton sees the performance as evincing the contradictory and poetic—
quintessentially Yugoslavian—character of the film, most critically in
the love and conflict between Lewis and Johnny Depp. In this film the
Lewis performance incarnates the long-lived presence of the "holy
fool," raising our attention to the delicate interface between pragmatics
and metaphysics, between political and economic realities and the al-
gebra of need and pain.

The European obsession with Lewis is the subject of Marcia
Landy's penetrating study "Jerry Agonistes." Jerry Lewis has been relegated to a relatively insignificant position in American film history
and has attracted dismissive, even hostile, reviews and critical comment. Accepted as an *auteur* in Europe, however, he is read as expressing Americanness in a sophisticated way. He can be understood, then,
as reflecting the essence of America as it is perceived through a European focus. He has also been labeled a postmodernist, holding up a mirror to the spectator but offering only a fragmented and incoherent reflection in return. Is it possible, Landy asks us to consider, that the
America Lewis signifies onscreen is true in a way Americans themselves cannot fathom? By examining not only the appreciative French
reaction to Lewis but serious considerations as well from Britain, Italy,
and Germany, Landy suggests how Lewis's films are regarded "as an
assault on American culture and politics, exposing a banality that
masks more aggressive designs."

In "Flaming Creature," Craig Fischer looks at Jerry's "mercurial"
performance style, contrasting his work in *Hollywood or Bust* (1956) with
Dustin Hoffman's in Barry Levinson's *Rain Man* (1988). While the two
films are structurally identical in many ways, the Method performance
that underlies Hoffman's Raymond Babbitt is grounded in the idea of
the consummate actor, while Lewis's multifaceted and unpredictable
style in *Hollywood* structures a performance that "threaten[s] to reduce
the tropes of traditional narrative organization (classical Hollywood

storytelling rules, the oedipal narrative trajectory) into an incoherent collection of attractions." This "collection of attractions," moreover, renders Lewis something of a "flaming creature," calling to mind the filmmaking of the gay avant-garde artist Jack Smith, who worked contemporaneously to, and sometimes with, Andy Warhol at around the time *Hollywood or Bust* appeared.

The mediated self of Jerry Lewis has led many observers to the presumption that the man is nothing if not an obsessive performer, relentless in his appeal to an audience. Krin Gabbard's exploration of the rarely considered (and even more rarely seen) Lewis adaptation for television of *The Jazz Singer* (1927), "The Day the Clown Quit," traces the roots of the characterization of a cantor's son who finds a career in show business from its origins in the 1920s through the many modifications it has seen. Lewis's version, with the protagonist finally performing "Kol Nidre" *in clownface*, is shown to be peculiar in particular ways that bring new light to his concerns as son, American Jew, and performer.

If Lewis's films and screen performances bring to light performance and charade, skin and substance, his work is also reflective of social processes, a structured world, and a set of human relations. Part 3, "Jerry Lewis and Social Transformations," attempts to look at Lewis in terms of ideological or cultural formulations. In Lewis's career, in his characterizations, and in the situations his films continually stage we see embodied a distinct view of the social world, if not analytical then at least critical and artfully described. The essays in this part approach Lewis's presentations in terms of their treatment of male bonding, of the role of intelligence and stupidity in social life, of illness and diagnosis, of cultural difference, and of the construction of mediated social reality.

First, Frank Krutnik's "Sex and Slapstick" explores the intense and immensely popular relationship between Dean and Jerry in terms of its legibility as a continuing instantiation of *liveness*. The sense of Martin and Lewis that audiences of cabaret, television, and film had during the 1940s and 1950s, he suggests, was that their relationship went far beyond the conventional opposition of gagster and straight man into a bond that was genuine, personal, and emotive. That sense of reality and spontaneity to one degree or another carried through the sixteen films the two made together and permeated their other work, so that the filmic identities seemed reflective to the audience of a relationship that was going on in real time. While Lewis is (perhaps too) easily readable as offering a "grotesque spectacle of homoerotic desire," nevertheless, for Krutnik, the "precarious intimacy" of Dean and Jerry made available to audiences of the time "a dizzying array of emotional and covertly erotic intensities between men."

Next, Mikita Brottman's "Imbecile Chic of Jerry Lewis" examines the social formulation of humor with particular attention to the role of stupidity and intelligence in Jerry's characterizations in early Martin and Lewis films such as *The Stooge* (1953). His screen postures and gestures are seen as grotesqueries, in some sense imitations of mental deficiency, and the production of this kind of screen material is considered in light of psychoanalytic theories of laughter, on the one hand, and the trend in the 1950s and 1960s for deinstitutionalizing both psychoanalysis and mental deficiency in a time of burgeoning public order and control, on the other. The success of Lewis's performances is seen as a reflection of widespread feeling that the hegemonic order was as problematic as it was difficult to question openly.

In "Sick Jokes: Humor and Health in the Work of Jerry Lewis," Lucy Fischer presents an analysis of *The Disorderly Orderly* in light of the "A Little Fun to Match the Sorrow" episode of the television show "Ben Casey," suggesting that underlying much of Lewis's work is a fascinating tension "between comic distance and empathetic intimacy." Being a comedian, she suggests, is often expressly not about being empathetic, nice, kind, or genteel, and from that perspective it is revealing to study these two incidences of Jerry performing a medical role without the capacity to be as distant from his patients as gagmen must be from their marks. The link between medicine and professional comedy opens a serious reconsideration of the reception of Jerry's comedy as "spastic"; we may find a far more complex structure of identification and distancing in the screen "Jerry Lewis" than has been illuminated by analysis uninformed about clinical practice.

David Desser's essay on *The Geisha Boy* (1958) sets the precedent of seeing this transitional film not only in terms of its Orientalizing context but also as a reflection of the "feminized" Jewish male discussed by Daniel Boyarin. Like many other films of its time, *Geisha Boy* actively romanticizes and feminizes the Orient—specifically Japan—while establishing Jerry's character as a noteworthy example of an unmilitarized, sensitive, and attractive male, the precursor in comedy of the types that Jim Carrey and Adam Sandler now play onscreen. The plot structure of *Geisha Boy* affiliates Jerry's Great Wooley with maternity and unaggressive masculinity, but does so by placing him in a Japanese culture that Hollywood prerogatives reduced to a setting in which "the exoticized 'Asian' woman came to be seen as a counterpoint to the (allegedly) increasingly strident, unfeminine American woman."

One of Jerry Lewis's most stunning and most troubling performances onscreen—and a performance to which I believe insufficient attention has been paid—is given in one of Martin Scorsese's most stunning and most troubling films, *The King of Comedy*. J. P. Telotte's essay "Jerry in the City" examines Jerry in this film as a figuration of what Paul Virilio calls "derealization," the cultural development through which the screen has come to represent the locus of reality and that has thus blurred the distinction between imagination and everyday experience. For Telotte, *The King of Comedy* explores the human topology that results from our pervasive preoccupation with celebrity. Jerry Lewis, with his totally mediated self, creates the perfect incarnation of Jerry Langford, a man whose every presence is a distance.

Scott Bukatman considers Jerry in light of Marshall McLuhan's analysis—contemporary with many of Jerry's own productions in the early 1960s—of society changing from a mechanical, industrial, and local paradigm to a global and electronic one. Jerry, he says, is "performing a body racked between these two paradigms," with a subjectivity that, while no longer definable in purely mechanical, static, traditional terms, yet remains uncomfortable with its "dispersal into global circuitry." The stammering, stuttering, shuddering dance of Jerry Lewis onscreen is, for Bukatman, something like the hallmark of contemporary man managing to eclipse a "unitary" and perduring past but not yet fully fragmented or fully energized in a shocking, fragmentary future.

The concluding part, "Jerry-Built," contains essays that focus on particular films as coherent thematic works rather than packages for the Lewis performance, as they frequently are taken to be. These essays consider films made by Lewis himself, or that were under his controlling influence.

Peter Lehman and Susan Hunt give consideration to the particular masculinities constructed in *The Nutty Professor*, a film they take to be an essay on our cultural splitting of masculinity into what they call the "mind guy" and the "body guy." Intellectual men, they point out, are taken in our culture to be poor lovers, whose mentality is developed at the expense of physique. The body guy, by contrast—in *The Nutty*

*Professor*, Buddy Love—has that indefinable "something" that makes him unfailingly attractive to women, even though he is capable of abusing them. In following the narrative of *Nutty Professor* through the various transformations of nerdy, sensitive, brilliant Julius Kelp into Buddy and back again, Lehman and Hunt offer some challenging conclusions about our deepest convictions about masculinity as reflected by this film. While the predilection for the body guy is both widespread and critically deconstructable, they suggest, nevertheless beneath such criticism resides a lingering analytical deprecation of the analytical type. As a statement about gender, *The Nutty Professor* signals a difficulty in representing masculinity through a stable and positive ideal.

In "Working Hard Hardly Working," Dana Polan is interested in the theme of labor in Lewis's own productions, with specific focus on *The Ladies Man*. Polan suggests that Jerry Lewis's films, although belonging to the genre of comedy, are not necessarily grounded in the premise of "funniness." An important premise of this particular film deals with the nature of labor and work, and they serve as ideological challenges to the centrality of alienation in everyday life. Polan analyzes what he calls the "comedy of laborious failure," in which the world of work is the setting for spectacular mishaps and miscalculations. This kind of comedy can function at the worker's expense, making fun of his inabilities to succeed, or may deride the controlling class, operating to critique social dominance. Polan also examines the "comedy of success in work," in which the job is typically carried out to excess. He shows how in Jerry Lewis's films there is a "constant emphasis" on the "moral benefits of labor."

In "Hello Deli!" Barry Keith Grant studies *The Delicate Delinquent* with a view to establishing the largely unheralded significance of this film directed by Don McGuire (under the tacit control of Jerry Lewis). Pivotal in Lewis's career, *Delinquent* exhibits all the manifestations of the performer's mature style, but at a time when he had not yet begun to make films of his own. The film reflects contemporary social concerns about what was called the "adolescent subculture." Further, the Lewis performance in this film is seen as a choreography of tensions between delicate civility and delinquent unruliness, between Jerry as The Idiot and Jerry as The Serious Man, a dualism that calls up generic codes of the then new teenpic genre that represented adolescents as either wild or mild. While this is in part a reflection of the awkward transition from youth to adulthood—both for the character and for the performer as filmmaker—the dualism of the character Lewis plays also points to Lewis's scars from his recently terminated relationship with Dean Martin and suggests the purely performative character of screen identity. One of the important features of *The Delicate Delinquent* is its foregrounding of the tensions between contradictory versions of masculine identity and thus its dispelling the notion that we can read Lewis's films and performances as being grounded in realism.

Finally, in my own essay on *The Errand Boy* (1961), I suggest a reading of a fascinating film either too little studied or too swiftly passed over as simple parody. We are presented in *The Errand Boy* with a systematic critique of capitalist culture as engendering and maintaining a "lack" among the powerless. Rather than follow Laura Mulvey's phallocentric use of the word *lack*, I examine the mechanics of social production and social class to see Lewis's Morty S. Tashman struggling against his lack of linguistic competence in a particular social scene—the movie studio—where language has particular and vital utility. Far from being little more than a self-reflexive backstage romp, then, *The Errand Boy* is a subtle and carefully constructed study of language and power in a contemporary context.

A collection such as this always has a number of drawbacks. Not everyone who has something valuable to say can be included, nor can anyone who is included find a voice for saying absolutely everything that is relevant and valuable. Many worthy or fascinating filmic moments are not given the consideration some reader will surely want: because if there are Jerry Lewis haters out there, to whom this book is respectfully addressed as an invitation, there are also Jerry Lewis fans, whose attachment is profound and knowledgeably grounded. To be found here are—in the truest sense of the word—essays on Jerry Lewis, attempts to understand him and come to terms with the body of his work (and his body *in* his work), written in the playful spirit the subject requires. The multivocal nature of the book is an intentional reflection of Lewis himself onscreen, a man of many postures, many voices, many faces, many feelings.

The book also cannot give—as no book can give—a sufficiently replete description or rendition of the real screen presentations the essays evaluate. The reader is encouraged to become a viewer and to take pleasure in knowing that many of Lewis's films are at least in current video release. The frontispiece images with each chapter are intended not so much as documentations as clues. Lewis is a man whose every moment onscreen is photographable and in some way memorable, but in this book we have made choices and committed ourselves to speaking in some depth about only a few such moments.

Finally, it is a sad feature of scholarly prose analysis that it is scarcely ever, in itself, lighthearted or blunt. Addressed to a subject such as Jerry Lewis, serious analysis can seem a bad fit. But if one need not be laughing to appreciate Lewis's work, as I have suggested, it is also true that philosophy need not inhibit laughter and joy. In hopes that they will find the rich accomplishments of Jerry Lewis sufficiently drawn in its pages to suggest new horizons or to open new doors, this book is given to those for whom insight is inseparable from pleasure.

### NOTES

1. Jerry Lewis invented the video assist for use on *The Bellboy* (1960) and according to Neibaur and Okuda it is currently used on virtually every movie set. . . . The production camera for the shoot was rigged at that time with an industrial type RCA Vidicon camera mounted near the lens, and can reproduce on a television monitor near or distant from the camera an image that fairly exactly duplicates what the camera is filming. This makes possible extremely quick evaluation of shooting, as well as technically facilitating certain strategic blocking problems if the director is also acting in the scene. The video camera on the set is now, according to Peter Bogdanovich, "a standard part of the production kit, whether the film is being made for theatrical distribution or for television. But very few people, even in show business, know that the inventor of the monitor, now commonly called the video assist, was Jerry Lewis." (2002, 3)

2. In this light, consider his casting the mezzo-soprano Helen Traubel as Mrs. Wellenmellen in *The Ladies Man* (1961), and offering her an exquisitely dramatized moment of silence in which she can bellow, in purest Wagnerian style, "Good morrrrrrrrrrrrrrning, Jerommmmmmmme!!!!" By allowing for her amplitude, Lewis suggests the musicality of the human voice (and thus of his own voice); but by using the trained opera singer, he raises for consideration the issue of professionalization. Why must only a trained, disciplined singer sing loud? Why may not any human voice be raised, whether or not it has been bounded and shaped through the strictures of traditional training?

PART I

# JERRY AND ME

"What we really laughed at in Jerry's films was not the otherness of the suffering but the sameness to our own." Mobsters stretching the "big mouth" (Jerry Lewis) in *The Big Mouth* (Jerry Lewis, Columbia, 1967). Frame enlargement.

# I

# Whatever Happened to Jerry Lewis?

*"That's* Amore ..."

Leslie A. Fiedler

I WAS NO more than five or six and not yet able to read when my mother, because a baby-sitter failed to show up, felt obliged to take me with her to a showing of *The White Sister* (1923), starring Lillian Gish. This premature venture into the world of adult magic made me an addict of moving pictures. Indeed, in the years since, I have seen more movies than I have read books, though it is for doing the latter that I have come to be paid. From the start, however, I wanted not to be just a passive watcher of films but to participate in making them. This seemed possible since, as was true of many Jewish American families, members of my own had played a part in the production of Hollywood's ready-made dreams. A cousin of mine was a property man; his two sisters worked in casting; and his daughter, whose first visitors after she was born were Charlie Chaplin and Theda Bara, had led the MGM lion onto the set for the first time. All these relatives, however, had not created films but had only done the small chores that made it easier for the directors, scriptwriters, choreographers, musicians, and actors to create them. Although some of these jobs required skills I did not have, there were two I felt at least qualified to try. Some of the stories I had published had been optioned, and for two of them screenplays had actually been written. But neither *The Second Stone* nor *Nude Croquet* had made it to the screen.

For a while it seemed as if I might have more luck as an actor, since my performances in several amateur productions and a semi-pro off-Broadway one had been favorably received. But none of my stage appearances was filmed until, in the late 1950s, I began to be invited to participate in talk shows, in which I appeared so often (and was paid scale) that I had to join AFTRA (the American Federation of Television and Radio Artists). On these shows, however, I played only the same role I lived offstage, that of an anti-academic academic and a part-time social critic—called by the producers of such programs a "nut," as were Allen Ginsberg and Norman Mailer, who were their first choices. But finally these shows gave me a chance to diversify my act. One night when I confessed before the cameras that I desperately longed to play any other part, someone apparently had listened. As I opened the door to my home in Buffalo, the phone was ringing; and when I picked it up I heard a strange voice asking if I could come to Hollywood for six or eight weeks to play the part of a gypsy caravan driver in a full-length film. I said immediately, "Yes, yes, yes," and before I knew it I was in California wearing tights and a plumed hat and rehearsing my lines in what turned out to be a movie called *When I Am King* (1981). It was so badly written, directed, and edited that though it had in the cast competent veteran actors like Aldo Ray and Stuart Whitman, it never made its way into any theater, and its producers eventually disappeared without a trace.

Nevertheless, thinking back I find that time to have been one of the most satisfactory in all my life—mostly because it was so unreal. I was put up in a room in the venerable Roosevelt Hotel, looking down from whose windows I could see the tourists gathering before the even more venerable Grauman's Chinese Theater. From there I was picked up every morning and driven to a location familiar to me from a thousand sleazy Westerns, in one thousand and one of which John Wayne had starred. My driver was a fellow actor, a dwarf and former circus clown who arrived each day already drunk and got even drunker from the beers he gulped as we sped down the freeway. From the start I had the sense of being in not a real Hollywood but a mythic one that existed only on the pages of Nathaniel West's *The Day of the Locust*. It was as if the Screen Actor's Guild contract I had been given was a passport into that magic space behind the movie screen that I had longed to penetrate.

That visit to Neverland, however, turned out to be my last as well as my first. A couple of years later my name appeared in the credits of a much better film called *Exposed* (1983), starring Rudolf Nureyev and Nastassja Kinski, but I never appeared in the flesh. What the camera did close in on, in an opening scene, were some lines from my *Love and Death in the American Novel* being written on a chalkboard by a professor played by the director of the movie. In a later scene the book itself was shown pressed to the breasts of his students, including Nastassja.

Yet, though I never participated in the making of any other movie, I did continue to watch them and even, reluctantly, to write about a few of them, such as *Beyond the Valley of the Dolls* (1970), *The Immoral Mr. Teas* (1959), and *The Birth of a Nation* (1915); all of them works that annoyed someone or other enough to be condemned, picketed, or banned. I did not, however, deal with any of the films of Jerry Lewis until I was asked to contribute to this collection and realized that he, who was once a super-best-seller, had become virtually taboo because he had treated the crippled and handicapped as ridiculous rather than pitiful.

His defense by European snobs who typically like only what Americans despise proved to be a kiss of death. Moreover, his American detractors were not convinced by the French defenders, who defended him on aesthetic grounds rather than on the ethical ones on which he was condemned in his own country. They seem not to have been aware of what I would have pointed out: that the portrayal of cripples as laughable is one of the three main ways in which writers have traditionally treated such unfortunates. Homer, for instance, portrays all malformed characters as appropriate targets for ridicule, whether they are mortal monsters such as Thersites or immortal ones such as Hephaestus. Nor is such portrayal of the disabled as comic absent from the culture of our own country. In fact, the minstrel show, a form of popular theater unique to America, began with "Daddy" Rice "Jumping Jim Crow," which is to say, doing a wild dance that he claimed was based on that performed by an old black slave so crippled by rheumatism it was both wonderful and funny that he could dance at all.

The second traditional way of portraying the handicapped is as monsters, ugly in their souls as well as in their bodies. Best known of these is Shakespeare's Richard III, to whom he gave a hunchback he never really had but who turned out to be not just hated and feared but loved and admired by actors and audiences. So, too, in the later nineteenth century, malicious amputees such as Long John Silver and Captain Hook fascinated as well as terrified small boys and their fathers. But in Victorian England and America there was a sentimental backlash against the negative portrayal of the disabled as vicious and ridiculous. This created a vacuum that was filled to overflowing by a third way of presenting the handicapped, as beautiful souls trapped in unbeautiful bodies. The best remembered of these saintly cripples is Charles Dickens's Tiny Tim. It was largely because of him that *A Christmas Carol* became a best-seller and has remained one right down to the present. By the end of the century in which it first appeared, however, more sophisticated readers began to feel, and were candid enough to confess, that all of Dickens's cripples moved them not to weep but to laugh. Given the choice, they found he was truer to himself when he portrayed the handicapped as comic or grotesque than as pathetic, as in the case of Quilp, the character whom he once said was the closest thing to a self-portrait he had ever created.

Jerry Lewis, by contrast, never forgot his primary obligations as a comedian: to keep the audience laughing all through his movies and to leave them feeling happy. Since the kind of comedy he wrote was slapstick farce, in which violence is present everywhere, this was not easy to do. Yet he somehow always managed to make the poke in the eye, the slap on the face, the kick in the ass, the hit on the head, and the pratfall, which was his trademark, seem not to matter. In any case, he presented them so that the audience did not respond with gasps of horror but continued to giggle and chortle, as also did the other characters on the stage. Only the protagonist never laughed but responded with a wordless cry of anguish, at which the laughter of everyone else was doubled.

To some of his critics it seemed that he did this by exploiting the shameless tendency of us all to be more delighted than dismayed by the calamities that befall others. It seems to me, however, that what we really laughed at in Jerry's films was not the otherness of the suffering but the sameness to our own. We are all cripples, he seemed to be saying, both those we call handicapped and we whom they call TABS, meaning "temporarily able-bodied."

The same message is contained in the riddle the Sphinx poses to Oedipus in Sophocles' tragedy, when she asks, "Who walks on four legs in the morning, two legs in the afternoon, and three legs in the evening?" Oedipus correctly answers, "Man"—which is to say, all humans, who begin crawling abjectly on all fours in our infancy, then stride proudly on two legs in our prime, and, when we are old, hobble unsteadily with the aid of a third leg, a crutch or a cane. To be sure, this melancholy thought is more compatible with tragedy, whose final words of wisdom are "Let no man consider himself happy until he is dead," than with comedy, which concludes with "happily ever after."

Jerry's typical endings, however, though they are not tragic or even melodramatic, are not what most people call happy either. It is hard to find any proper name for his endings, since they do not end with a victory for the protagonist; and what victory would be possible for the nerds who are the anti-heroes in the stories Jerry tells? Defined from the very beginning as losers, they cannot kill a dragon, find the Holy Grail, and become saints or kings; nor can they be convincingly portrayed as overthrowing a tyrant and freeing his oppressed people—or even getting rich and being elected Lord Mayor of London. The world in which Jerry's protagonists find themselves is one in which politics and religion play no important role. State houses and churches seem to be permanently closed, and the only well-lit places are the classrooms, gymnasiums, laboratories, and auditoriums of seedy second-rate colleges flanked by sleazy nightclubs, bars, and soda parlors to which the students flee when school is out.

The potholed streets over which these protagonists move from place to place seem much to me like those of Newark, New Jersey, a city that began to die before it began to live. It was there I once worked in a shoe store side by side with a crew of losers, one of whom was Danny Levitch, Jerry's father. Although he boasted constantly about his rosy prospects in the theater, he always seemed to end up working as an extra salesman. His father's habitual failure must have haunted Jerry and fueled in him a relentless desire to succeed, but that desire is not shared by the comic creeps who survive in his films. None of them seems to be dreaming of success or, indeed, any other fully adult goal. Instead they yearn for what is called, in the jargon of the young, "popularity," hoping to be accepted, applauded, and loved not for what others believe and they fear they really are—namely, wimps—but as sleek and loveable hunks, which they hope they can become or at least seem to become by finding the right style of dress or shade of lipstick or way of dancing. The reward for thus renewing themselves is perhaps the oldest of all happy endings: "getting the girl." Sometimes they modernize this dream of their fathers and grandfathers by making it "getting the girls." The shift from singular to plural, however, makes no real difference, since whether they strive to have and to hold just one woman until death do them part or to bed down many, their beloved turns out to be the same bubble-headed blonde shiksa, whom his protagonists think they desire but whom Jerry himself probably could not have stood for a single minute.

There is a slight note of irony in all his portrayals of such females, as he did not realize fully, until Dean Martin had become his inseparable stagemate, that he really thought of those women as rivals for his true love, who was not a woman at all but a glib, sexy, self-confident male much like Martin. The series of movies in which Jerry explored in depth his ill-fated relationship with Dean and Dean's rejection of him—from *My Friend Irma* (1949) to *Hollywood or Bust* (1956)—are not only the saddest and funniest he ever made but absolutely unique.

To be sure, the concept of male couples joined by a sublimated passion "which passeth the love of a woman" yet is "indifferent to men and their erections" is central to many American works, from the minstrel show to such classics as *The Last of the Mohicans*, *Moby Dick*, and *Huckleberry Finn*, about which I have written at length. But the love that joins Jerry and Dean is in many ways different from that which joins the paleface audience to the black actors in the minstrel shows and Huck Finn to Jim, Ishmael to Queequeg, Natty Bumppo to Chingachgook. These all have a racist, political dimension, since in all of them a white and a nonwhite male, though their people back at home are fighting each other, discover it is possible in the wilderness or at sea to find temporary peace and love in a relationship physical but not fully sexual. But Jerry and Dean both would have been more likely to be considered black than white by the WASPs who wrote those books, since one was a Jew and the other Italian, and both therefore too swarthy to be placed on that high rung of the evolutionary ladder WASPs occupied. Of course, the first generation of Italians and Jews were deeply suspicious of each other because of their different religions and cultures, but their children born in America began by playing together on the streets of their neighboring ghettos and, in their quest for upward social mobility, ended up with similar careers as gangsters, boxers, or actors. It was in the theater that Dean and Jerry entered into their bond, which, like many such theatrical unions, they announced to the world by fusing both their names into one, calling themselves Martin and Lewis. But unlike Abbott and Costello, Laurel and Hardy, Burns and Allen, they were as drastically different from each other as the stereotypes of their races: the kike Jerry Lewis (née Joseph Levitch) sober, modest, hard-working but afflicted by self-doubt, chiefly sexual; the wop Dean Martin (née Dino Crocetti) charming, articulate, and talented but with an unfortunate propensity for getting drunk. One thinks of him primarily, however, as he apparently thought of himself: as one of the mythological Italo-American lounge lizards like Rudolph Valentino and Frank Sinatra.

There were no such mythic erotic role models for Jerry, yet it was he who truly loved, rather than Dean, who would only let himself be loved. And it was Dean who ended the marriage, of which Dean never seems to have been fully aware. So, too, he was not aware of how traumatic was their final separation, which sent Jerry back to his legally married wife and family. But even there Jerry could never forget the cruel words Dean had spoken to him at the moment of what Jerry felt as a divorce: "You can talk about love all you want. To me, you're nothing but a dollar sign," Dean said and then continued his career as leading man and singer of schmaltzy Neapolitan love songs without interruption.

Jerry, however, made fewer and fewer movies, filling his growing hours of idleness with busy work as national chairman for the Muscular Dystrophy Association, whose activities on behalf of victims of such neural disorders climaxed in a Labor Day telethon that since the 1960s has collected millions of dollars. But life has not otherwise been kind to Jerry. As he has grown older he has suffered other disasters, including prostate cancer, a heart attack, and a general failure of his body—which he felt for many years was invulnerable. Especially his buttocks and lower back, on which he had fallen hundreds of times, were wracked by pain so bitter that he turned to Percodan for relief. Instead of giving him a surcease of pain for which he hoped, that drug left him only with an addiction that lasted for fifteen years. Nevertheless, I do not like to think that Jerry ever regretted the tortures to which he submitted his flesh for so long, since they had given real pleasure to so many. Among these I count myself, to whom his routines seemed so attractive that I learned how to do some of those falls myself to entertain friends and break up dull parties.

Despite his multiple afflictions, Jerry kept trying to compose a movie with a happier ending than the one that seemed to lie ahead of him in real life. To do this, he was aware he would have to exorcise the ghost of Dean Martin, which continued to haunt him, by rewriting the story of their love. Ultimately, he did so. As late as 1982, Jerry agreed to appear in Martin Scorsese's *The King of Comedy* (1983), which contains an account of his relationship with Dean Martin, with their roles reversed: that is, Scorsese cast as the unattractive loser, hitherto portrayed by Jerry himself, Robert De Niro, who is of the same ethnic origin as Scorsese and Dean Martin. He then used Jerry to play the part of the successful "king" of showbiz, who rejects De Niro/Jerry.

But Jerry years earlier had made, in *The Nutty Professor* (1963), a more radical revision of their relationship in which only one member is real. The Jerry-like protagonist is called Professor Julius Kelp, while the Deanlike character, called Buddy Love, is not the real antagonist he seems, only an imaginary alter ego. When the film starts, however, nobody seems to know this, not even the professor himself, who feels that to win the heart and hand of the woman he thinks he loves he must turn himself into that younger, more attractive male. The woman is also convinced that it is the nonexistent Dean-figure she really loves. In the end, however, she discovers that she wants and needs someone much more like the unbeautiful professor, and it is that professor she is about to marry when the movie ends.

This seemed to me such a totally satisfactory ending to the story that I could not imagine why anyone would or could add anything to it. I was therefore astonished and a little dismayed when, as we entered the third millennium, I saw a notice in the *TV Guide* that another movie called *The Nutty Professor* (1996) was playing on cable. When I actually saw it, I discovered it was indeed a continuation of Jerry's original film, though his name was not listed as one of the writers or actors but only as one of its executive producers.

It had, moreover, a new ending in which the professor turns out to be a double winner, getting both "the girl" and "the girls." He can do this because, in the new version, he is a kind of Dr. Jekyll, able to turn himself into Hyde with the chemical compound he has invented.

This makes it possible for him to be shown, as the action draws to a close, asleep in a bed where he has earlier made love to three lusty bimbos and then, on waking, dressing himself in the proper garb for a marriage to the blonde young starlet he was always convinced he desired. She, however, has changed too, being now no longer a bubble-head but a serious graduate student and also, despite her yellow hair, black. So are most of the other major characters, including the professor, who is played by Eddie Murphy, an African American actor much admired by young people both white and black and whose name alone seemed to guarantee a large audience for the film. This time, moreover, the professor comes onscreen looking not like a medical textbook figure or a terminal victim of muscular dystrophy but instead a grossly fat, aging man destined apparently to get even fatter—a disability at which it is possible to laugh without stirring up the strong negative reactions prompted by Jerry's earlier mocking of the maimed.

These multiple changes make clear what Murphy realized was always true, though less evident earlier: that the major theme of this movie was not disability or interethnic male bonding or even race but reality and illusion. This play on what is and what merely seems Murphy made even more complex by announcing to the audience in publicity releases that he himself was a kind of shape-shifter who would be playing not only the professor but some six or seven other characters. He does indeed play them in full sight in the most hilarious scene of the film, which takes place at a family dinner for the professor: Murphy is made up as the professor, sitting in the midst of three generations of his family, clearly also played by him. This involves, of course, Murphy appearing simultaneously as male and female, old and young.

This kind of age- and gender-bending, as well as the trifling with illusion, seems more characteristic of high art than of pop. Certainly, it is to be found in the Mannerist literature and painting of the fifteenth century and also in the avant-garde schools of art of the twentieth century, such as Surrealism, Dada, Futurism, and Postmodernism. But it is also to be found in the popular minstrel show, in which nothing is as it seems and the audience knows it. Those who pretend to be black turn out to be white, and those who come on in the garb of women turn out to be men, and that which seems a typical Southern plantation is revealed finally as a stage of the theater actually located in Buffalo or Boston or New York

City. To be sure, so that the movie audience does not miss this affinity, Murphy in the key dinner-table scene makes his characters speak, move, and relate to one another and to the audience in ways much like those characteristic of a style first used by blackface minstrels and later transmitted to the purely white audience of vaudeville, musical comedies, and "talking movies" by an older generation of Jewish American actors such as Al Jolson, Eddie Cantor, and, to be sure, Jerry Lewis. It is Al Jolson whom we best remember, but Murphy reminds us that Jerry actually made a best-selling record of the minstrel-show tune "Rock-a-Bye Your Baby with a Dixie Melody" some thirty years after Jolson had made it a hit.

But thirty more years after that release, Jerry seemed about to disappear not just from the stage and screen but from the memory of the audience; or worse yet, it seemed as if he might end up being remembered only as the celebrity announcer who every Labor Day presides over the Muscular Dystrophy Telethon and whose picture is displayed, between those genteel money-raising orgies, on posters everywhere in this country.

On those posters, he who was once accused of slandering the disabled is portrayed as their smug and kindly benefactor. Lest anyone miss the point, he is shown hugging a photogenic child purported to be a victim of muscular dystrophy. Typically these victims are girls, usually white, and always scrupulously clean and with the fixed smiles of professional models. Though they have come to be officially known as "Jerry's Kids," I think of them as "this year's Tiny Tim," and of the portly, solid citizen who beams down on them as this year's Scrooge: not the earlier Scrooge who is almost indistinguishable from a "stingy old Jew" but Scrooge after his conversion into the professional founder of the feast for all the deserving poor.

Thanks to Eddie Murphy, however, Jerry has been delivered from this ignominious fate, his older, truer self having been resurrected, as it were, and displayed once more on screens, actually being watched by a new audience that includes the young as well as the old and the black as well as the white. It seems, in fact, that Jerry will not die again for a long time, since the box-office success of the first blackface version of *The Nutty Professor* was so notable that it has been followed by another, *The Nutty Professor II: The Klumps* (2000). This seems to me to be the single-handed accomplishment of Murphy, who was cool enough to appear before the cameras pretending to be a white man pretending to be black—or rather, perhaps, pretending to be a Jew pretending to be a white man pretending to be black. We therefore owe him thanks for having restored to us in a strange new form the original Jerry Lewis, one of the makers of that mulatto culture that is America's gift to itself and the rest of the world.

Jerry Langford (Jerry Lewis) prepares to let loose on the presuming schmuck
Rupert Pupkin in *The King of Comedy* (Martin Scorsese, Twentieth Century
Fox, 1983). Frame enlargement.

# 2

# Being Rupert Pupkin

Shawn Levy

FROM THE TIME I left a San Diego boat basin red-eared in the spring of 1993 to the morning that I'm writing these words, I have borne an invisible Jerry Lewis tattoo.

Certain things you just don't get over, ever. Being dressed down on a yacht by a roaring legend of showbiz is one of them; being the guy who dared try to capture all the contradictions of said legend between the covers of a book is another. Although in virtually every meaningful way I have moved past Jerry Lewis—the nightmares, the daily concern with book sales and his health, the sense that our lives and careers were somehow intertwined—I can never entirely shake him.

Come Labor Day, I am drawn to the telethon like a recovering alcoholic who can't resist thumbing through a wine list. When word of another ill-tempered, politically incorrect Lewisian outburst hits the news wire, I gobble it up, immediately tracing in my mind connections to similar faux pas of decades past. I meet people—some quite famous—whose own attraction to Lewis makes them eager to ask questions and share stories. Old acquaintances tell me, "I was thinking of you the other day," and then describe flipping channels to a half-remembered Lewis film or a bit of the telethon. Strange—and some *deeply* strange—people call or write to share their passions; thanks to Jerry, indirectly, I will never again have my home number listed in the phone book.

Writing a book is always an ordeal: I know that now for certain with two others behind me. But writing *King of Comedy: The Life and Art of Jerry Lewis* was, I think, a unique burden, conditioned by the still-evolving and potent impact of my subject in the living world and by the fascinating, bizarre, magnetic hold that Jerry—and the image and idea of Jerry—still has on so many people.

When I first chose to write about Lewis in mid-1992, it was because I couldn't interest anyone in publishing a book about Pedro Almodovar. One New York publisher liked my clippings and tried to interest me instead in writing one about Spencer Tracy. Rather than respond with a flat-out no, I thought it would be smart to counteroffer some other names and started searching around for suitable subjects: movie folk who intrigued me but who'd never been given the full biographical treatment. I was exploring the possibility of some personal favorites— Peter Lorre, John Garfield, Peter O'Toole—when a little birdie trilled the name "Jerry Lewis" in my ear.

I presently discovered that there had been no book at all on Jerry since his 1982 autobiography *Jerry Lewis in Person*, and none before that other than the dubious 1974 Arthur Marx twin bio of Jerry and Dean Martin, *Everybody Loves Somebody Sometime (Especially Himself)*, and that fine bit of paperback reportage from 1964, Richard Gehman's *That Kid*. I wasn't then nor had I ever really been a tremendous fan of Jerry Lewis—a year or so earlier, in fact, as senior editor of *American Film*, I had rejected a proposed article about him. But I knew he was a plenty ripe subject for a book. Off the top of my head, I could list a half dozen or more things about Jerry that would make fascinating research and reading and, I reckoned, a suitable backbone for a biography: the Borscht Belt, slapstick comedy, Martin and Lewis, the early auteur years, the telethon, *The Day the Clown Cried* (1972, unreleased), the aborted Broadway play "Hellzapoppin,'" *The King of Comedy* (1983), and that increasingly unpleasant, slick fellow who popped up now and again alongside David Letterman or Larry King. I reckoned, I told my then agent, we had stumbled onto a gold mine.

Well, there are gold mines and there are gold mines. The people who wanted the Spencer Tracy book took a pass on Jerry, but the next place we went with the concept, St. Martin's Press, thought enough of it to ask to see a proposal and, in early 1993, to offer a modest advance. I was an unemployed freelance writer living with my wife and two kids in a cramped apartment in a new town; I took the job. I'm not sure what St. Martin's had in mind when they commissioned the book—they publish an awful lot of show-business titles of varying size and attitude. But I always knew exactly what *my* intention was: a full-scale, soup-to-nuts, authoritative life with passages of criticism—Richard Ellmann's *James Joyce* recast with Jerry Lewis in the lead. It was a vast and emblematic story I was exploring, I reckoned, and I intended a last-word sort of result. (I was asked to deliver sixty to eighty thousand words—not exactly an all-encompassing length—but fully intended to ignore that limit and, in fact, wrote more than triple the maximum called for in the contract.)

And so began my work, which included library and archive research on both coasts, digging up hard-to-find films, and, of course, making contact with potential interview subjects—a list of colleagues, acquaintances, employees, family members, and business associates, up to and including Jerry himself. A friend of mine was chummy with Suzanne Pleshette and suggested I write her. She, upon receiving my letter, called to speak with me and, among other things, to tell me that she had contacted Jerry to tell him about my project—something I was hoping to put off for a little while longer so as to get myself more steeped in the material before we spoke. Thus warned, I wrote Jerry myself to tell him about me and the book I had in mind.

As I recounted at length in the epilogue to *King of Comedy*, he called, we met, we seemed to get along, we met again, and, in a completely different atmosphere, he like to have chewed my head off. Sitting in close quarters in the salon of his yacht, Sam's Place, he gave me merry hell about my line of questioning (I had asked about his absence from the screen after the debacle of *The Day the Clown Cried* [1972]), about my personal lack of tact and humanity (he dubbed me an "insensitive prick"), and about my professional failings (he seemed to think that hero worship had made it difficult for me to talk with him without being insulting; whatever). He grabbed the cassette out of my tape recorder and told me he'd return it with his tirade erased (he did), and I left, ears ringing, swoony, stunned.

I drove north from San Diego numbed and tingly at once. I had never seen anything like Jerry's behavior—or had I?

It was a few days before the feeling of déjà vu took a shape that I could recognize: I realized that I had lived through a scene from *The King of Comedy* (1983), the one about halfway through the film when Jerry—playing a Jerry and wearing his own clothes and telling anecdotes from his own life and tending his own dog—lets loose on the presuming schmuck Rupert Pupkin (Robert De Niro) and chases him from his Long Island mansion. Rupert has insanely thought that he'd been invited to the house to work on his comedy material; a mortified, pissed-off Jerry has been summoned from the golf course to chase the intruder away, leading to one of the great angry outbursts in the movies: "I made a mistake," Rupert wheedles, chastened. "So did Hitler!" Jerry bellows back, acting from a place deeper in his thorax than he ever had before or afterward—thoroughly chilling stuff.

The legend of the making of that scene, as attested to by Jerry and director Martin Scorsese, is that De Niro had spent the morning baiting Jerry with anti-Semitic remarks, trying to coax something sincerely angry out of him, working him toward a climax that was as real as the little details of Jerry's life—such as the childhood photo on the mantelpiece—that Scorsese had used for verisimilitude and to make the veteran comic comfortable in a substantial straight role. As so often in real life, when the thin membrane of his defensiveness was punctured, Jerry responded by comparing the person who made him uncomfortable to a Nazi. And like so many things in the film, the shouting was nauseatingly real: "Jerry has three sets of teeth," a journalist ready to interview him was once warned, and, like poor, deluded Rupert, I certainly felt I'd been nipped by all of them.

But Rupert is crazy—criminal, even—a dingbat loner who resorts to a felony as a means of getting a foot in the door of showbiz. I was merely a writer trying to tell the world—or remind it—that Jerry Lewis was a figure worth its regard. Had I been so awful as all that? Or had a lifetime of pokes and prods by a largely condescending press conditioned him to lash out with peremptory strikes at the merest whiff of negativity? I soon had lunch with the fellow who provided my introduction to Suzanne Pleshette, and he told me, more or less, that being hollered at by Jerry was a good thing: "You'll hear a lot of bad stories about him," he said, roughly (he grew up in a showbiz family during Jerry's heyday and must've heard plenty), "and now you'll have a better idea if they're true or not."

And that was more or less accurate. I came across a lot of stuff about Jerry over the next couple years—some of it laudatory, some of it scandalous—and developed what I felt was a fairly trustworthy internal Geiger counter for what was true and what wasn't. Astounding revelations and charges came from odd places, and my instinctive reactions to them on first hearing proved more and more accurate as the months and years of research and writing went by.

In fact, I developed an unofficial protocol for verifying the claims of interview subjects or some of the more scurrilous printed materials I discovered—a system the efficacy of which was borne out by the extensive legal review that the manuscript underwent prior to publication: thirty-five hours on the phone with a nit-picking libel lawyer that resulted, for the most part, in cutting or significantly rewording material that was potentially hurtful to *other people*; most of what I had to say about Jerry stood up to severe scrutiny.

And, of course, severe scrutiny was called for: Jerry had made it clear to me in our final phone conversations (the last parting dance steps after his tirade on the yacht) that he would hold me liable for besmirching his name, and he put St. Martin's on similar notice. (At the same time, after cutting me off, he continued to give his approval to presumably trusted friends whom I approached for interviews; predictably, most—but not all—of what they had to say was favorable.)

I went ahead researching and writing under a couple of threatening clouds. There was the sheer difficulty of producing a first book and the anxiety of working on deadline for money (for none of which I expected or received anybody's sympathy); but there was also the grotesque burden of waking up every morning and spending the day thinking about someone who'd caused me real pain. I knew I had to keep my personal biases—and I'm still not entirely sure what they are—out of the text; indeed, I felt that the marshaling of oceans of data was the only way to hold back raw opinions. I remember telling someone that I felt entitled to speak my mind out loud once for every dozen factual discoveries. But given the frame of mind in which I lived those months, the responsibility to present something like a blank face to the world was a tremendous challenge.

The book was finally published in the spring of 1996—almost three years after Jerry and I last spoke.

Reviews appeared in a surprising number of high-profile publications: *Time*, the *New York Times*, *USA Today*, the *Los Angeles Times*, the *Boston Globe*, and so on. (An editor friend had assured me early in my process that every showbiz journalist in America would like to write a Jerry Lewis story and my book would be the occasion for them to break down their editors' resistance: canny fellow.) Virtually all of what was written stressed at some point the very issue that most concerned me: fairness. To a one, critics were satisfied that I had given Jerry his due and then some, even with the provocation to trash him that he gave me.

"Spot-check him on individual topics," wrote the *New York Times*, in a typical evaluation, "and you find the author striving to be scrupulously fair." (My favorite variation on this theme was published by *Screw*, which I didn't even know was still in existence, much less in the business of reviewing books: "A remarkably fair portrait of a great American asshole," declared its critic, a sentiment that I bootlessly urged St. Martin's to use in advertising or at least on the paperback edition.)

Jerry, naturally, didn't concur with these assessments. His first response was to wag a finger at my publishers, however cryptically: he forwarded to my editor a copy of *my* original letter to *him*, with various of my statements—presumably the ones he felt I'd violated—highlighted.

Then I heard from him, in a fashion.

One day in May, a FedEx envelope arrived at my home. It was postmarked Las Vegas, but within it was another envelope postmarked Akron, Ohio. In that envelope was a letter from a physician in Lawrence, Kansas, to Jerry. It seems that Jerry, who was engaged in his nationwide tour of "Damn Yankees," had brought his wife to see this doctor for treatment, had paid with a personal check for $93, and had then rolled on to Ohio and other points. The doctor was writing to tell Jerry that he wouldn't be cashing the check but was rather having it framed "as a momento [*sic*] of someone who not only is a celebrity but also a 'star' in the world of humanity."

Jerry made a copy of the letter and then—in an idiosyncratic typescript familiar to me from having read scores of his memos in the papers he donated to the University of Southern California—typed out the following message at the bottom (all punctuation and spacing as they appeared):

MR.LEVY
ISN'T LIFE WONDERFUL—
HOW DIFFERENT PEOPLE-
HAVE DIFFERENT PERCEPTIONS OF ONE ANOTHER—
I AM TRULY BLESSED—
WHAT HAVE YOU ACCOMPLISHED ??
JL.

I was, naturally, dumbfounded. The image of the man sitting in a hotel suite or dressing room in the Midwest, receiving a letter that most of us would regard as a nice compliment, then thinking something like "That fucking Shawn Levy! I'll show *him*" and dashing off this note and sending it to his Las Vegas office for forwarding to me— well, it was about the damnedest thing I could imagine. I had suffered nightmares of Jerry pulling up in front of my house in a rented Lincoln Town Car and trying to punch me in the nose, but this! It made me feel as if I had only begun to scratch the surface of his neuroses and paranoia in the book; I couldn't imagine that it would ever end. Would Jerry forward *every* praising letter he received? And for how long?

In all other respects, though, the "Damn Yankees" tour, which had preceded publication of the book and coincided with and continued on well past the publicity tour I did for it, was a boon. Jerry, despite himself, sold books wherever he went. In addition to the admirable job that St. Martin's and its publicists did in beating the drum and generating press, I heard from journalists in California, Colorado, North Carolina, and Florida who had asked Jerry about the book, gotten a rise out of him, and written about it. Inevitably, I was assured by the publishers, books sold in those cities.

Typical was Jerry's appearance in my own hometown, Portland, Oregon. He gave a press conference to local print and electronic media. (I didn't have the stomach to attend.) Someone brought up the topic of me and the book, and Jerry lit up, accusing me of being, among other things, "tasteless, untalented, and insensitive." His attack made the TV news and the papers. Sales shot up immediately at Powell's, the city's biggest bookstore.

But never did I or my publisher hear from a lawyer suggesting that the book was libelous or that the unpleasantries it detailed were not true. The book may or may not have been biased and may or may not have been fair; Jerry might feel entitled to malign me in public or declare, as he did through his son, Chris, on his own Web site, that the book was "10 percent" factual; but the reality was that the book was— with two or three minor errors that had nothing to do with Jerry's personal life—scrupulously truthful, not to mention the first full-length work ever published in this country to argue seriously for Jerry's contributions to American culture.

But whether I told the truth or not or was sufficiently laudatory had seemingly nothing to do with another phenomenon, one I had passingly intuited during the years I worked on the book: the untapped, even maniacal passion for Jerry Lewis out in the great wide world.

From the moment the book appeared I started getting the most astounding letters and phone calls: fans, acquaintances, relatives, and ex-employees seemed to latch onto me as a chance to unburden themselves of their experience of Jerry. There were maybe twenty—hardly a groundswell—but the tenor!

There was a woman who claimed to have been raised by Jerry's business manager—and who certainly had some unique knowledge about Jerry's personal and professional lives—and who would call my house to read passages of the book to me and amplify and expand on them. Sometimes she called late in the night Pacific Time; uninterrupted, she could yatter for thirty to forty minutes.

There was the grandson of a comic legend—a performer whom Jerry had greatly admired during his own rise—who phoned with hair-raising stories about Jerry's sex life and its impact on his household. There was a scary smack of truth to his claims, but even *listening* to them made me feel like calling a libel lawyer to confess myself.

Another man with ties to the Lewis family called with similarly disturbing stories along the same lines—family secrets, resentments, grudges—again with a nauseating aura of credibility.

Collectors rang seeking rarities—including the tape of Jerry chewing me out. Academics with specific interest in Jerry's work called for help tracking down this or that bit of material I'd uncovered or reported on. One or two people phoned just to comment on the book itself—a grateful respite.

And it wasn't only kooks, cultists, and scholars whom the book drew out.

In my newspaper work I would occasionally come across Hollywood professionals who knew the book and had stories or insights about Jerry to share: the directors Martin Scorsese and Richard Linklater, comic Harry Shearer, and Tom Hanks, who told me that all of his comedian friends had read the book and that Martin Short did a knockout impression of Jerry throwing me off his boat. Other people in the business, knowing I had written about Jerry, would let me know how they felt with a knowing look and a pointed "You know how he is. . . ." (Alas, I did.)

I began to develop the impression—not unusual among biographers, I'm sure—that Jerry and I had become like Holmes and Moriarty, hands wrapped around each other's throats, tumbling over the Reichenbach Falls, linked inextricably forever. "When he dies," I would moan to friends, "people will think of me, and when I die, people will think of him."

Of course, that was an overstatement. Like any first-time author, I was living through an exaggerated impression of the impact my book had made on the world. After months of isolation in a room with a pile of research materials, a computer, and one's own chaotic thoughts, the jolt of air that is publication can impart an illusory sense of omnipotence—as well as a sense that you've been exposed naked to the world's caprices, obsessions, and prejudices. In time I came to understand that what I endured was a mere glimpse of the sort of publicness that people like Jerry live constantly and utterly within. No one was ever going to write a biography of *me*, but I had a wee taste of what it might be like—and I didn't care for it. My wife and I had our telephone number changed and unlisted, and I stopped returning phone calls from people who found me at the newspaper and claimed they "just had to" talk to me about Jerry Lewis.

And there was another lesson. Through the time I was working on the book, I had a specific interest in the phenomenon of Jerry's French reputation, probably the single biggest cliché about both the career of Jerry Lewis and the cultural tastes of the Gallic people. For sure, I thought when dreaming at the keyboard of the riches that would accrue to me as the result of my efforts, I would swim in royalty checks made out in French francs.

Fat chance.

In part, *King of Comedy* was too big a work—about 250,000 words—on too cultlike a subject to interest other publishers, even those in England who didn't have to pay a translation fee on top of buying the publication rights.

But in part, sadly, too, nobody in France was interested in publishing it because the French had given themselves over to other tastes, other fashions, in the decades since crowning Jerry "Le Roi du Crazy." Just as Jerry would tell the world that the French mania for him was nothing compared to the love he enjoyed from Swedes, Belgians, Brazilians, and Japanese, so did the French seem to want to hide their much-belittled national enthusiasm for him behind an arras. Jerry might be a Chevalier of the Legion of Honor—a living national treasure, as he likes to remind people—but the people who accorded him the honor didn't seem to want to pay for the privilege of reading about him.

*King of Comedy*, I note from perusing Amazon.com, is currently out of print; the royalty checks (talk about modest!) have long stopped coming. Jerry still pops into my head: mouthing off in the press about lady comedians or the people who have the nerve to question his fund-raising techniques; announcing this or that movie or TV deal in Army Archerd's *Variety* column; inhabiting the upper reaches of the cable dial in performances that span fifty years; and, like the tax man, Santa Claus, and the prophet Elijah, making a reliably annual appearance in homes all over North America via the telethon.

My attitude when I encounter these various incarnations of the man is more and more amused, in a way that has a small savor of beneficence. A half decade, two books, and countless life experiences separate me from working on Jerry Lewis, and I no longer feel tethered, Prometheus-like, to him: no bad dreams for years! But there's still this nagging thing I have in mind, a residual doubt, characteristic, for all I know, of all biographers or maybe unique to anyone who tries to pin down so protean a character. I experienced some close encounters with someone, became familiar with the work and chronological career of someone, tracked down details of the life of someone, tied myself— emotionally, intellectually, financially, and by reputation—to someone, and I still really can't say who I was dealing with or if it was even a single human being. The scrim of individual identity, even more than that of fame, keeps the essential Jerry—if there is such a critter—at an impassable distance.

He remains beguilingly, mockingly apart, outside, distant: part ambitious kid; part comic innovator; part savvy Hollywood player; part pioneering director; part faded movie star; part humanitarian; part son, husband, father, lover, employee, business partner, boss, elder statesman, crank, crab, and icon—a man like all men, maybe, and yet undeniably one of a kind.

# PART II

# JERRY LEWIS, FACES OFF

A badge of maturity: Jerry Lewis (l.) becomes an Eskimo holding the halibut both he and Johnny Depp (r.), also an Eskimo now, have longed for inside the eponymous dream sequence of *Arizona Dream* (Emir Kusturica, Warner Bros., 1993). Frame enlargement.

# 3

# Dreaming of Jerry Lewis's Arizona Dream

Andrew Horton

I did it because it was off the wall.
> —Jerry Lewis on why he appeared in *Arizona Dream* (Levy 1996, 457)

## HOLLYWOOD MEETS THE BALKANS

Fade in on Jerry Lewis in one of the most unusual films he ever made:

It's an Arizona roadside landscape seen in a haze from a passing car.

In the distance we see him, in his late sixties, doing a little comic shuffle along a line of Cadillacs mounted on posts like some kind of kitsch roadside art similar to Stanley Marsh III's "Cadillac Ranch," ten cars sticking out of the ground along one Texas road. Jerry shuffles along with a broom in hand, doing a little strut as if this were a vaudeville stage routine or a comic dance number in one of his early Martin and Lewis films. The total effect is engaging and comic and yet strange and dreamlike as well. Is this real or some kind of surreal moment?

Question: If you could name one film that seemed to be a Hollywood comedy shot by a kind of Salvador Dali from the Balkans, starring an aging comic playing a Cadillac salesman, what would it be? The answer is the subject of my investigation and perhaps the most neglected of all of Jerry Lewis's works: Emir Kusturica of the former Yugoslavia's carnivalesque *Arizona Dream* (1993). The scene described above is Jerry's first appearance in this unusual opus in Lewis's long

43

career. "Arizona" is a real place, but "dream" suggests that "other" world. Thus the title clues us to the mixture of moods and modes, tones and textures, genres and genders that this unlikely Balkan Hollywood movie serves up.

Lewis was sixty-seven at the time he signed on with Bosnian-Yugoslav director Kusturica to play Arizonan Leo Sweetie, who tries to sign up his nephew from New York, Axel (Johnny Depp), to get into the car-sales business. Comedy and pathos mix with realism and surrealism in this engaging but unlikely tale woven by Kusturica with the help of an American screenwriter, David Atkins. "I like Emir so goddamn much," Lewis recalled several years afterward. "He's such a sweet man—thirty-five years old, energetic, enthusiastic, wonderful man" (Levy 1996, 457).

My thesis is simple: Lewis clearly enjoyed his involvement with *Arizona Dream* because it allowed him to stretch beyond the "nutty" professors, bellboys, and other wacky male figures he had made a living playing onscreen. Jerry's role here is a mixture of a crazy uncle, a father figure, a hero, and a "holy fool" in a film that is much closer to being a Balkan absurdist comedy than a Hollywood slapstick farce like the comedies Lewis became famous for. His biographer Shawn Levy agrees that in this phase of his career Lewis "was pushing toward a stage in his life when he could truly play a living legend, adding grace and weight to projects without the onus of carrying them on his back" (458). We can point to a few other films that have been part of this phase, especially Martin Scorsese's *The King of Comedy* (1983), which may well have been the "prototype" that inspired Kusturica to cast Lewis in a nonscrewball role ten years later.

Before going any further, however, we need to suggest a working definition of *Balkan*. We are certainly speaking of those countries that geographically exist in an area of southeastern Europe stretching from the former Yugoslavia to Turkey and including Bulgaria, Romania, Greece, Albania, and the various countries that now make up the former Yugoslavia. Yet the term *Balkan* means much more than a location on a map, as film scholar Dina Iordanova has explained in her recent study *Cinema of Flames: Balkan Film, Culture and the Media*. According to Iordanova, "The Balkans is not a geographical concept but one that denotes a cultural entity, widely defined by shared Byzantine, Ottoman and Austro-Hungarian legacies and by the specific marginal positioning of the region in relation to the western part of the European continent" (2001, 6). Put simply for our discussion, the cinemas of these countries reflect a complex set of cultural influences that have meant they have a very different look to them than films produced by Hollywood. Even more specifically, we will see that Kusturica's cinematic vision is "Balkan" in its unusual mixture of realism and surrealism, pathos and comedy, and, finally, a sense of triumph over all adversity in a manner that acknowledges that "real" life offers no such victory.

For example, in Emir Kusturica's well-celebrated film about the clash of Stalinism with a freer sense of "third world" Communism during the 1950s, *When Father Was Away on Business* (1985), the young male protagonist "triumphs" over a series of disasters in his life in Sarajevo by walking in his sleep and, in the final shot, dreaming of sailing out over the city, past all the problems he has ever faced, joyously rising, rising, rising.

We can now return to Jerry Lewis's pleasure in being in a film in which he did not have to "carry the whole show." This situation is exactly the case for *Arizona Dream*, since Johnny Depp's character, Axel Blackmar, is our main protagonist. In fact, Axel sets up the whole film, for what we literally see is his story, told in voiceover to "us." But what becomes clear long before the film is over is that, as Axel's crazy uncle, Leo (Jerry Lewis) is the "hero" of Axel's life and thus the spiritual main protagonist of the film, even if he is only onscreen about 15 of the 142 minutes of the released American version.

Kusturica begins and ends the film as an Inuit (Eskimo) dream within Johnny Depp's sleeping mind and restless soul. The "real" story of *Arizona Dream*, which takes place in New York and Arizona, is inseparably touched and fused with this bracketing dream, thus becoming Kusturica's one "Hollywood" story that reflects what I have called "Balkan magic realism" (Horton 1988, 72).

Axel prepares us for this mixture of dream and reality in his opening voiceover monologue:

> Daydreaming was a long way from life's truths, but what's the point in breathing if someone already tells you the difference between an apple and a bicycle. If I bite a bicycle and ride an apple then I'll know the difference. Thinking about what to do makes you more tired than the actual doing.

This speech would already help us understand the title of the film, but Kusturica has scripted a deeper insight into this complex mixture of dream and reality that unfolds before us:

> I remember my father once said that if you ever wanted to look at someone's soul, look into their dreams and that would allow you to have mercy for those swimming in deeper shit than your own.

As we shall see, what Axel has just described is what is actually revealed onscreen; for it is Leo who is clearly in deeper "shit" than Axel.

Finally, Axel makes the film very personal as he establishes a direct relationship with us:

> My name is Axel Blackmar and I work for the Department of Fish and Game. Most people think I count fish but I don't, I look at them. I look at their souls. And read their dreams. Then I let them into my dreams. People think that fish are stupid. But I was always sure that they weren't because they know when to be quiet, and it's people that are stupid. They pretend they know everything and don't need to think. Sometimes I look into a fish's eyes and see my whole life. I love them for that.

Lewis's expressed admiration for Kusturica would, I suggest, involve the director's all-embracing vision as expressed by Axel. "Joy includes everything: happiness and sorrow," Kusturica has said (Horton 1988, 64). And each of his films has reflected a wide spectrum of emotions and structure. Before we turn to a closer look at Lewis's character and performance in *Arizona Dream*, it is helpful to understand both how "Balkan" this film is and how typical it is of Kusturica's work.

*The Time of the Gypsies* (1989) won many international awards as a moving, hilarious, and absurd comic drama based on true stories of Yugoslav gypsies today, who sell their children to make money. Kusturica was part of the late 1960s and early 1970s generation of Yugoslav filmmakers who studied film at the famous Czech National Film-Art-Music University of Performing Arts and Theatre (FAMU) film school in Prague and managed to make films that not only reflect their troubled culture but also wink to a world audience with cinematic references "borrowed" from the cinemas of the world (Horton 1998, 173).

That said, *The Time of the Gypsies* blends a true story with a "makeover" of Francis Ford Coppola's *Godfather I* and *II* (1972, 1974). A young gypsy man, Perhan, who comes increasingly to resemble Al Pacino in Coppola's works, leaves his native Yugoslav town to work for a gypsy "godfather" in Italy. Central to the story is a young man coming of age who has a love-hate relationship with a kind of uncle or father figure. As in South American "magic realism" in the fiction of writers such as Gabriel García Márquez, a Balkan surrealism exists in this and other Kusturica films as objects and images fly through the air, including images of a dead mother and a dead pet turkey. By film's end, neither love nor his chosen illegal "godfather" business fare well, as our "Pacino" figure is murdered and his young son steals coins from his dead father at the funeral.

Finally, one should realize that Kusturica's films elicit a lot of laughter as well as tears. As he explains above, such a double vision of "joy" is very "Balkan." Even psychologists suggest that laughter can be a healthy and transcending way to deal with pain and horror (Horton 2000, 15). Thus, while most people living outside the Balkan nations know only the chilling images of wars and murders in Bosnia, Kosovo, and Macedonia in recent years, those familiar with the poetry, music, drama, art, and cinema of this area between western Europe and the East recognize how much Emir Kusturica belongs to a tradition of comic dramas or dramatic comedies that manage to transcend the horrors of "reality."

*Arizona Dream* is directly related to all we have just mentioned. There is Axel's pain at having lost both parents in a wreck in which Uncle Leo was the driver, generating at the center of the film a huge love-confusion relationship between Axel and Leo. Leo has basically raised Axel as his son after his parents died. But there is also conflict, clearly in large part inspired by Leo's guilt at having—albeit accidentally—caused the death of Axel's folks. And there is a sense of magic realism, since the whole film grows out of and returns to Axel's dreams of an Eskimo father and son.

Add the fact that *Arizona Dream* is full of cinematic allusions to other works—ranging from the classic French short *The Red Balloon* (1956), *Gone with the Wind* (1939), and Alfred Hitchcock's *North by Northwest* (1959) to Robert Flaherty's *Nanook of the North* (1922) and old Hollywood silent comedies. Most important, however, is the casting of Jerry Lewis; for while we get to see quite a modified version of Jerry's usual screen persona, the film nevertheless has moments when Jerry gets to be the Jerry we all know and appreciate. Faye Dunaway is cast as Axel's love interest, Elaine Stalker, a crazed woman old enough to be his mother (a point that is mentioned several times). In the same way that we as viewers "negotiate" our memories of a much younger Jerry with the aging car salesman we see before us in Kusturica's film, so we remember the Faye Dunaway of *Bonnie and Clyde* (1967) and other, earlier works as we apprehend this woman before us, obsessed with flying.

## A COMIC FISH-OUT-OF-WATER TALE

Our first real look at Lewis makes us laugh out loud. Jerry comes running down the steps of his pale pink Arizona hacienda, grinning from ear to ear, dressed in his underwear, white cowboy boots, and a half-finished strawberry-pink tuxedo top, with a harried tailor trying to keep up with him while measuring and pinning. But Jerry, looking completely absurd, is in a hurry to greet Axel, who has just arrived from New York. Thus Kusturica starts us off with a very familiar pratfall and slapstick figure. This is Jerry the clown.

Greetings with Axel are exchanged, and the dialogue brings us up to speed on Jerry's upcoming wedding and his desire for Axel to be his best man. It's a theme of this film and of all of Kusturica's works that most relationships are mismatched. This is certainly true of Jerry and his bride-to-be (played by a sexy Paulina Porizkova), who is young enough to be his daughter and clearly would be a better match for Johnny Depp. That, as we have noted, Johnny Depp's diegetic girlfriend is old enough to be his mother plays off well with this theme that everyone in the film appears to be a fish out of water. Axel himself is such a creature, to be sure, and is identified as such when first we meet him as a young man with a special affinity to fish out of water, since it is his job to haul them up from the local wetlands and measure them for the City of New York.

Kusturica makes this literally and visually clear, as an Arctic fish does apparently "fly" through America, at least in Axel's dreams. A flying halibut becomes the central motif for the film, with all the possible symbolic and religious echoes it may arouse in a viewer. Halibut means "holy," for instance, and Christ was, after all, "a fisher of men." Of course, the average viewer of the film is not likely to pick up on this symbolic "echo" that goes throughout the film, but the fish is a holy dimension in Kusturica's tale, "sailing" beyond all the problems and tensions that humans create through the narrative. This theme is also amplified in one of the songs in the magnificent soundtrack by the much-admired Bosnian composer Goran Bregovic, in which a repeated line is "The fish knows EVERYTHING."

Jerry Lewis is directly linked to all these playful and suggestive elements in the final dream sequence of the film, as he becomes an Eskimo holding the fish both he and Johnny Depp, also an Eskimo now, have longed for.

A consideration of Jerry in this closing scene can clarify our understanding of his role in the rest of the film. By the end of this Balkan Hollywood tale, Jerry has died and young Axel is totally depressed. But that's only the "real" story in the film! Axel breaks into Leo's showroom late at night some time after the funeral, the place now something of a wasteland, with its great glass windows shattered. He speaks to us again in an off-camera voice:

> I couldn't say life was beautiful anymore, and all I could hope for was that the Eskimo boy in my dreams would rush out to me and hug me. And even though I no longer felt like a fish and realized I knew nothing, I was happy to be alive.

At this point Axel has climbed into the couch shaped from one of Leo's Cadillacs inside the showroom. But Axel suddenly sees a red balloon pass in and land on him—the same red balloon we saw being made from the intestines of a halibut fish in the opening credit sequence. Dream and reality thus finally fuse in Axel's imagination as this "balloon fish" floats into his vision.

There is the sound of wind in Leo's office, howling mournfully, and a red light, and then the camera begins to rise through smoke and windy clouds as we journey back to the frozen land of the Eskimos. We now hear Jerry's voice saying, "*Honika veeki!*" which a subtitle translates as "What a wonderful fish!"

Axel's and Emir Kusturica's "happy ending" now joyfully begins, as we see Jerry Lewis and Johnny Depp as Eskimos huddled around an ice hole, fishing. It is impossible here to convey how funny and yet how touching this dream ending is. Jerry with his hooded parka is a perfect Eskimo Yoda–guru–father figure for Depp, who is the eager young

Eskimo son-student-youth, also hooded in his parka under the bright Arctic sunlight. Jerry says he will catch the fish, and then he attempts to explain to Depp why both eyes of the fish are on the same side of its head. Jerry gives us his idea that the eyes are originally on two sides until the fish becomes an adult. At that point, Eskimo Jerry explains, one eye moves over to join the other: "It's a badge of maturity!" chirps Jerry as Depp nods eagerly.

They catch the fish, and Jerry hits it with a hammer to kill it. One of their sled dogs watches them carefully, and Jerry speaks more about what the moving of the eyes might mean as he holds this huge flat fish in his arms. Just as the fish suggests something holy, the dog's piercing and seemingly understanding glare suggests that this is no ordinary dog. In fact, remembering the beginning dream of the dog as savior of its master, we sense the dog is also a "more-than-natural" force. Suddenly, to Leo and Axel's wonder and amazement, the fish sets off out of his arms, flying off into the distance.

We end this Balkan fairy tale not with Jerry Lewis or Johnny Depp but with a flying fish. It is a vision of triumph and beauty, and as the film's title suggests, it is a dream. In reality, Leo has died; Axel has split up with Faye Dunaway; and Dunaway's obsessed daughter, Grace (Lili Taylor), has committed suicide. But we must emphasize again that such a transcendent ending—the Eskimo dream sequence—is in keeping with a Balkan sense of triumph over adversity, a sense in which memory of past joys is not obliterated by experiences of present tragedy. The Yugoslav film voted by the Yugoslav critics as the best film of the twentieth century in their country was Slobodan Sijan's *Who Is Singing Over There?* (1980), which is an ensemble social comedy about a bus ride through Serbia in 1941 that ends with everyone except two gypsy singers dying as the Nazis bomb Belgrade (Horton 1999, B11). To relate the plot makes it sound tragic, and yet the laughter at every screening I've ever been to is very real indeed. *Arizona Dream* reflects such a surreal cultural as well as cinematic vision.

## JERRY LEWIS AS A "HOLY FOOL"

One of the real strengths of Jerry's role in Kusturica's film is that he becomes much more than Jerry Lewis doing his old tricks. He becomes, in fact, a "holy fool," a figure unknown in the United States but thoroughly understood in Orthodox Christian countries, including the former Yugoslavia, Russia, Greece, and other Balkan nations. Such figures are those persons who appear to live in their own unique oneiric world and who thus seem to be "touched by God—half crazy and half admirable" (Horton and Brashinsky 1992, 188). Once again, as with the flying fish, an element of spirituality crosses with humor as such a tradition acknowledges that laughter can be inspired by a higher spirit.

A scene soon after we first see Jerry/Leo in his half wedding suit brings out this dimension. Leo confesses to Axel that he not only brought him out to Arizona to join in the wedding celebration but also wishes to draft him into the Cadillac business. Yet Axel makes it clear that he does not wish to sell cars. Then Leo has a monologue that suggests how far gone he is:

> You're damn right, and that's success. And in order to obtain that success, you have to sell cars. Do you realize my father had the first Cadillac dealership in Arizona in 1914. His dream was to sell as many cars as he could and to stack them one on top of the other until he could climb up and reach the moon, isn't that beautiful?

Axel points out that the cars would topple over before they reached the moon. Leo responds, "Yeah, that's what I told him, but he wanted me in the business." When Axel repeats that he just doesn't want to sell cars, Leo looks depressed.

What is revealed is that Leo's father must have been pretty crazy himself, as he brought Leo into his "dream" and judged it as "beautiful." At this early point of the narrative, we know that Axel is a dreamer, too, but the two dreams—an Eskimo dream and a Cadillac dealership dream—simply don't mesh.

We wouldn't necessarily call Leo a holy fool if this were the only suggestion of his deviation from what most would consider to be reality. But as Leo lies dying at the end of the film, he tells Axel that he is climbing the cars and should soon reach the moon. A clown is silly and funny because of what she or he does physically. What the concept of holy fool introduces is that this individual is both comic and touching because he sees the world differently. As Leo is dying, he is clearly in another reality, joining the dream his father passed down to him, as impossible and improbable as that might be. At least in his dying moments, Leo is finally fulfilling his father's wishes.

In an eerie but touching way, one feels Kusturica has brought out a dimension of Jerry Lewis's own personality for which he has not been able often to find a screen equivalent: the holy fool. Note that the term embraces the whole spectrum of the human experience. Lewis's career has been built on being the goofy fool, full of jokes and physical comedy. But while a comedian like Chaplin had the chance to use close-ups of his sad face to suggest that deeper "spiritual" or emotional side to the Little Tramp, the "Jerry" clown was never really given the chance to go beyond pratfalls. My strong feeling is that *Arizona Dream*, even more than *King of Comedy*, should be the film that those who have dismissed Lewis as less than a major comic should see. And it is the "Balkan touch" that Kusturica brings to the project that has, I feel, "liberated" Lewis and allowed him to touch us as holy fools do: there but for the grace of God go you and I.

But two more dreams in the film appear as "real" yet are, in retrospect, Axel's imagination once more. The first is the seemingly "real" scene of Leo dancing by the mounted roadside Cadillacs, and the second is the rising of the ambulance with the dying Leo into the night sky, headed for the moon. The arc between the two is important for gauging Axel's changing relationship to his uncle. The first "vision" of Leo is one of a clownish figure who seems totally unaware of anyone or anything around him as he dances among cars that are clearly not leading him into the sky, as his father suggested they could if stacked one on top of the other. Yet the second vision is Axel's effort—in his imagination and fantasy—to give this dying loved one the wish fulfillment he never had. We have no "classical" cutaway to Axel "dreaming" to explain the *E.T.*-like shot of the ambulance rising into the sky. However, given all the dream references throughout the narrative from the beginning, such a reading seems reasonable, even inescapable: Axel is dreaming his uncle to the heavens.

## JERRY AS HERO FIGURE

Johnny Depp in voiceover once more tells us that Leo was his childhood hero. And it is important that this information reaches us in the scene immediately following the prenuptial scene described above, when Axel and Leo are watching old black-and-white home movies. What we see on the screen is Leo clowning and mugging for the camera and literally taking some falls as he plays with a very young Axel—that is, the Old Jerry doing the same tricks and pratfalls he used to do in his early films. We also see that both Leo and Axel are moved almost to tears recapturing, as movie viewers themselves, such happy days. Axel explains, "One thing I was sure of, my Uncle Leo was definitely the hero of my childhood. The smell of that Old Spice cologne carried me back further into that lost childhood than the old home movies did."

Then the next few lines confirm the kind of holy fool–hero figure that Leo became for the youth. According to Axel, "Leo was the last dinosaur with that cheap cologne, and he believed in the American dream. I was crazy about him because he always believed in a miracle. He always looked like a ten-year-old boy whose sleeves were too long."

At this point, Leo watches a younger version of himself hugging Axel. It is telling that there is no footage of Axel's father hugging him. Thus "old movies" reveal truth: Leo was and remains Axel's hero. And yet we return to the fact that Axel's parents died in an accident caused by his "hero." Nothing is simple in the Balkans or in *Arizona Dream*. Near the end of the scene Axel tells us, "Leo could never shake his guilt of what happened six years ago. Four days after the funeral I caught the first train to New York. And if anyone asks now why I don't get up and leave now, it's because you can't say 'No' to your childhood hero. One thing I was sure of, I was never going to become my uncle, and I was never going to sell Cadillacs."

Leo followed his father's dream about selling cars, and it basically drove him crazy. Axel has learned from this. He can see Leo as his hero without needing to imitate him. Yet, to return to the ending of the film, while Axel is unwilling to sell cars as his uncle wishes him to do, he nevertheless gives him a higher honor, making him his father and teacher in his dream.

This celebration of Leo as Eskimo father-hero is clear to us, for Jerry Lewis does not appear in the opening Eskimo dream that sets up the film. What we see there is an Eskimo father with a sled and his children running around. Then, the father with his sled team falls into freezing water as the lead dog and the whole sled break through the ice. Yet the father does manage to catch a large halibut. Then we see the father warming himself by a fire and drinking some booze. Quite drunk, he falls over and is about to die but is saved by his lead sled dog, who pulls him onto the sled with the fish on top of him. Back in the igloo, the wife revives her husband as a young boy looks on. The father awakens and opens the fish, pulling out the bladder and blowing it up to create a red balloon, which he hands to his son as a gift. As the dream ends and the red balloon begins to float through the sky toward New York City and a sleeping Johnny Depp, we see that the Eskimo's boat in the background is NANOOK 111—a wink to Flaherty's famous documentary about Eskimo life in the 1920s.

The father in this opening dream is a real Eskimo, but he is no hero. He would die if his dog and wife did not save him. Thus yet another transformation has taken place in Kusturica's ending of *Arizona Dream*. Axel transforms this figure into Leo in the final episode, which is literally a dream taking place in his mind while he is in Arizona; hence the title, *Arizona Dream*. The real Leo is dead by film's ending, but Axel gives him lasting life as his Eskimo hero as he captures a fish that, finally, has the sacred power to fly away and leave the humans to do what humans do.

## THE NIGHTMARE OF RELEASING *ARIZONA DREAM*

Jerry Lewis makes it clear in interviews that he enjoyed working with Emir Kusturica and playing Leo Sweetie. But he was also aware of the nightmare that the making and release of the film became. Clearly, the mix of a Hollywood production mentality and a star European director was not a smooth one.

Jerry recounts that Kusturica had a script that was 265 pages long, which after a rewrite emerged as 294 pages (Levy 1996, 457). "It was then," Jerry comments, "they realized there was no fucking way" it could be made. The budget soared from $19 to $32 million, and the studio (Warner Bros.) cut off production before Kusturica was finished shooting. Finally, during the editing process, the film was taken out of Kusturica's hands, and they forced him to cut his original nine-hour version to two hours and forty minutes; but then they cut another twenty minutes, so that the released version was nowhere near what the director wanted it to be.

The result was that the film never got a regular theatrical release. It went straight to video in 1995 after playing a few film festivals. In a sense this makes Jerry Lewis's performance, along with those of Johnny Depp, Faye Dunaway, Vincent Gallo, and Lili Taylor, all the more intriguing. It's not worth going over all the lapses in plot, continuity, and structural logic at this point. The wonder is that the film is as intriguing as it is. And so much of this effect is because Jerry does touch us with his crazy uncle–mad car salesman–holy fool figure. He is onscreen so short a time, and yet each scene counts, so that we do come to sense the holy fool nature of Leo, whether he is dancing with a broom through a line of Cadillacs or watching old home movies with Axel and reliving the past. In short, rather than some kind of has-been, Lewis emerges as an aging man who has never realized his inner dreams.

One viewer expresses his admiration for the film this way:

> The film, at first, absorbs the viewer into a translucent though engaging tale of exploration into the mind and soul. This makes the viewer believe momentarily that the film that they are watching is going to be fanciful and mystic. Hence there at first is no bond between the characters and the viewer. However, reality becomes less and less of a point or actuality in the film as it paces through the lives of the characters centering on Johnny Depp's character. . . . Jerry Lewis also makes the film great. And the sadness at the end is alleviated by the theme that life goes on, almost in circles. To anyone who has not yet been seriously touched by a film, watch this. It might change your mind. (Barclay 1999)

Even a popular critic such as Leonard Maltin gives it a strong rating (two and a half stars), despite its obvious shortcomings given its production difficulties, stating that the film "boasts exceptional performances—one of Lewis's most impressive" (2000, 59).

## LOVE BEYOND SUICIDE: JERRY GIVES UP ON LIFE

*Arizona Dream* is like many contemporary films that mix genres. It has elements of comedy, but it is suffused with the melodrama of individuals who give up on life. Lili Taylor, the daughter of Faye Dunaway, clearly feels she should have been Johnny Depp's lover rather than her mother, and so, in the closing moments, she shoots herself. And Depp plays a game of Russian roulette in an earlier scene, obviously suggesting that his life has touched bottom and he is willing to die. No laughter rings out in these scenes or in Jerry Lewis's overdose suicide.

There is no long speech at Leo's demise. We see the empty bottles and Axel arriving with the ambulance to carry him off. Leo obviously sees himself as a complete failure. He has married a woman young enough to be his daughter, and she has had an affair with Axel's friend (Vincent Gallo). Leo had wanted to help Axel's parents but wound up killing them. And he tried unsuccessfully to rescue Axel from Faye Dunaway.

That failed rescue scene is one of the best Jerry Lewis scenes I can remember. Kusturica shoots in close-up as Jerry sits at a table outside Dunaway's ranch, trying to explain to her why she must let go of Axel. After talking in metaphors about old cars and new, he finally comes out and says, "But you are old enough to be his mother." His face is pudgy, his clothes out of style, and his hair obviously dyed. In short, we feel sorry for this sad and frustrated figure.

Dunaway shoots him a look that could kill and retorts, "But I'm not his mother. I'm his lover. And I must tell you, your nephew is a wild animal in bed. Perhaps he can give you some lessons."

The head-twisting, shoulder-wrenching reaction Jerry gives to this is an amazing piece of acting. At this moment, Jerry Lewis as Leo absolutely conveys his complicated and conflicted love for Axel. Lewis uses all his skill at physical comedy to capture not laughter at this point but inner turmoil. Then Leo lets out, "My reaction is one of regret for my nephew. I had hoped that his sexual awakening would have been with someone who knew the difference between making love and *fucking*." Dunaway then proceeds to knock everything off the table and chase Leo off her property with a shotgun.

Leo has done everything he can, and it hasn't been enough.

In the ambulance scene, a weeping Axel tries to comfort him. He even tells his uncle he will sell cars. It is then that Leo, with an oxygen tube stuck in his nose, shakes his head no and tells his nephew, "Nobody drives the big models anymore."

Axel's reaction is to simply say, "I love you." The scene is held longer than usual to let us take in Jerry dying and Depp crying over this man he loves who has just killed himself. The cut is to the ambulance going down an empty Arizona street and then taking off into the night sky, headed for the moon. We then cut to the next morning and a close-up of Depp waking up in a convertible, the dream of a flying ambulance evaporating in the light of day.

The daily news on television and in print has not brought us many happy stories from the former Yugoslavia, especially during the 1990s. The breakup of the country, the Bosnian and Kosovo wars, and the threatened splintering of the former Yugoslav Republic of Macedonia have left scars that will be slow to heal. The suicide of Leo Sweetie, a Cadillac salesman in an age when no one buys the big models anymore and a man who clearly wanted to be loved by his father and those around him, is clearly a Balkan ending. Yet, once more, Emir Kusturica defines life and joy not just as being one emotion but as embracing a full range; thus a smile and a tear as Depp's loving embrace of his dying uncle helps Jerry feel, at least in his dreams (and in Depp's too), that he is flying toward the heavens.

If Kusturica begins *Arizona Dream* by evoking laughter from his audience when Jerry comes skipping across an Arizona landscape doing a soft-shoe routine with a broom, unaware that his nephew is watching him, he ends Lewis's life within this tale by evoking tears of love from Axel, who is losing the one man he truly admires. It is that stretch between two such opposites that Jerry Lewis bridges in a remarkable performance that deserves more attention than it has received. As Shawn Levy notes of this performance, Lewis "had set out to become Charlie Chaplin and he almost had" (1996, 458).

Now, the tragedies surrounding the terrorists' attacks on September 11, 2001, have added new dimensions to our viewing of *Arizona Dream*: for as Axel begins the film telling us about the soul of fish, we see New York and a glimpse of the twin towers of the World Trade Center behind him. Thus the Eskimo dream at the end, as Jerry Lewis "lives" on, is even more of a triumph against the hardships of realities that have crushed in upon us all since the film was completed.

Lewis's films can be seen as "an assault on American culture and politics, exposing banality that masks more aggressive designs." Prof. Julius Kelp (Jerry Lewis) shelved by his students in *The Nutty Professor* (Jerry Lewis, Paramount, 1963). Frame enlargement.

# 4

# Jerry Agonistes

## An Obscure Object of Critical Desire

Marcia Landy

THOUGH HE WAS a commercially popular film star with Dean Martin in the 1950s and in the 1960s on his own, Jerry Lewis has mainly been relegated to a relatively insignificant position in American film history. Until very recently, North American reviews and critical commentary on his work have been hostile, peremptory, or emphatically dismissive, if not altogether negligible. For example, Richard Kozarski's *Hollywood Directors, 1941–1976* (1977) has no chapter on Jerry Lewis or on Frank Tashlin (with whom Lewis worked extensively). Andrew Sarris, despite his championing of auteurism, held no brief for the French elevation of Lewis to the rank of auteur, his disdain expressed in the hostility with which he dismisses Robert Benayoun, the pioneering French critic to write on the comedian, as "a *Positif* critic who so resembles Jerry Lewis that hero-worship verges on narcissism" (Levy 1996, 333).

In *American Cinema*, in a section titled "Make Way for the Clowns," Sarris compared Lewis unfavorably to Blake Edwards, whose "*The Pink Panther, A Shot in the Dark*, and *What Did You Do in the War, Daddy* are funnier than all the Lewis-Tashlin movies" (1968, 241). Among the twelve reasons for his skepticism about Lewis's "talent as a creator" Sarris listed that Lewis's "aspirations exceed his ability"; that his work reveals a disjunction between a "verbal sophistication in nightclubs and sometimes on television and . . . [a] simpering simplemindedness on screen" (241); and that his comedy lacks "verbal wit" and appeals mainly "to audiences in the sticks and to ungenteel audiences in the verbal slums" (242). Sarris faulted Lewis for his weaknesses of narration and found the "feature-length film an inappropriate vehicle for farce," also commenting that in Lewis's remakes he has played "the innocent" with themes of "effeminacy and transvestitism" (242). Critical as well of Lewis's "conformist, sentimental, and banal dialogue," he suggested that "he has never put one brilliant comedy together from fade-in to fade-out" (244).

In his review of *The Patsy* (1964), Bosley Crowther described the film and Lewis's directing as an "idiot brand of clowning . . . another form of mishmash in which Lewis falls all over himself" (1964, 24). And commenting on *The Family Jewels* (1965), the same critic found "no jewel in the lot" (Levy 1996, 335). In a different and slightly more sympathetic vein, Howard Thompson found *The Ladies Man* (1961) to "percolate amusingly at first," but "after half an hour it all folds like a tent" (1964, 26). Of *The Nutty Professor* (1963) he proclaimed that "Lewis is trying for something different this go-round," and it "may leave a lot of people thinking and hoping for such more experiments" (1964, 8). Not so generous, Gerald Mast wrote in *The Comic Mind*, "Jerry Lewis's primary failure is that he never discovered who he was" (1979, 303). His gags "do not flow from any human or personal center" (303) and he "cannot manage a plot" (305). In one sense Mast's comments, and Sarris's even more, are neither wrong nor arbitrary. Rather, they are indicative of the substitution of judgment for analysis. They stop at evaluation where they should begin with examination. As John Russell Taylor summed up "Anglo-Saxon" critics in the 1950s, "When they were not moralizing about the overstressed sexuality of Elvis Presley and the dangers of his effect on the young, [they] were likely to be tut-tutting about Jerry Lewis's spastic humour and claiming that his moronic screen persona made cruel fun of the afflicted" (Lloyd 1982, 84).

In the case of much of this "tut-tutting" on the part of North American reviewers and critics, the reaction to Lewis was based on his raucous and brassy behavior, the continual and unremitting strings of gags and lack of coherent narrative in his films, and his mugging and clowning. The uneffacing intrusion of his own persona and the gaudiness (read "vulgarity") of his comic world have also been considered aversive, perhaps threatening sexual and gender decorum. In reading American reviews and critical commentary on Lewis's films, one finds the focus formalist, centering largely on technique, on the character of the gags, and on negative comparisons of Lewis to the "great" comedians of the past: Harold Lloyd, Stan Laurel, and Charlie Chaplin. Are the negative reactions by U.S. critics, as opposed to his popularity with audiences, indicative of a critical failure properly to identify the sources of Lewis's comedy? Do they represent a critical refusal to confront the uncomfortable yet illuminating images of American culture and society that Lewis offered audiences in the 1950s?

In the 1980s, Dana Polan was one of the first North American critics perceptively to diagnose these opposing critical reactions to Lewis. In his essay "Being and Nuttiness," he commented that there were two Jerry Lewises, "the Id (short for Idiot and also suggesting the roots of comic idiocy in a primal unreason) and Jerry Lewis the Serious Man (with capital letters, *s'il vous plaît*)" (Polan 1984, 43). Polan attributed the double reaction to Lewis to the "all too common cliché that the French love Jerry Lewis" and the Americans do not (43), suggesting that the "Las Vegasy" world to which Martin and Lewis belonged was also a factor in the negative treatment of Lewis's work in North America. Most important, Polan observed that "what the French find in Lewis is an analysis that corresponds to their image of America that may be missed by Americans" (46). Thus the question is, "What is this image of America that 'may be missed by Americans?'" Is it actually "missed" by Americans, is it suppressed, or is it willfully repudiated?

A reading of French writings on Lewis's work reveals how seriously his films have been regarded there, while American critics and reviewers have often viewed his acclaim in France with incomprehension, if not derision. French critics have hailed him as a serious comic actor and a "total" filmmaker. In particular, a large (though not unanimous) part of the French reception to Lewis has constructed a mythology to insert Lewis into the pantheon of "total filmmakers" along with other Hollywood auteurs, mainly as a consequence of his work with Frank Tashlin, a man eventually deemed a worthy auteur by French critics. Most notably, Robert Benayoun and Jean-Louis Comolli can be credited with creating and publicizing the "massive adoration of Jerry Lewis" in France (Sikov 1994, 192).

Many of the French critics working from the theory of auteurism in relation to genre analysis granted a privileged status to directors who carved an individual niche for themselves in the "impersonal" and formulaic system of Hollywood filmmaking. According to this view, these individuals produced serious works in a recognizable and personal style that shed light on cinematic practices, spectatorship, and

American culture despite Hollywood commercialism. Yet auteur criticism has been two-sided. In turning consideration toward works that have been regarded as trivial escapist pabulum for the masses, these critics have offered a corrective to the cliché-ridden dismissal of genre films and their creators, at the same time eroding the traditional divide between high and low culture.

The French have celebrated Lewis as a comic artiste and have compared him to Chaplin, Laurel, Buster Keaton, and Jacques Tati. He has been granted an elevated stature in the world of comic burlesque, some French criticism regarding his brand of comedy affirmatively as "anti-culture"—as expressing the foibles of American culture or at least embodying its excesses. Lewis is, according to Bérénice Reynaud, "our alter ego on the screen" who draws on many elements of popular culture (1989, viii). Reynaud's comment on Lewis's reception suggests the national character of the veneration of Lewis by French critics. Their interest in Lewis's work is thus an opportunity to view perceptions of America from the European perspective. If American critics have been unable to situate Lewis's comic persona and to understand its locus in American culture, French critics have created an identity for him to occupy, often in the image of the European intellectual as cineaste. His work has been regarded as aligned to surrealism and to avant-garde forms of filmmaking. These French critics' conceptions of American-ness are restricted to the cinema and do not—beyond generalizations—treat historically inflected conceptions of American society.

An essay contributed by Jacques Aumont, Jean-Louis Comolli, André Labarthe, Jean Narboni, and Sylvie Pierre to a volume on the films of Frank Tashlin is exemplary of this eclectic and textually based thematic and social mode of analysis. Focusing on Lewis's comedy and detailing the particular elements of his style, this encyclopedic essay shows that his work contained "themes, traditions, myths and techniques of the American cinema [that] recur again and again" (Aumont et al. 1973, 91). The critical method is a formal (psychoanalytic) discussion, exemplary of other treatments of that work in French criticism, that focuses heavily on Lewis's uses of the body—as do European critics more broadly—describing it as aphasic, if not catatonic, and indicative of dislocated identity.

In particular, the critics lay great emphasis on his juvenilized persona and on "regressive tendencies"—his adoption of the fetal position, his hiding, his wearing short pants, and his articulation through a perpetually changing voice (Aumont et al. 1973, 92) They also note his clinging trousers, his transvestitism, and a way he has of relating to objects that betrays his weakness and clumsiness (99). They stress that the settings in his films are grand hotels and colleges, places of passage in space and time, and note how often the prologues and epilogues are reminders that one is about to see or has just seen a film. The films are metacinematic in that they are heavily interspersed with quotations from other films, parodies of film genres, gags lifted from other films, self-quotation, walk-ons from prominent entertainers, and invitations for actors to play themselves (105). Moreover, the films reveal a society with a high level of technology.

Placing Lewis's comedy in the tradition of the great comedians of show business, Robert Benayoun established many of the themes of Lewis criticism in France (and in Europe more generally), highlighting the importance of a number of Lewisian traits (Benayoun 1972, 23–24, 150). For Benayoun, Lewis is a "child man," a "great auto-didact" (73). The Lewis persona exemplified by films such as *The Ladies Man* is a creation emerging "toute pièces par le matriéchat américain" (entirely from American matriarchy) (265).

French writings on Lewis have not been restricted to film critics and historians. The philosopher Gilles Deleuze has written eloquently on Lewis's ingenious and unique contributions to the cinematic image, particularly pointing to the ways in which the comedian's films can be seen to belong to the post–World War II regime of the "time-image." Here, "the image no longer refers to a situation that is globalising and synthetic, but rather to one that is dispersive. The characters are multiple, with weak interferences and become principal or revert to being secondary." This cinema of the time-image no longer expresses the power of character to determine and overcome situations. Instead, character and situations constantly splinter (as in a dream) and metamorphose into different perspectives and milieux (1986, 207). Deleuze also sees Lewis taking up "the classic figure of American cinema, that of the Loser, of the born loser, whose definition is 'he goes too far.' But it is precisely in the burlesque dimension that this 'too far' becomes movement of a world which saves him and will make him a winner" (1989, 65). The new burlesque with which Deleuze associates Lewis belongs not to the Bergsonian comedy of the mechanical but to the electronic world: it "arises from the fact that the character places himself (involuntarily) on an energy band that carries him along. . . . The comic is no longer something mechanical" (1989, 66). Lewis is situated not as star, personality, or individual but as a process. In comparing Lewis's films to those of Tati, Deleuze—like Bergson—seeks to identify the character of this new automatism that seems to transcend a national context. For him, Lewis becomes postmodern; his work precludes certain kinds of analysis (e.g., psychoanalysis) where unconscious motivation continues to play a role and reveals a dream world where boundaries between the real and imaginary dissolve. This regime of the time-image is symptomatic of a different form of cinema that exposes, if not undermines, the classical cinema of action and character of the pre–World War II era.

But the French are not the only Europeans to appreciate Jerry Lewis, and contrary to reigning mythology, he is not the sole property of French critics, although other Europeans who have written about him have done so with some indebtedness to the French. In Italy, for example, there is a growing literature on Lewis's work, best exemplified by Mauro Marchesini's comment that he is "the last of the great expressionist comics in cinema who think with their bodies and express themselves in spasmodic muscular acrobatics." His Jewishness has also been frequently addressed in the European context, and Marchesini connects it to the Diaspora and to the long-standing role of the Jewish comic as adopting "the character of clown and schlemiel as a response to the hostility of the New World" (1983, 153).

Like Marchesini, Giorgio Cremonini links Lewis's persona of the schlemiel to the world of the ghetto. Cremonini echoes the frequent focus on Lewis's body and on its grotesque and excessive character, describing it in terms of an "afasia gestuale" (1980, 23) and also in terms of exemplifying the "logic of non-sense" (30). Cremonini applies Mikhail Bakhtin's notion of the carnivalesque to Lewis's films (37). Both critics also focus on the theatricality of the films, the cinematic world depicted as stage or screen, the role of doubling, and the influence of figures such as Chaplin and Billy Wilder. (They also acknowledge the importance of Tashlin.) In relation to situating Lewis's films in the context of American society, Cremonini has written that this is a cinema of suffering American individualism similar to the work of Jules Feiffer (Cremonini 1980, 76). In contrast to Chaplin and Keaton's world of transformation, Lewis's comic world is closed. Lewis rebels subtly, not blatantly, against capital (79).

From the 1970s to the present, German critics have provided their own perspective on the Lewis persona; as early as 1971 there was a Jerry Lewis festival in the Munich Leopoldkino that lasted a full year. For example, Rainer Werner Fassbinder acknowledged Martin and Lewis's work in *In a Year of 13 Moons* (1978), where he uses a segment from *You're Never Too Young* (1955) in elaborating the character of Anton Saitz (Gottfried John) and his contemptuous relation to the sexually transformed Erwin/Elvira (Volker Spengler). Yet Anton is a devotee of mass culture, and his attraction to Jerry Lewis invokes a number of suggestive motifs concerning Hollywood, a culture that is hardly innocent but reveals the darker dimensions of gender and sexuality. Thomas Elsaesser describes *Thirteen Moons* as "about outsiders: marginals, deviants, foreigners, outcasts, and social failures" (1996, 200). In the context of this film, the depiction of Martin and Lewis takes on critical resonance as a form of sexual politics, suggesting the more complex cultural dimensions of their comedy.

In a lengthy article in *Filmkritik* in 1974, indebted to Benayoun, Rainer Gansera discusses a range of Lewis's films. Gansera, too, rehearses Lewis's biography, stressing his Jewish "immigrant origins" and his experiences of anti-Semitism as a youth (1974, 149). However, Gansera does not isolate the Lewis solo films but discusses the films made with Dean Martin, here diverging from most French critics, who seem more inclined to favor Lewis alone. He places particular emphasis on the films about military life made both before and after the breakup. Nevertheless, for German as well as for other European critics, the films Lewis made with Tashlin and those directed by Lewis himself get the largest share of critical attention. Gansera, like other European critics, invokes Woody Allen; however, he also compares Lewis to Hitchcock (168) and suggests that if under Tashlin's direction Lewis was relatively controlled, in his own work he has experimented more with style and expressive modes of performance (172). Humanist, sentimental, careerist, or individualistic, the typical Lewis comedy is located as a continuation of slapstick, characterized by variety and by nuanced accommodation to sound, music, and color. Gansera also notes that Lewis, like Tashlin, draws on cartoon and op art. Moreover, Tashlin's films are characterized by attention to timing and to camera work, as are those of Jerry Lewis (162). And both directors experiment with narrative. In the case of *The Bellboy* (1960), Lewis constructed a text that relies on gags, not on narrative, and the result is "unbelievably realistic" (162).

Gansera singles out Lewis's relationship to women in his films, finding that in the films made with Martin the men's relationship is central, with Martin largely being an older brother to Lewis (153). The solo films, however, raise challenges about the character's relationships to women and also about his relationship to American society. In grandiose terms, the author suggests that an understanding of Lewis's comedy would require an investigation of "the pre-history and history of mankind and of American society" and of nature expressed often in terms of the relationship to material objects and to animals, "the material of great comedy" (173). When Lewis is being "The Kid," Gansera sees him as kindly; when he recognizes that he is being laughed at, he seeks to turn the laughter to his advantage so the audience will adopt him. As "Id," Lewis is more isolated. He tries to enlist the audience, even to make them laugh *at* him, since that is preferable to being isolated. He is the "ugly duckling" who becomes a swan.

A more recent German review by Georg Seesslen differs from other European assessments in focusing on both Martin and Lewis (1996, 23). In his essay, Seesslen stresses Freudian psychology, commenting on the oedipal character of the Martin-Lewis films by an allusion to Woody Allen's *Oedipus Wrecks* (1989). He identifies the oedipality in the frequent presence of a range of father figures and in the disappearance of the mother—who returns "as matronly dominatrix, criminal virgin, the sickest of all women, and the indeterminate superwoman." Seesslen affirms Lewis's role as child-man and his flight from women. The team of Lewis and Martin, he notes, functioned at a particularly "neuroticized time" in American culture, where the relationship of the two men, their friendship, relies on the feminine as Other (24). In the separation of the comedy team, Martin headed in the direction of the "hedonistic" character in his Westerns (26), his identification with the Rat Pack, and his entertainment on television and in nightclubs. Lewis, on his own and with Tashlin, moved in the direction of developing the metacinematic and sexual dimensions of his films. Citing *The Ladies Man* and *The Nutty Professor*, Seesslen comments on the resemblance they bear to the films of Fellini (31).

Raymond Durgnat is one of the British critics appreciative of Lewis's comedy. He has commented on how Lewis, basically a city comedian, "thinks with his body" in an "every-which-way style suitable to the Tranquilizer Age" (1970, 234). He represents "imbecility sunk to the level of genius." Writing particularly on *The Ladies Man* and *The Nutty Professor*, Durgnat asserts that "if *The Ladies Man* was a fantasia on American misogyny, *The Nutty Professor* is a fantasia on the themes of virility and self-assurance" (1963, 31). While these assessments do not provide a specific sense of Americanness, they do reveal Durgnat's grappling to understand the cultural character of "the American" as conveyed through the Hollywood cinema. As French and Italian commentators did, Durgnat sees Lewis's work as an interrogation of the nature of the comic, exemplified by *The Patsy*, in which Lewis is "a very lovable misfit in a world of people who love him really. . . . his failures are not failures of mediocrity or slickness, but of inventiveness and sincerity" (1970, 235, 238).

Creating an auteur of Lewis was conducive to a radical rethinking of popular cinema, in which the work of particular directors was situated in a specific genre and milieu and in relation to a particular mode of critical filmmaking. In much the same way, writings on other directors (e.g., John Ford and Douglas Sirk) produced a reevaluation of the Western and the melodrama. Yet, while bearing the marks of auteurism, Lewis's fame in Europe extends beyond the mere phenomenon of cultural capital and aestheticism. In the way it holds up "uno specchio posto davanti agli spettatore" (a mirror before the spectator) (Cremonini 1980, 3), Lewis's image is identified with certain characteristics of American culture as perceived in Europe, a culture that can be considered hostile toward European cinema, especially the tradition of quality and the unquestioned alignment with realism. Closely tied to the ideological conflicts between realism and artifice is the emphasis on the power of Hollywood. What most endeared Lewis's films to the Europeans from the 1950s to the present was their explicit illusionism, their anti-realistic realism, and their self-conscious and playful exploration of media. Lewis's fantasies, his use of slapstick and gags, are interpreted as a critique of realism and therefore as a critique of a naive belief in the world as seen.

These European critics regard Lewis's films as an assault on American culture and politics, exposing a banality that masks more aggressive designs. In particular, in the childlike character that so many of his critics have commented upon, his persona raises the juvenilization of American culture to the point of absurdity. In singling out this character of the "child-man," whose innocence is alluded to so often in the literature of and on "the American," European critics highlight the contradictory nature of the long-standing myth of the "innocent abroad." Moreover, in their emphasis on the grotesque uses of Jerry's body, on his "imbecility sunk to the point of genius," and on his fear of women, they have also exposed the problematic but self-conscious image of cinematic masculinity conveyed through Lewis's panorama of characters. Lewis's critical focus on the "aphasic gesture," on gibberish, and on the contortions of the body generally provides an avenue for understanding the obvious and unresolvable dissonances that are central to his character.

According to Ed Sikov, most French critics (but especially Benayoun) have "noticed the consistency with which Lewis's characters fragment into doubles and/or distorted aspects of themselves" (1994, 192). The focus on his body and on the issue of *dédoublement* (the elaborate process of creating and proliferating doubles) has proved a major (psychoanalytic) source for identifying the schizoid world Lewis and his characters inhabit and his frenetic and dissonant responses to it. Doubling pervades every aspect of Lewis's work and its critical reception. From a schizoid split between Lewis the personality and Joseph Levitch–become–Lewis, the time-honored figure of the double extends to the eruption of a range and diversity of comic characters, to the structures of the films themselves, and to the ubiquitous motif of mirroring life and entertainment. Gérard Recasens describes Lewis as a "bicephalic personality" (1970, 5), and in fact, the figure of Lewis in the European context seems doubled in yet other ways—he both exemplifies and exposes the foibles and follies of American culture.

On the level of doubled narrative, Lewis films are often remakes of earlier films—*Scared Stiff* (1953) (*The Ghost Breakers* [1940]); *You're Never Too Young* (*The Major and the Minor* [1942]); *Living It Up* (1954) (*Nothing Sacred* [1937]); *The Nutty Professor* (*Dr. Jekyll and Mr. Hyde* [1931]); *Cinderfella* (1960) (*Cinderella* [1950]); *The Patsy* (*A Star Is Born* [1937]). His films are also characterized by framing devices (*The Errand Boy* [1961] and *The Patsy*, films that begin and end with the real-life image of the successful comic star), and doubling is typically central to the Lewis character: in *The Errand Boy* he plays the role of Morty and also appears as himself; in *Living It Up* he assumes a role that was originally written for a female; in *The Bellboy* he doubles as Stanley and also as himself; in *The Patsy* he is Stanley, the schlemiel, but he finally emerges as himself, as great comedian and director; in *The Nutty Professor* he is Buddy Love and Julius Kelp, Don Juan and his desexualized opposite; and in *Cinderfella* he is the scullery boy, the son rejected by his stepmother and the lover finally of Princess Charming. In *The Disorderly Orderly* (1964) the duality consists in Jerome's phobia, an inability to confront pain that inhibits him from becoming a doctor like his father. This phobia is linked to his attachment to Susan, a popular high school cheerleader. Once released from her, he is free from obsession and may pursue a career in medicine.

The characters in Lewis's world proliferate and fracture further: fictional characters mingle with real-life personalities—Milton Berle, Ed Sullivan, Harry James, George Raft. He consorts with puppets (*The Patsy* and *The Errand Boy*), fairy godfathers (*Cinderfella*), and talking birds (*The Nutty Professor*). He is also divided between the indignities and frustrations of his past and his desires in the present, and he moves between the nonentities of the work world and the upper echelons of the entertainment world. His names in these films—Morty, Jerome, Julius, Stanley, and Herbert—imply a division between the "sissy" and his opposite, the virile heterosexual male. As critics have often noted, these characters are split into losers and winners, competents and incompetents, children and adults, and females and males (a doubling often achieved through behavior, not costuming). As in *Cinderfella*, when he parodies the suave Hollywood star as he glides down the stairs, his appearance undergoes transformations, from the infantile to the ostensibly feminine and to a parody of virility.

Like a ventriloquist, Lewis has multiple voices—his Donald Duck–like squawk, his high-pitched nasal drone, and the sober voice of the "adult" "Jerry Lewis." He can mime other languages or babble, leaving sentences dangling. Comparing Lewis to Chaplin and to Stan Laurel, critics have pointed to the nonverbal dimensions of his language. Thus another duality, between verbalization and silence, inheres in the Lewis persona. The noncohesiveness of character implicit in doubling has been part of the difficulty in the critical evaluation of Lewis on both sides of the Atlantic, as scholars have worked to trace the different lines that constitute the texture of his schizoid milieu. These lines divide between Jew and Gentile, mama's boy and motherless child, male and female, child and man, the incompetent and the braggart, loser and winner, victim and aggressor.

But how are we to interpret this image of the American expressed through Lewis's various comic incarnations? He is naive, unable to contend with his mistakes. Although he is a loser, a schlemiel, he struggles to overcome that characterization and to be recognized. He "tries too hard," as shown in *The Disorderly Orderly*. His duality is also evident in his relationships to his work, where he is constantly struggling to overcome the stigma of failure, stupidity, and endless mistakes. A creation of Hollywood and mass culture, he lives in an artificial world peopled by equally incongruous characters—principals, fortune hunters, gangsters, spies, oversized football players. For the most part he is de-eroticized, has little sexual desire for women or rather fears them. He has never matured and is a polymorphous creature of sentiment and nostalgia. He is not highly articulate: his body expresses the range and intensity of his fears and desires. While he is compared to the silent-film comedians in the consummate use of gesture and gags, he is, after all, the creator of his own fantasies, derived from another time and milieu.

Above all, he is an American Jewish director, a product of the Hollywood system who expresses the figure of the American to Europeans. One side of his accomplishment seems to reside in his "genius" in capturing the character of Americanness as seen through a European lens. This establishes the terms for a further investigation of his frequent dismissal by North American critics; until recently no full-length American study did justice to the nature and impact of Lewis's films in the North American context. Ed Sikov's *Laughing Hysterically* (1994) profitably locates Lewis in the milieu of the 1950s and 1960s, and Frank Krutnik's *Inventing Jerry Lewis* (2000) seeks to take account of Lewis's reception in Europe, in addition to offering serious readings of individual films and also maintaining Lewis's position as auteur against critical opposition. Krutnik and Neale's study of popular film and television has also sought to locate Lewis's comedic persona in the context of "comedian comedy" (1990), a form that has

a structure of address in which an audience is witness to a live (or would-be live) performance, and in which the performance itself is directly and explicitly aimed at those listening and watching. When they appear in films, therefore, these performers bring with them not just an extra-cinematic persona, but a style, and a style of performance, established in cinematic terms. . . . Devices like direct address to the camera, references to the fictional nature of the films in which these performers appear, quotes from, or references to, other films, and references to the world of showbiz outside the fictional universe of any one film, are all endemic to comedian comedy. (104)

Without disparaging European critics' ascription of an avant-garde character to many of Lewis's films, this designation of comedian comedy helps account for the sources of the films and the ways in which they violate narrative continuity and coherence. Particularly in the case of such films as *The Errand Boy* and *The Patsy*, which celebrate "entertainment," these films can be seen to belong to a particular style associated with numerous gags, wisecracks, jokes, interruptions, digressions, repetition, self-referentiality, and direct address, traits dismissed by earlier North American critics and reviewers as characteristic of the actor-director's personal, egomaniacal, and familiar fantasies. Moreover, much like the venues for comedian comedy, these films are set in big hotels, are peopled by celebrities, have nightclub scenes, and are often a parody of other films. Unlike other types of comedy—romantic comedy, screwball comedy, silent slapstick—comedian comedy is explicitly associated with "entertainment," a form unfortunately assumed to be mindless, obvious, self-congratulatory, and devoid of meaning. That this negative critical assessment may have signaled a lack of understanding or more a self-conscious depreciation of popular entertainment is shown in Peter Bogdanovich's comment, praising the work of Frank Tashlin (and by extension Jerry Lewis in Tashlin's films), that "too many American critics cannot see the often bitter comment under the brassy façade" (1973, 61). What was denied Tashlin and Lewis was a position in American culture, a regard for their work as creating a world that offered an insight into American entertainment and its ethnic linkages.

Lewis's films have eluded the usual serious assessments accorded such comic directors as Ernst Lubitsch, Frank Capra, and Preston Sturges, who are considered to exemplify the quintessential character of Hollywood comedy and the creative role of the auteur within the studio system. Further, Lewis's work has not played a prominent role in studies of the musical. Nor do his films seem to make the connection with American culture of the 1950s and 1960s exemplified in serious studies of the melodramas of Douglas Sirk, Vincente Minnelli, and Nicholas Ray. These melodramas have been analyzed for their treatments of social class, gender, and sexuality as this genre dramatizes serious postwar transformations in American culture. If the study of North American popular culture has selectively looked to find "meaning" in signs of "resistance" and "subversion," Lewis's work has not seemed to offer an easily accessible cultural critique, although situating Lewis in the context of the cinema of the 1950s and early 1960s could link him to a number of motifs that are part of 1950s media culture. His "new burlesque," for instance, is characterized by excess in relation to its representations of the family, masculinity, the "feminine mystique," youth, music, and television.

Part of the problem in linking Lewis's work to these issues is the difficulty of analyzing comedy, the fact that there do not seem to be cohesive notions of comic genres that can lead us easily to a social critique. As Krutnik and Neale assert, "perhaps the most striking thing about comedy is the immense variety and range of its forms . . . probably greater than that of any other genre" (1990, 10). And surely one of the most difficult dimensions of comedy to assess is slapstick. Whereas comic narrative is comprehensible within the conventions of other genres, slapstick poses enigmatic issues concerning the uses of the body, objects, and relationships to the milieu that are often independent of diegetic meaning. As so many European critics have noted, Lewis's persona, his uses of his voice, his physical contortions, and his infantilism are key to his films; yet these were the characteristics that disturbed and antagonized earlier North American critics and reviewers. In recent North American criticism, however, Lewis's "misdirected and disconnected gestures" are no longer abrasive and meaningless; instead, they bespeak "a spectacular dissolution of identity" (Krutnik 2000, 8) and a "movement toward delirium and lunacy as well as an obsessive concern with male paranoia" (Sikov 1994, 221). While the films are not seen as a "reflection" or "realistic" portrait of the 1950s, they are historical in that they are an enactment of the affective texture of a world often described in contemporary studies of melodrama and science fiction. Scott Bukatman, reflecting Deleuze's concerns, has made a compelling case for regarding Lewis's films from a postmodern perspective, as a refusal to occupy "a fixed subject position" (1991, 200). He writes, "Spectators are placed in the radical position of searching into the mirror's depths, only to find reflected back the incoherent and fragmented, multiplied yet elusive image of Jerry Lewis" (203).

What are we to do with this elusive, multiplied image? Is it the return of history in a new form as film, or a revelation of the as-yet-unfinished critical project of understanding relationships between past and present and of the impact of the cinematic image in its various permutations? What is clear is that these recent attempts to introduce historical methods into the study of Lewis's films illuminate not only the schizoid character of those films but also schizoid aspects of critical evaluations of them from both sides of the Atlantic, and perhaps, too, the schizoid character of American culture and politics.

In *Hollywood or Bust* (Frank Tashlin, Paramount, 1956), the naïf Malcolm Smith (Jerry Lewis) gives a movie review: "Part of it was shot in Lower Tasmania." Frame enlargement.

# 5

# Flaming Creature

## Jerry Lewis and Screen Performance in *Hollywood or Bust*

Craig Fischer

DIRECTED BY AUTEUR Frank Tashlin and released by Paramount in 1956, *Hollywood or Bust* was the last film to star Dean Martin and Jerry Lewis before they dissolved their partnership. Most of the film's 1956 reviewers were unimpressed. Bosley Crowther of the *New York Times* found the movie "repetitious" and a "mild disappointment," while *Variety* called it "uneven" (Neibaur and Okuda 1995, 114). Later commentators are split over both the film's inherent value and its reputation among other critics. Ed Sikov ranks *Hollywood or Bust* with Tashlin's best works, calling the film a trenchant exploration of "the extreme artificiality of the United States and its populace" and lamenting that Tashlin's brash, cartoony approach to sex and association with Jerry Lewis make his films unpalatable to modern audiences (1994, 181–182). James L. Neibaur and Ted Okuda, however, argue that *Hollywood or Bust* has been lavished with praise in "various film journals," despite the fact that the film is "devoid of any genuine merriment or satiric punch" (1995, 110). *De gustibus non est disputandum.*

Thirty-two years later, Barry Levinson directed *Rain Man* (1988), a film whose production and reception were the epitome of New Hollywood prestige. Packaged by Michael Ovitz at Creative Artists Agency, complete with a cast that includes Dustin Hoffman and Tom Cruise, *Rain Man* grossed $65 million at the box office, received good notices, and won Oscars for Best Original Screenplay (written by Barry Morrow

and Ronald Bass), Best Actor (Hoffman), Best Director, and Best Picture.[1] It continues to be an audience favorite. Currently it is number 172
on the Internet Movie Database's "Top 250 Movies as Voted by Our
Users" poll.

My descriptions of *Hollywood or Bust* and *Rain Man* make these
films sound radically different from each other, and in many ways they
are. *Rain Man* lacks *Hollywood or Bust*'s strongest asset: a Great Dane
named Mr. Bascom who drives a car, French-kisses Dean Martin, and
develops a crush on Anita Ekberg's toy poodle. Yet the two films share
some pronounced narrative affinities—most notably a road-trip plot
that links two disparate characters—and a prolonged look at the differences and similarities between *Hollywood or Bust* and *Rain Man* reveals
that Jerry Lewis was one of the most radical stars in mainstream Hollywood history. While the norms of Hollywood storytelling and acting
emphasize hierarchy and consistency, Lewis developed throughout his
career a wildly unpredictable, volatile performance style, one that
destabilized the notion of "character" as conceived by Hollywood and
pointed to the innovations of the experimental filmmaker Jack Smith.


## SCHIZOPHRENIA, STARDOM, AND UNDERWEAR: DUSTIN HOFFMAN AND JERRY LEWIS

In this section, I list various similarities between *Hollywood or Bust* and
*Rain Man*. An inevitable question arises from this comparison: Does
*Rain Man* mirror the Martin-Lewis-Tashlin movie? My answer is in two
parts. First, of course *Rain Man* recycled material from *Hollywood or
Bust*. No two movies could be that alike by accident. Second, "plagiarism" of this sort is what allows Hollywood to keep up with the entertainment demands of an entire world. Various techniques (including
the unity of classical Hollywood storytelling, stylistic norms, genre formulas, remakes, and sequels) optimize serial manufacture while trading on audience appreciation of the tried and true. Martin and Lewis
built their careers on just such "plagiarism." As Neibaur and Okuda
point out, many Martin-Lewis films emulate the work of previous comedy teams (like the Three Stooges, Laurel and Hardy, and Abbott and
Costello before them, Martin and Lewis starred in a horror comedy) and
borrow their plots from previous movies. Hollywood's *modus operandi*

has always been to find fresh aesthetic and financial promise in familiar tropes, so complaining about *Rain Man*'s "plagiarism" of *Hollywood or Bust* is a bit like complaining about the dampness of the ocean.

The similarities, then, between *Hollywood or Bust* and *Rain Man* include the following:

Each film features a handsome swindler, a wheeler-dealer whose very name reflects his untrustworthiness. In *Hollywood or Bust*, for instance, Dean Martin plays Steve Wiley, a two-bit hood with gambling debts, while in *Rain Man*, Cruise plays Charlie Babbitt, a foreign-car importer who lies to his customers. At the beginning of each film, the swindler is in financial trouble, and both scheme to sell cars in order to pay off their debts. Wiley rigs a raffle to win a car that he plans to sell to pay off his bookie, while Babbitt procures foreign cars for rich and impatient customers.

Further, each swindler has a relationship with a woman who objects to his insensitive nature. Steve's girlfriend is Terry (Pat Crowley), a dancer he meets while traveling cross-country. At the beginning of *Rain Man*, Charlie is in a shaky relationship with Susanna (Valeria Golino). Both couples split up, primarily because the woman gets fed up with the swindler's mistreatment of the next character I'll describe, the character who is in many ways central to each story: the naïf.

Each swindler is improbably paired with an innocent who is unable to process and respond to the world in normal ways. In *Hollywood* the naïf is Malcolm Smith (Lewis), a *nebbish* who honestly wins the car raffle at the beginning of the film. In *Rain Man* the naïf is Raymond Babbitt (Hoffman), an institutionalized autistic who is revealed to be Charlie's brother. Both naïfs are media junkies—not unlike Jerry Lewis himself. Malcolm is given to spouting detailed information about the production of his favorite Hollywood movies (particularly movies starring Anita Ekberg), while Raymond compulsively sings game-show jingles and schedules his day religiously around the late-afternoon airing of "The People's Court." Both naïfs are also obsessed with underwear, representative of the sexuality accessible to the swindlers but not to them. In *Rain Man*, Raymond insists that Charlie buy him boxer shorts from one particular Kmart in Cincinnati, while Malcolm expresses his lust for Anita Ekberg by fantasizing about her "undies" hanging on a laundry line.

Both *Hollywood* and *Rain Man* are "road pictures" in which the swindler's financial schemes force him to join the naïf on a cross-country driving trip that begins in the east (New York City, Cincinnati) and ends in California (Hollywood, Los Angeles). In *Hollywood*, Steve uses a counterfeit ticket, claims to be a co-winner of the car, and goes along for the ride when Malcolm insists on driving out to California to meet Anita Ekberg. In *Rain Man*, Charlie plans to bring Raymond to Los Angeles and wheedle inheritance money out of him, but Raymond refuses to fly, and the two must drive to L.A. Both pairs of partners travel in convertibles and follow a route that passes through Las Vegas, where in each case the naïf uses uncanny abilities (Malcolm's "lucky feeling," Raymond's limitless memory and mathematical wizardry) to win enough gambling money to get the swindler out of debt.

Both films conclude with the swindler redeeming himself by treating the naïf with honesty and compassion. In *Hollywood*, Steve tells Malcolm the truth—that he cheated in order to win the car—and in *Rain Man*, Charlie vows to become closer to Raymond after he realizes that the autistic savant is his brother. With this redemption, the swindler wins back the love of his girlfriend. By the end of *Hollywood*, Steve has reformed, and he and Terry have reignited their affair. *Rain Man*, however, defers absolute romantic closure; Susanna remains narratively and literally out of the picture, though we see Charlie talking to her on the phone, making sincere promises to fix their relationship.

Although these two films are structurally similar, anyone who's seen both *Hollywood or Bust* and *Rain Man* knows that they feel like profoundly different movies. Much of this difference in tone is undoubtably due to differences in genre. *Rain Man* is a drama peppered with serious conversations and surprising revelations about family ties, while *Hollywood or Bust* is a comedy full of hay bales stuffed with beautiful girls, phallic ten-gallon cowboy hats that spout oil, and other wacky violations of dramatic plausibility. Yet another key difference lies in the films' diametrically opposed notions of character consistency. Raymond as a character is defined by his *rigidity*, his autistic inability to respond and adapt to new situations. Malcolm, however, is prone to expressing a wild range of character traits that run the gamut from good-natured childishness to gibbering perversity.

Raymond spends much of the first half of *Rain Man* explaining to Charlie the precise rules that govern his life at Walburg Hospital: he watches "Jeopardy!" at five o'clock; he doesn't go out when it rains; and it's lights out at eleven o'clock. And if variations disrupt these rules—as they do, violently, when Raymond is confronted with his first highway accident, his first airplane flight, or the wail of a smoke alarm—his response is helpless panic. The second day Charlie and Raymond are on the road, Raymond refuses to wear Charlie's underwear and repeatedly insists that they buy boxers at "Kmart in Cincinnati, 400 Oak Street." Charlie loses his cool, stops the car, and springs into a screaming tirade where he expresses doubts about the nature of his brother's mental illness: "I think this autism is a bunch of shit! You can't tell me you're not in there somewhere." But Ray isn't "in there" in any normal sense. The film's plot and Hoffman's emotional flatness defy the traditional Hollywood character arc by shaping someone who is, by definition, incapable of growth and change. Raymond's true function is to catalyze Charlie's change. Director Levinson and screenwriters Morrow and Bass give us reason to hope that Raymond is changed by his cross-country journey with Charlie; Raymond dances with Susanna in a Las Vegas elevator without panicking, and he even proves capable of making a wan joke ("Kmart sucks!") at film's end. But he also begs to be reinstitutionalized, removed from the world of flux and contingency.

When he is first introduced in *Hollywood or Bust*, however, Lewis's Malcolm exhibits a remarkably inconsistent and fluid personality. Malcolm and Steve (and Steve's bookie [Maxie Rosenbloom]) stand in line outside the theater where the car raffle will be held. They strike up a conversation about the movie fan magazine that Malcolm is reading, and a medium close-up features Lewis's face as he shows the magazine's nonnude centerfold of Anita Ekberg to Steve. In this close-up, Lewis's facial expression and smile are curiously sedate and "normal," as if he were just a regular guy bonding with another guy over the spectacle of a pretty woman. This sense of macho camaraderie is reinforced by the dialogue that immediately follows this close-up:

> MALCOLM: I saw her last picture six times.
> STEVE: It couldn't be, with a body like that.
> MALCOLM: What couldn't be?
> STEVE: Her last picture.

Yet our first impression of Malcolm as a lusty and somewhat dorky all-American boy is entirely misleading. Over the course of *Hollywood or Bust*, Malcolm's hunger for Ekberg blossoms into an almost fetishistic perversion. Later in the film, Malcolm obsesses about Ekberg's "undies" hanging next to his own, while biting his knuckles, arching his eyebrows, and making guilty faces like a boy caught masturbating in the bathroom. Malcolm's immediate response to Steve's "last picture" comment is sexually oblivious, however: he launches into a detailed explanation of Ekberg's last movie (*The Lavender Tattooer*, a dopey pun on *The Rose Tattoo* [1955]) that out-savants anything Raymond mutters in *Rain Man*:

> It was produced by the Nathan Brothers and directed by William B. Hoffmeyer. Part of it was shot in Lower Tasmania—that was directed by Howard Raznovich—costumes by Patricia Wonderstone. The screenplay was by Willie Rachauer, Harry Jones and Florence Hershfield—that was for the woman's touch—from a play by John and Betty Stetson, based on an incidental remark dropped by a waiter at Sardi's, name of Nicholas Blaney, in Technicolor and VistaVision.

Malcolm follows this insanely nuanced description with a brief wince—as if exhausted by the level of erudition he's exhibited—and then proceeds to demonstrate Ekberg's "Bali-Bali dance." Malcolm's knees bend; he takes tiny steps forward and backward as his arms stick out at right angles from his body and his hands move in alien geometric patterns. He ends the dance by grimacing and rubbing his head, a gesture that invokes Lewis's usual "spastically" desperate performance style. In this brief scene, Malcolm veers from lusty male to movie-fan idiot-savant to feminized Balinese burlesque clown, as mercurial as Raymond is rigid.

Yet Malcolm's erratic identity(ies) might point to a broader similarity between Malcolm and Raymond: both might be seen as mentally "disabled." At the risk of taking a comedic character too seriously, Malcolm's personality shifts are supplemented by abnormal behaviors and delusions; he pretends to be a matador instead of simply running out of a bull pen, for instance, and he buys a ridiculously expensive necklace for a woman he barely knows (but whose undies he has fetishized). This combination of behavioral incongruity and Lewis's twitchy, "spastic" performance style has led journalists and critics to see his career as a humorous reenactment of physical and emotional trauma—even as he raises money to help people with muscular dystrophy. As journalist Leslie Bennetts writes:

> It has always seemed ironic that Lewis, who spent virtually his entire professional career working to help people with neuromuscular dis-

eases, built that very career through a stage persona that was so spastic as to seem disabled, so dopey as to appear retarded. He developed that character very early in life; even in school he was known as "Id," short for the idiot. Later, when he became famous, the internationally known character named Jerry Lewis often seemed like one endless, increasingly unfunny joke on people who actually had progressive degenerative diseases. (1993, 28)

Rae Beth Gordon interprets Lewis's career in a slightly different "medical" way, arguing that Lewis's popularity among the French is based on long-standing connections between medical and pseudomedical discourses and the Gallic theater. For Gordon, Lewis's "spastic twitches and grimaces" descend directly from the epileptic performers in late-nineteenth-century French theater and early film, while Lewis's obsession with doubling signifies "the triumphant emergence of the lower faculties, replete with the automatisms of idiocy, epilepsy, and hysteria" (2001a, 206–208): Jerry as id(iot) who enacts multiple personality traumata across the two characters he plays in *The Nutty Professor* (1963), the seven he plays in *The Family Jewels* (1965), and the four he plays in *Three on a Couch* (1966). If Malcolm in *Hollywood or Bust* changes personality on the slightest of whims, *The Nutty Professor*'s Julius Kelp is so self-contradictory that he fractures into two entirely different characters, as psychically fragmented as Raymond is autistic.

Frank Krutnik sees a similar schizophrenia not only in the characters Lewis plays onscreen but also in the other, nonfilmic images that Lewis has cultivated throughout his career. According to Krutnik, there are at least four different Jerrys, all of whom I see clearly on display in *Hollywood or Bust*:

(a) the Idiot-Kid, the familiar Lewis-figure;
(b) Las Vegas Jerry, the slick showbiz professional, increasingly evident in nightclubs and on television (as in Lewis's work as guest host for NBC's "Tonight" show in 1962 and his own live ABC show in 1963);
(c) Jerry Lewis, Hollywood director, another "successful" persona;
(d) Telethon Jerry, the persona that ascended with the decline of Lewis's film career, but prefigured in the sentimental didacticisms of films like *The Errand Boy* and *The Nutty Professor*. (Krutnik 1994, 19)

Despite Krutnik's claim for the latter-day "ascendance" of Telethon Jerry, I would argue that these different Jerrys operate not as a hierarchy or historical progression but as a simultaneous, Bakhtinian babble of voices. Lewis began his showbiz career as an off-the-cuff *tummler* at a Catskill hotel, and Shawn Levy, in his fulsome Lewis biography, points out that the Martin-Lewis partnership gelled during after-hours, ad-libbed jam sessions (1996, 20–34, 64–65). In his subsequent films, TV appearances, and live performances, Lewis has been endlessly capable of leapfrogging from Idiot Jerry to Vegas Jerry to Telethon Jerry to other uncharted territories of mugging, overacting, and improvisation. Note the precredit sequence of *Hollywood or Bust*, where he plays movie spectators from around the world, from a stuffy Britisher to a buck-toothed "Oriental" to a suave Frenchman making out with his *fille* in the cinema.

My favorite account of Lewis's mercurial performance style is Bill Barol's "I Stayed Up with Jerry," a hilarious report of the author's experience sitting in a Vegas audience and watching all twenty-one and a half hours of the 1987 Muscular Dystrophy Association Telethon. Excerpts from Barol's article make it clear that all the various Jerry personae diagnosed by Krutnik bubble up during the MDA festivities:

> 6:41pm: "This gentleman is durable," Jerry says, "because he only does quality. And he only does quality because that's the way he thinks. Mr. Paul Anka."
>
> 12:30am: . . . Mr. T climbs up into the audience. Jerry tells him to sit, because he's going to introduce "one of the brothers—Sammy Davis Jr." Sammy is in midnight blue this trip. Jerry: "You got something for me? Lay it on me, man." Jerry and Sammy may be the only two people in America who talk this way.
>
> 5:29am: Jerry thanks Fuji Photo Film in a zany Japanese dialect.
>
> 11:52am: The toteboard turns over to $22,301,614. "Yeah!" Jerry cries. "Go, and do! With the thing!"
>
> 11:53am: Casey [Kasem] mentions "La Bamba" and Jerry starts babbling in mock Spanish.
>
> 3:14pm: Jerry sits alone at center stage. The toteboard reads $39,021,723. "It's been a long day," Jerry says quietly. "A good day. A good day for mankind. My *God*, what a good day for mankind. He's singing "You'll Never Walk Alone." The big, the final Standing Ovation, and he's gone. (Barol 1987, 66–68)

Malcolm's character in *Hollywood or Bust* is similar to Lewis's hosting of the 1987 Telethon. Both display Lewis's career-long compulsion to improvise and his willingness to create performances so unsettling and unpredictable that when they appear in movies, they threaten to reduce the tropes of traditional narrative organization (classical Hollywood storytelling rules, the oedipal narrative trajectory) into an incoherent collection of attractions. He can even make a variety show like the telethon—a parade of attractions—into something surreal and unpredictable, a self-conscious parade-of-attractions on parade.

## "BLOW IT UP REAL GOOD": WHY JERRY LEWIS IS A FLAMING CREATURE

One of my favorite sketches on the old SCTV comedy show was "Farm Film Celebrity Blow-Up," where two farmhands in bib overalls, Big Jim McBob (Joe Flaherty) and Billy Sol Hurok (John Candy), inexplicably held interviews with famous celebrities in a barn. The punch line of each skit was that the interview ended with the celebrity blowing him- or herself to bits. One of their guests was a living hall of mirrors: Martin Short impersonating Dustin Hoffman impersonating Michael Dorsey impersonating Dorothy Michaels in full drag from *Tootsie* (1982). Big Jim and Billy Sol try to conduct the interview, but Short/Hoffman/Michael/Dorothy is interested only in maintaining his illusion of femininity. His Method acting techniques have led him to empathize with the *Tootsie* role too much. "I'm such a craftsman, I now understand what a woman feels," "Hoffman" says, beginning to sob. "And I envy them, man . . . I envy their ability to have a child, man. I wish that I could bear a child!" When the "Farm Film Celebrity Blow-Up" hosts tease him, "Hoffman" replies: "No man understands how vulnerable a woman can feel . . . unless he's a consummate actor like myself."

This notion of the "consummate actor" further defines the differences between the real-life Hoffman's Method approach and Jerry Lewis's more fractured performance style. In his classic book *Stars*, Richard Dyer defines a star image as a *structured polysemy*, a cultural sign that generates "multiple but finite meanings and effects." Yet Dyer acknowledges that some stars are more polysemic than others. There are, for instance, actors and actresses who specialize in carrying the same persona—and who essentially play the same character—from film to film, and these stars create a relatively stable set of meanings over their careers. Dyer writes of one of these:

> John Wayne's image draws together his bigness, his association with the West, his support for right-wing politics, his male independence of, yet courtliness towards, women—the elements are mutually reinforcing, legitimating a certain way of being a man in American society. (1999, 63–64)

Seemingly more polysemic is the performer who uses Method techniques to "get lost" in a role. Dustin Hoffman has appeared in roles strikingly different from one another (Benjamin Braddock in *The Graduate* [1967], Michael Dorsey/Dorothy Michaels in *Tootsie*, Willie Loman in a TV version of "Death of a Salesman" [1985], Raymond in *Rain Man*, slick producer Stanley Motss in *Wag the Dog* [1997]), and these roles stretch his acting abilities even as they undermine a consistent image across his *oeuvre*. Yet, clearly, Method performances establish a locus of meaning grounded in the idea of the "consummate actor." When I watch *Rain Man*, I never believe that Hoffman is an autistic person; rather, I am struck by how Hoffman creates a repertoire of gestures, tics, and vocal inflections that imitate the autistic experience and present Raymond as a believable character. The extradiegetic notion of Hoffman as a "consummate actor" gives audiences an interpretive hook ("Wow, that guy can play anything!") that helps them make sense of his disparate roles and diverse career.

There is, however, no such commonsense interpretive ground that spectators can bring to Lewis's career. He is not a Method actor, but as we've seen, there are many different Lewises, among them "Retarded" Jerry, Idiot Jerry, Las Vegas Jerry, Auteur Jerry, Telethon Jerry, and even "Good Actor" Jerry, the Lewis who was commended for his performances in such "straight" films as *The King of Comedy* (1983) and *Funny Bones* (1995). And each of these roles can erupt whenever and wherever Jerry appears: in a film, at a press conference, during his telethon gig, and during his Broadway run in "Damn Yankees" (1995). Yet, to appreciate how radically Lewis rewrites the traditional relationship between a star and his or her audience, we need to look at the one Jerry persona most analyzed by critics: gay Jerry.

Ed Sikov calls Lewis a "gay icon from Hell," asserting that the homoerotic romance between Dean and Jerry is a central convention of the Martin-Lewis films, capable of erupting into wild, campy farce. Here is Sikov's description of a series of scenes from *Money from Home* (1953):

> Within twenty minutes of the credit sequence Jerry/Virgil has gotten himself into a dress—a flaming red Arabian number with innumerable gauzy veils. Almost immediately—in fact, as if in response—he gets jabbed in the butt with a hot shish kebab skewer with the meat still on it. Soon after—again, as if in direct response to the skewer—he's performing the dance of the seven veils for the pleasure of a tubby sultan who proceeds to advance on Jerry with a lascivious grin. (1994, 187–188)

Krutnik likewise argues that although the Martin-Lewis partnership follows a dialectical logic—Martin as masculine handsome man and Lewis as his feminized, spastic monkey—their films also contain homoerotic moments that push through attempts at repression and "resonate with nuances and longings" (2000, 81).

These longings and tensions surface in *Hollywood or Bust*. The world that Malcolm and Steve inhabit is one fraught with sexual confusion. During the musical number "There's Nothing as Gay as a Day in the Country," women's bodies are used to mount a hilariously exaggerated sexual spectacle, but Malcolm also sings about the prettiness of wild daffodils. Late in the number, Lewis warbles a lyric about "the cute little guy / who's casting a fly / at a trout leaping out of a brook"; the "cute little guy" is really a blonde bombshell, whose hair falls around her shoulders as her fishing cap falls off and she reels in a catch. Similar confusion occurs when Terry is first introduced—she drives by Steve and Malcolm, kicking up a dust cloud, and Malcolm's response is to complain about "what that guy did to our shiny new car."

Yet, while these first impressions of women may seem uncertain, the one complete certainty in *Hollywood or Bust* is the absolute and immediate fondness Malcolm has for Steve. After the car raffle, Steve ingratiates himself with Malcolm, who says, "We'll be pals, just like Burt Lancaster and Katharine Hepburn in *The Rainmaker*." This comment refers to how the Lancaster character exploits Hepburn and her fictional family—yet a subplot in *The Rainmaker* (1956) involves the Lancaster and Hepburn characters' having a brief affair before Hepburn ends up with the local sheriff. This theme of "friendship" is developed a little later in the film, immediately after a scene where Malcolm drives off without Steve, briefly stranding him at a gas station. Malcolm returns, and Steve yells at him for driving away without him. Malcolm replies, "You were scared that somethin' happened to me," and expounds on Steve's virtues, winding up with "You gotta stop worryin' so much about us, Steve—but I guess that's difficult for you, since you're such a kind man." Lewis punctuates this line with a quick, furtive, appraising glance up and down Martin's body—the sort of glance conventionally reserved for indisputably heterosexual types like Dean to apply to beautiful "guys" like Terry.

Steve also seems to have Malcolm on his mind, particularly during *Hollywood or Bust's* most disturbing scene. As Steve sexually assaults Terry and pushes her to the ground, he says, "Just like Burt Lancaster and Deborah Kerr in *From Here to Eternity*, produced by . . ." This dialogue connects to the earlier mention of Burt Lancaster—perhaps indicating that both *Hollywood* scenes might have a sexual charge—and Steve's words reveal that as he is attacking Terry, he is also thinking enough about Malcolm to imitate him. At the finale of *Hollywood or Bust*, Steve is paired off with Terry, but spastic sissy Malcolm is present too, a reminder that in the Martin-Lewis world, sexual desire and gender roles are wacky, fluid, and open to constant revision, and that in this tightly bounded zone of male friendship, Lewis and Martin can never be far apart. Not so, of course, in *Rain Man*: Raymond remains resolutely Raymond; Charlie and Raymond can't hug without panic setting in; and at film's end, Raymond is safely back in the hospital. Everything in *Rain Man* is rigid and safe, especially in the performance of the naïf. To find queerness and performativity like Lewis's in his rendition of Malcolm, we can more productively cruise in the wilds of the avant-garde.

The queerness and schizophrenic pileup of personae in Lewis's films make his work very similar to that of queer filmmaker and performer Jack Smith, who started his film career collaborating with Ken Jacobs on several experimental films beginning around the time *Hollywood or Bust* was released (*Little Cobra Dance* [1957], *The Death of P'town* [1961], and *Blonde Cobra* [finished 1963]). After an acrimonious break with Jacobs, Smith filmed his best-known work, *Flaming Creatures* (1963), a pan-sexual, Orientalist fantasia that proved popular with underground audiences before being busted for obscenity by the New York District Attorney's Office in 1964. During this time, Smith made other contributions to New York's avant-garde culture, publishing several articles and photo spreads in *Film Culture* (most notably his pioneering statement on camp aesthetics, "The Perfect Film Appositeness of Maria Montez" [1962]), dabbling in live performance art, and appearing in several Andy Warhol films (*Batman Dracula* [1964], *Hedy* [1965], *Camp* [1965]). Throughout the 1970s and 1980s, Smith focused on live performance ("Sacred Landlordism of Lucky Paradise" [1973] and "Penguin Panic in the Rented Desert" [1981]), while occasionally screening footage from *Normal Love* (1964), *No President* (1969), and other unfinished films. He died of AIDS in 1989 at the age of fifty-seven.[2]

There seem to be profound affinities between the careers of Jerry Lewis and Jack Smith. Both fashioned "sissy" star images that portrayed homoeroticism (covertly and unconsciously in Lewis's case, quite consciously and overtly in Smith's) as an emotion to be celebrated rather than ridiculed and feared. Both Lewis and Smith were directors interested in innovative mise-en-scène: one of Lewis's aesthetic prides was the sixty-room multilevel set for *The Ladies Man* (1961), while Smith, on a much smaller budget, still managed to make opulent mermaid costumes and a pink-and-white layer cake strong enough to support a crowd of naked revelers in *Normal Love*. Both were also experts at fracturing their star images and creating multiple characters; some of the personae that circulated throughout Smith's *oeuvre* include Sinbad Glick, a self-proclaimed "oily" actor who appears a more decadent version of Vegas Jerry, and Inez (a.k.a. Yolanda la Pinguina), a feather-and-bra-wearing statue of a penguin that Smith used in his live performances to lampoon femininity and fashion. Further, Smith's work reinterpreted real people into expressions of his own particular worldview: he called Jonas Mekas "Uncle Fishhook," the ultimate capitalist robber baron, and Maria Montez was Smith's personal muse, the quintessential representation of the absurd joys of artificiality and glamour. And just as Lewis's performance style embraced chance and improvisation, Smith's live performances focused on his minute-to-minute, ritualistic improvisations with the elements of his set. As Stefan Brecht writes:

> All of Smith's gestures are hesitant. The simplest lifting of an object or
> securing of a string is a serious task which he will accomplish, but

which he does not seem quite to know how to go about. He tries various approaches—in front of you—perhaps gives up some lines of approach too quickly. He is figuring out how to do it while doing it. (Brecht 1997, 43)

According to Ken Jacobs, Smith claimed to have a "nostalgia for the forties," a nostalgia that manifested itself as love for such figures as the Andrews Sisters and Judy Canova (MacDonald 1998, 372). If this love did not include Jerry Lewis himself, it certainly focused on the exuberant but repressed era in which the electric bond between Jerry and Dean was born.

If Lewis never affiliates consciously with the queer "camp" of avant-garde filmmakers, that group—at least one of its leaders—surely adopted him. Jerry makes a star turn in Andy Warhol's *Soap Opera* (1964). *Soap Opera* splices together short filmed skits about love and lust put on by Warhol's Factory stars with found footage culled mostly from television ads. About halfway through the film, Warhol drops a muscular dystrophy commercial starring Lewis into the mix. Lewis stands over a boy dressed in a cowboy outfit sitting in a wheelchair; as Lewis delivers his best Telethon Jerry pitch, the little boy shoots at him with a toy gun. At the conclusion of the commercial, Lewis stops talking, makes his right hand into the shape of a gun, and fires back at the kid: Idiot Jerry blasts right through the treacle of Telethon Jerry, manifesting an ability to shed and switch personae that is of a kind with both Jack Smith's performances and the improvisations of a Gerald Malanga or Pope Ondine.

Perhaps I'm trying too hard to drag Jerry Lewis into the company of queer avant-garde filmmakers. His influence on other queer performers is already obvious; indeed, while watching *Hollywood or Bust*, my four-year-old son kept pointing at Lewis and saying, "He looks just like Pee-Wee Herman." And at the very least, Lewis in *Hollywood or Bust* has given us an alternative to the rigid Method acting and liberal pieties of *Rain Man*. Raymond is defined as both distant and asexual: he passively calls Susanna's kiss "wet," and he screams when Charlie hugs him—the perfect innocent abroad for the era of AIDS and the conservative gender ideology of the Reagan epoch. Malcolm buys Anita Ekberg an extravagant necklace in order to declare his love. Raymond is attracted to a prostitute only because of the pretty shine thrown off by her necklace; he is not allowed to think about anyone else's underwear but his own. And in *Rain Man*, we never believe that Hoffman is truly autistic. But Lewis, both on- and offscreen, is wild, chameleon-like, "abnormal," sissified, and thus more "dangerous," vibrant, and authentic to us. At the end of *Rain Man*, Raymond is back at the hospital, while Malcolm at the end of *Hollywood or Bust* is roaming free, arm-in-arm with Anita Ekberg but still casting an eye in Steve's direction. Clearly, both Malcolm and Raymond are coded as monstrous Others, but given the choice between an autistic, droning Other and a spastic, sissy, sexualized, and incessantly zany one, I know which I'll choose.

### NOTES

1. A good survey of *Rain Man's* production and reception is in Prince 1999, 170–171.

2. The information for this autobiography was taken from "An Anecdoted Chronology" in *Flaming Creature: Jack Smith: His Amazing Life and Times* (Leffingwell, Kismaric, and Heiferman 1997). For Smith's key writings, including "The Perfect Film Appositeness of Maria Montez," see Smith 1997.

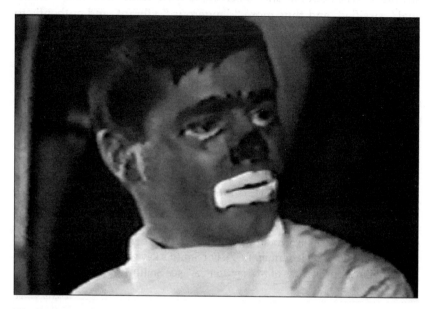

The integrity of show business expressed in clownface. Joey Robin (Jerry Lewis) applies makeup in "The Jazz Singer" (Jerry Lewis Enterprises, 1959). Frame enlargement.

# 6

# The Day the Clown Quit

## Jerry Lewis Returns to *The Jazz Singer's* Roots

Krin Gabbard

THE 1959 TELEVISED version of "The Jazz Singer" that starred Jerry Lewis departs radically from other versions of the story. On one crucial level, however, the Lewis version is more faithful to the original screenplay of *The Jazz Singer* (1927) than was the film itself. Samson Raphaelson gave birth to a rich tradition in American mythology when he wrote a short story about a cantor's son who disappoints his father by becoming a jazz singer. Raphaelson wrote "The Day of Atonement" in 1922 after seeing a road-show production of "Robinson Crusoe," in which Al Jolson played the part of Friday in blackface. (See Carringer 1979 for Raphaelson's short story and the shooting script for the first *Jazz Singer*, as well as an essay on the literary background of the film.) Knowing that Al Jolson was born Asa Yoelson, the offspring of a cantor who migrated from Lithuania, Raphaelson created Jack Robin, a cantor's son "previously known" as Jacob Rabinowitz. "The Day of Atonement" reaches its climax when the Jolsonesque protagonist must choose between performing at the opening of his first Broadway show and replacing his dying father on Yom Kippur, the Day of Atonement and the most holy day in the Jewish calendar. As in all versions of *The Jazz Singer*, the son is the only person other than the father who can bring the requisite feeling to his rendition of the "Kol Nidre," an essential part of the Yom Kippur service. In Raphaelson's narrative, Jack Robin chooses the temple and reconciliation with his father, walking out on his Broadway debut and giving up a promising career as an entertainer.

When Raphaelson turned "The Day of Atonement" into a stage play in 1925, it bore the title "The Jazz Singer" and starred an obscure vaudevillian named George Jessel. Both the play and the subsequent screenplay for Warner Bros. end with the son singing in the temple rather than in the theater. There is a hint in the short story, however, that Jack Robin might yet gain some fame as a cantor in the secular world, not unlike Josef Rosenblatt, the real-life cantor who sings as a screen performer in the 1927 film. Because cantors (unlike priests and rabbis) are not clerics bound by religious vows, they have historically sung in secular venues before audiences that could include gentiles as well as Jews. With a beautiful voice and a reputation as an accomplished performer, Rosenblatt was offered a large salary by Warner Bros. to appear in the original *Jazz Singer* as Jack Robin's father, an old cantor on the Lower East Side of New York City. Rosenblatt's personal religious convictions prevented him from wearing makeup and playing a fictional character, so he turned down the part of the father but nevertheless agreed to sing on camera as himself (Rosenblatt 1954, 289). In a crucial scene, a homesick Jack Robin attends a performance by Rosenblatt while he is on tour in Chicago. Inside the theater, the cantor's performance is intercut with reaction shots of Jack, whose pained expression clearly suggests that he is recalling his old life in New York and his father's singing. The scene was probably meant to prepare the audience for the climactic scene in which Jack replaces his father in the synagogue.

Like the short story, Alfred A. Cohn's published screenplay for the first *Jazz Singer* ends with a degree of ambiguity. Jack had been encouraged in the early stages of his career by the attractive blonde dancer Mary Dale, a more established performer and the gentile love interest who is an essential element in *The Jazz Singer*'s fable of assimilation. In the screenplay, she and her producer follow Jack to the Rabinowitz apartment and later hear him sing "Kol Nidre" in the temple while his father is close to death. Mary Dale tells the Broadway producer, "Don't you understand? It's his last time in there. He *has* to come back to us" (Carringer 1979, 133). The final page of the screenplay brings the ghost of the old cantor next to Jack. He raises his hand as if to give his blessing and then slowly disappears. The executives at Warners wanted something more overtly pleasing to audiences, however. Although they included scenes of Jolson singing "Kol Nidre" in full cantorial regalia (and selling the song with a great deal of body

English) and set up the shadowy appearance of his father next to him, they added a coda that begins with the title card: "The season passes—and time heals—the show goes on." In the film's final scene, Jack Robin is on the stage of New York's Wintergarden Theater (Jolson's favorite venue) singing "Mammy" in blackface, in spite of the fact that his producer had assured him that he would never work again if he chose the temple over the theater on opening night. As he sings his thoroughly secular imaginings of an infantilized African American, Jack's mother and Mary Dale both watch with love in their eyes.

As the first successful film in which actors talked and sang on-screen, *The Jazz Singer* is a watershed in the history of the American cinema (for more on which, see Crafton 1999; Eyman 1997; and Weis and Belton 1985). The film's "Mammy" finale is crucial to that history in more ways than one. For Robert B. Ray (1985), the double ending—Jack in the temple followed by Jack in the theater—was typical of Hollywood's paradigm of inclusiveness that often involved a "single character magically embodying diametrically opposite traits" (58). For Rick Altman (1989), the ending inaugurated the subgenre of the backstage musical and defined its syntax; as in *Dames* (1934), *Strike Up the Band* (1940), *The Band Wagon* (1953), and many others, the success of the show in *The Jazz Singer* is linked to the bonding of a romantic couple. For Michael Rogin (1996), the film demonstrates how whites have historically benefited not only from exploiting the surplus value of African American labor but also from exploiting (here in the happy ending) the "surplus symbolic value" of blacks themselves (80). For Linda Williams (2001), the film registered an essential moment in American history when an entertainment industry heavily populated by Jews not only identified with the suffering of African Americans but actually made it "the very energy and meaning of the nation" (156). The film essentially argues that the Jewish American hero can have it all—the love of both parents, a beautiful gentile woman, commercial success, unproblematic access to African American culture, and an unmistakable sexual presence—without abandoning his ethnic and religious roots. Nearly all subsequent versions of *The Jazz Singer* allowed the hero to remain true to his past and still assimilate as a successful entertainer in mainstream American culture.

The one exception is Jerry Lewis's "The Jazz Singer," in which the cantor's son clearly gives up show business.

## "TV'S FINEST HOUR"

The television play, broadcast on NBC on October 13, 1959, begins in a small nightclub in Chicago where Joey Robin, formerly Yoselle Rabinowitz, displays multiple talents—singing and playing the trumpet but specializing in jokes and sight gags. He is soon interrupted by the noisy arrival of Ginny Gibson (Anna Maria Alberghetti) with her obnoxious producer, an unwilling spectator at the tiny club. (In 1960, Alberghetti would appear as the princess in Lewis's *Cinderfella*. She had previously appeared opposite Dean Martin in *Ten Thousand Bedrooms* [1957]. In Lewis's "Jazz Singer," she directly corresponds to Mary Dale.) Although he aggressively heckles Ginny as well as her producer, Joey eventually apologizes and meets her for lunch, knowing that she is in a good position to help him with his career. Over lunch Ginny tells Joey that her brother had seen him entertaining American troops in Korea and that he had suggested she meet with him. Ginny then invites Joey to fly to Los Angeles and appear on her television variety show. Joey seizes the opportunity, in no small part because he has not been back to his parents' home in Los Angeles for five years and knows that he will be able to visit his father (Eduard Franz) on his birthday.

Although the father has disowned his son for refusing to join the family's five generations of cantors, Joey arrives at the Rabinowitz apartment hoping for the best. He is greeted lovingly by his mother, Sara (Molly Picon), and the many relatives at the birthday party. At first he is even embraced by his father. But after a series of arguments and angry rebukes, Cantor Rabinowitz expels Joey/Yoselle from the apartment. A few weeks later, the old cantor collapses rehearsing for Yom Kippur. In a bravura moment of television editing, the father's collapse rhymes with a quick cut to the son taking a pratfall while rehearsing for Ginny Gibson's TV show: when Franz falls in the temple, his head moves to the lower right of the screen; when Lewis falls on stage, he lands in a similar position, his head to the right. The rehearsal continues with a brief dance sequence that—according to Scott Bukatman's convincing analysis of the Jerry aesthetic (1991)—may redeem the entire program. In what Bukatman calls a moment of "temporary transcendence" (203), Lewis's dancing is typically fluid, graceful, and witty. Even when he feigns awkwardness, he is in complete command of his body.

Although Joey is ecstatic when stagehands and chorus girls enthusiastically congratulate him on his performance, his pleasure quickly fades as his uncle and then his mother arrive with the news that his father is gravely ill and that no one else can replace him in the synagogue on Yom Kippur. Joey argues vociferously about his need to continue with the show, but he has barely begun a dress rehearsal when he abruptly leaves the studio and hurries to his father's bedside, still in full makeup. As in the 1927 screenplay, the female star and her producer follow the protagonist to his parents' living room, conveniently located across the street from the synagogue. While the producer argues with Joey's uncle about the iron laws of show business, the jazz singer's father wakes up long enough to confess that he was wrong to meddle in the life of his son. Joey then steals away to the synagogue unnoticed. In the final scene he is singing "Kol Nidre," with no suggestion whatever that he will return to a career as a performer. Again as in the 1927 film, the old cantor hears his son singing across the street. In Lewis's version, however, there is no text about seasons passing and the show going on. The program simply ends with Joey in a temple of religion rather than in a temple of show business.

Lewis's version of "The Jazz Singer" was an episode of "Lincoln Mercury Startime," a variety series that ran for one season on NBC with episodes lasting an hour. One episode featured Mitch Miller and later became the series "Sing Along with Mitch." Dean Martin, who had ended his partnership with Lewis a few years before and who would later have a successful variety show on NBC, hosted two specials on "Startime." Other actors who appeared in the series included Alec Guinness, James Stewart, and Bert Lahr. The program immediately following Lewis's in the series featured Ingrid Bergman in an adaptation of Henry James's *The Turn of the Screw.* Billing itself as "TV's Finest Hour," the series mixed earnest drama with high-gloss vaudeville. In the credits for Lewis's "Jazz Singer," Ralph Nelson is listed as director, and Oliver Crawford is credited as the author of a teleplay, "based on Samson Raphaelson's 'The Jazz Singer.'" The return to Raphaelson's short story and the two other texts that predate the 1927 film is a striking revision of a narrative that has endured for seventy-five years.

But Lewis's "Jazz Singer" is also significant for leaving behind the racial dynamics so important to the 1927 original. Rather than perform in blackface à la Jolson, Lewis's Joey Robin is in clown makeup when he walks away from his debut. Most remarkably, he sings "Kol Nidre" in clownface as the film ends. Although Joey Robin completely yields to his father's demands at story's end, and although the program includes a brief moment of father-son reconciliation, the oedipal tension between them is stronger than in any previous version of the story.

Whether or not all these departures from the earlier *Jazz Singers* can be directly attributed to the artistic vision of Jerry Lewis is difficult to say. His caricatured image appears after the final credits with the caption "This has been a Jerry Lewis Enterprises production." Most commentators agree that Lewis himself would have had a great deal of control over anything released by his production company. He has definitely continued to exercise authority over the program, keeping it away from audiences ever since the 1959 broadcast. In a conversation with Murray Pomerance, Scott Bukatman reports that he seized an opportunity to watch a print of the program when he was given access to Lewis's archives. He was not, however, able to secure Lewis's permission to screen "The Jazz Singer" at a retrospective of the filmmaker's work he was organizing. Why Lewis made the decision to keep this print from the public is a difficult question. Critics were scornful of the program, even referring to it as "Rudolph the Red-Nosed Cantor." Perhaps at this early stage in his career Lewis had not yet begun ignoring the admonitions of critics, however much their words may actually have wounded him. His stated reasons for removing the program from circulation are not convincing. For example, Lewis maintains that the program fails because he was too young for the part of someone wrestling with "deep problems of life" (Neibaur and Okuda 1995, 262), in spite of the fact that the program dramatizes precisely the kind of crisis a young man might face in the early stages of a career. Lewis has also complained that he was not able to convince the executives at NBC that the program should run ninety minutes (the length of the 1927 film) instead of an hour, and that the broadcast should have been live rather than on tape. "I need the charge I get from a live audience," he told a newspaper interviewer (Levy 1996, 242). At any rate, there is no mention of the 1959 "Jazz Singer" in Lewis's autobiography. (After despairing of ever seeing the program in its entirety, I was able to acquire a multigeneration video copy from an obscure collector of all things Jerry.)

## RETURNING TO THE SCENE

Like many other performers, not all of them Jewish, Jerry Lewis felt compelled to return to the original *Jazz Singer*. Warner Bros. celebrated the twenty-fifth anniversary of the first film's release with a 1952 re-make starring Danny Thomas. Neil Diamond made his one and only appearance as a leading man in films when he returned to his own roots as a cantor's son and remade *The Jazz Singer* again in 1980. I have argued that another group of films can be considered unacknowledged or un-intentional remakes of the film (Gabbard 1996, 35–63). For example, most of the first biographical film about Al Jolson follows the contours of *The Jazz Singer*. *The Jolson Story* (1946) refigures the son's revolt against his cantor father's wishes, the unconditional love of the mother, the discovery of blackface performance, the successful wooing of a gen-tile starlet, and the attempts to maintain a Jewish identity while enjoy-ing the adulation of middle America.

Perhaps the most faithful remake—acknowledged or unacknowl-edged—is *The Benny Goodman Story* (1955). Once again, a Jewish son must overcome the opposition of a father to popular music while re-taining the loving support of a devoted mother and the attentions of a beautiful gentile, in this case an heir to the Vanderbilt fortune, Alice Hammond (Donna Reed). Neither the young Benny (Barry Truex) nor the mature Benny (Steve Allen) ever puts on blackface, but each has sig-nificant encounters with African American jazz musicians who, as much as Hollywood allowed in the 1950s, help him become a more sexually mature male. Just as Jolson found a new emotional language and a clever way of sexualizing himself by performing his fantasies of African American culture, Benny overcomes an early sexual humiliation when he encounters a group of Creole and African American jazz musicians who tell him, "We just play what we feel." Young Benny, who has never before heard jazz, quickly becomes an accomplished improviser, pre-sumably finding sufficient emotional expression in black music to tran-scend the wound to his masculine pride. Later on in *The Benny Goodman Story*, African American musicians are there to encourage the mature Benny at the crucial moment when he successfully romances Alice. The finale of *The Benny Goodman Story* is more economical than the ending of the 1927 *Jazz Singer*: While Jack Robin sings "Kol Nidre" in the temple and then returns to the theater for the performance of "Mammy," Benny Goodman does it all in the finale at Carnegie Hall. Although the music is almost always the familiar popular music of the 1930s, the film makes a point of featuring the unmistakably Jewish tonalities of Ziggy Elman's Klezmer trumpet solo, as if to prove that Benny has not left behind his ethnic roots even in the midst of a jazz concert.

Films as diverse as *Broken Strings* (1940), *Is Everybody Happy?* (1943), *St. Louis Blues* (1958), and *La Bamba* (1987) have all recycled crucial elements of the first *Jazz Singer*. The successful negotiation of the father's law while crossing over to mainstream culture seems to have an inexhaustible appeal for Americans, including blacks (*St. Louis Blues* is the story of W. C. Handy) and Mexican Americans (*La Bamba* narrates the brief life of Ricardo Valenzuela, later known as the pop star Richie Valens). Even "The Simpsons" devoted a half hour to parodying *The Jazz Singer* in 1991. Perhaps inspired by the histrionics of Laurence Olivier as the old cantor in the 1980 remake ("I HAF NO SON!"), "The Simpsons"' "Like Father, Like Clown" starred Jackie Mason as the voice of Rabbi Krustofsky. After seeing him perform in a nightclub, the old rabbi had disowned his son, soon to be famous as Krusty the Klown. Thanks to the interventions of Bart and Lisa, Krusty sings "Oh Mein Papa" as he is reconciled with his father on live television at the episode's conclusion.

The father-son reconciliation is not, however, as strong in the 1927 film as it is in "The Simpsons"' parody and most of the other remakes. As the old cantor in the first *Jazz Singer*, Warner Oland humiliates and beats young Jakie before the boy runs away from home. When he returns to New York as Jack Robin to serenade his mother (as Linda Williams [2001] points out, the real love affair in the 1927 film is not between Jack and Mary Dale but between Jack and his mother), the father puts a definitive end to the festivities with his one and only spoken line: "Stop." Only as he lies dying with his son at his side does the old cantor relent. A title card gives him the line "My son—I love you." The film implies that Jack is so moved by his father's dramatic, if sudden, change of heart that he goes to the synagogue primarily to please him, rather than his mother. In the 1980 remake, however, Laurence Olivier not only lives to hear his son sing "Kol Nidre" but is actually in the audience enjoying himself as Diamond sings his hymn to assimilation, "America."

The 1952 remake features an even more complete reconciliation. Anticipating his role in Lewis's televised version, Eduard Franz plays the father as the leader of a wealthy congregation in Philadelphia. Although he would prefer that his son join the five previous generations of cantors in the family, the father closely follows his son's career, at one point singing every word of a rapid-fire radio commercial that his son had performed. Seeking father-son harmony after a brush with death,

Franz's character releases his son from the obligation of becoming a cantor, even imputing a spiritual dimension to his son's profession, a connection that was crucial to the 1927 original: "Jazz singing is fundamentally an ancient religious impulse seeking expression in a modern, popular form" (Carringer 1979, 23). I have speculated that the easy reconciliation between Jewish father and son at the climax of the 1952 remake surely responds to the deaths of so many Jewish fathers a few years earlier at the hands of the Nazis (Gabbard 1996, 52). And as J. Hoberman (1991) has pointed out, the emergence of the State of Israel in 1948 drastically altered the issues of Jewish assimilation that are crucial to the film's plot. In the 1950s, Jews like the old cantor who refused secular modernity could simply move to Israel. Like the father in the 1952 remake, observant Jews who stayed surely found something to like in secular America.

Significantly, Eduard Franz plays a much more rigid patriarch in Jerry Lewis's 1959 version. The oedipal hostility between father and son is consistent and almost unrelieved until the end. By recasting Franz as the jazz singer's father, Lewis seems to be taking back the benevolence and understanding that Franz expressed with such sincerity in the 1952 *Jazz Singer*. A significant moment of pathos for Franz in 1959—and one of the more compelling pieces of screenwriting in the program—is a smooth transition between Joey Robin singing the ballad "This Is My Night" in the nightclub and the cantor's young pupil singing the Hebrew lyrics to A. W. Binder's song "Israel's Keeper," on which Joey's song is clearly based. The face of the boy replaces Lewis's in a carefully synchronized lap dissolve. The old cantor soon appears on camera to gently instruct the boy on the importance of singing from the heart. But even this tender moment is taken away quickly when the cantor brusquely denounces his son in a conversation with his wife while the young pupil is still present. Later, at his birthday party, the cantor publicly and violently humiliates his son when Joey begins to sing "This Is My Night." Because the song is a popularized version of "Israel's Keeper"—Joey admits that he has "jazzed up" the song—the father slaps his son in front of all the guests and insists that he leave immediately. In what Bukatman has called an "affectless performance" as the jazz singer (1991, 192), Lewis plays the scene as a loyal son deeply wounded by his father's anger and intolerance. Stopping to touch the mezuzah outside the door, Joey leaves the apartment, his head hung low. The touching spectacle of the rejected son is a rare moment when

Lewis achieves real pathos without seeming to apologize for it or in some way to undermine the seriousness.

Rather than arguing that jazz singing is just another way of addressing God, the angry cantor critiques Joey's revision of "Israel's Keeper" and his career as a comedian with the phrase "A thoroughbred from generations does not pull a junk wagon." The suggestion that telling jokes and singing jazz is a step down in social class is another significant change from the *Jazz Singer* tradition that began with the Raphaelson story and the 1927 film and continues through most of the remakes. The injection of a class dialectic into the 1959 version may have grown out of Lewis's distress at critical claims that his abilities were simply those of an overachieving working-class boy and not the result of real artistry. Although Martin Scorsese did not create *The King of Comedy* (1983) with Jerry in mind, perhaps Lewis himself is speaking when Jerry Langford solemnly tells Rupert Pupkin (Robert De Niro), "What looks so simple to the viewer at home, all those things that come so easily, that are so relaxed, and look like it's a matter of just taking another breath. It takes years and years and years of honing that." In 1927 the apology for the jazz singer's craft was presented as a title card at the beginning of the film: "Perhaps this plaintive, wailing song of jazz is, after all, the misunderstood utterance of a prayer." In 1952, Eduard Franz tells Danny Thomas, "Whenever you sing, always lift your head high and raise your voice to God, the way you did in the temple."

In Lewis's version, by contrast, the old cantor never regards jazz and popular music as anything other than a particularly déclassé version of sacrilege. The closest thing to a justification for the son's profession occurs when Uncle Nat—who corresponds most closely to the neighborhood friend Moishe Yudelson (Otto Lederer) of the original film—explains to the cantor that the Jewish people have always survived and often prospered because of laughter, thus bringing legitimacy at least to Joey's work as a comedian. The message in the 1959 version appears to be that one can speak to God only in the temple, even if the speaker is in clownface. The final orchestral flourish that supplements Lewis's "Kol Nidre" suggests that Joey Robin has made the right decision. Certainly, he seems to have retained more of his religious faith than the jazz singers who came before and after him, if only because we see Joey Robin touching the mezuzah at the door of his parents' apartment.

## LEWIS'S MINIMALISM

Anna Maria Alberghetti plays Ginny Gibson with a great deal of charm and warmth, but the casting of a brunette, Italian American actress pushes the production away from another of the basic *Jazz Singer* motifs—the Jewish entertainer's move into mainstream American society through the devotions of an American woman, the blonder the better. The gentile object of desire in 1927 was the blonde May McAvoy; in 1952 it was Peggy Lee. Perhaps by 1959 Jews were sufficiently clubbable that a white Anglo-Saxon woman was no longer an essential ornament. In the 1980 version, Neil Diamond is matched with a brunette Latina, Luci Arnaz.

In most remakes of *The Jazz Singer* there is little tension between the adoring mother and the gentile girlfriend. In 1927, May McAvoy and Eugenie Besserer, who play Mary Dale and Sara Rabinowitz, respectively, never exchange a word even though they are in the same room at the climactic moment when Jack must decide whether to spend his evening in the theater or the temple. In *The Benny Goodman Story*, Benny's doting mother (Berta Gersten) is uncomfortable with Alice Hammond, at one point telling her, "You don't mix bagels with caviar," a sharp contrast to the cantor's argument in 1959 that jazz singing is a step down on the ladder of class. By the end, however, Alice sits next to Benny's mother at the final concert and enjoys her full support when Benny asks for Alice's hand by means of a clarinet solo.

In 1959, by contrast, Sara Rabinowitz and Ginny are never more than acquaintances. Ginny commits a major faux pas by referring to Sara as "Mrs. Robin." But in this version, Joey is sufficiently enchanted by Ginny to fantasize about marrying her. In the 1927 film, shortly after telling Mary Dale that he regards his career as more important even than her, Jack Robin looks in the mirror in his dressing room and sees himself in blackface. The image is then replaced by a vision of his father in ceremonial robes before his congregation. In the corresponding scene in the 1959 version, Joey looks in the mirror and imagines himself marrying Ginny with the willing participation of his father and mother. He also imagines a marquee with his name above Ginny Gibson's, then with his name below Ginny Gibson's, and finally with his name alone. And unlike Jolson's jazz singer, Joey Robin is not given a long series of love scenes with his mother. Lewis's version is about a father and a son.

Although Jerry Lewis and his father both had a great deal of respect for Al Jolson, there is no blackface in the 1959 version of *The Jazz Singer*. Of course, one could argue that clownface—certainly in the American tradition epitomized by Emmett Kelly—is rooted in minstrel traditions and can be regarded as a continuation or at least as a displacement of blackface. Nevertheless, in 1959 and at the beginning of the twenty-first century, few Americans are likely to see an imitation of African American culture when someone like Jerry Lewis performs in clownface. The omission of a clearly marked blackface performance from the 1959 version leaves a hole at the center of the *Jazz Singer* narrative, even though the 1952 remake also dispensed with burnt cork. (The 1980 version restores blackface, but with the racist suggestion that only the white songwriter-hero can replace the jailed member of an African American singing group. And once the blacked-up hero is exposed by an angry member of an all-black audience, the white protagonist is allowed to throw the first punch, as if his newly acquired negritude authorizes his violence.) Minstrelsy was the dominant form of American entertainment for most of the nineteenth century (Lott 1993). For the first half of the twentieth century, blacked-up actors were a staple of the American cinema, beginning at least as early as Edwin S. Porter's *Uncle Tom's Cabin* (1903) and figuring prominently in D. W. Griffith's *The Birth of a Nation* (1915). After his debut in the 1927 *Jazz Singer*, Al Jolson wore blackface in several subsequent films. Charles Correll and Freeman Gosden blacked up to reprise their radio roles as Amos 'n' Andy in *Check and Double Check* (1930). A partial list of white stars who have also appeared under cork would include Eddie Cantor in *Whoopee!* (1930), Fred Astaire in *Swing Time* (1936), Mickey Rooney and Judy Garland in *Babes in Arms* (1939), and Bing Crosby in *Dixie* (1943). Larry Parks blacked up to play Jolson in two extremely successful biopics, *The Jolson Story* and *Jolson Sings Again* (1949). In 1951, Doris Day did a blackface imitation of Jolson in *I'll See You in My Dreams*, a film that also starred Danny Thomas and was directed by Michael Curtiz for Warner Bros. In 1952, however, when Warners remade *The Jazz Singer* with Danny Thomas as star and Curtiz as director, there was no blackface performance.

Although I have found no evidence of a decision-making process at Warner Bros. that resulted in a ban on blackface in the 1952 *Jazz Singer*, it is possible that groups such as the NAACP learned of the film in the early stages and convinced studio executives that the practice could be seen as offensive. It is also likely that the men at Warners decided on their own that times had changed and that blackface had become too provocative to be part of mainstream entertainment. After Keefe Brasselle blacked up to play Eddie Cantor in the 1953 biopic at Warners, and Joan Crawford appeared under a light coat of dusky body paint in MGM's *Torch Song* (1953), no films with blacked-up actors appeared again until *Black Like Me* (1964), which, of course, took the practice in an entirely different direction.

Lewis surely shared the views of many liberal Americans in the 1950s who would have found blackface to be offensive to African Americans. He would probably have refused to perform in burnt cork if it had been suggested (although I have located a still photo of Lewis wearing blackface at what appears to be the same time as his "Jazz Singer"). In addition, Lewis has taken little of his singing and dancing style from African American traditions. Like Danny Thomas in 1952, Lewis is scarcely a jazz singer and certainly not a minstrel man. Unlike Thomas, however, Lewis does wear heavy makeup at the end of the film. As he prepares for the final rehearsal of his big number just prior to the evening broadcast, Lewis applies a white rectangular mouth, a dog's nose, white eyeliner, and exaggerated marks around his eyes and eyebrows. Although he lectures Uncle Nat and then his mother on why he cannot walk away from the broadcast, he sings only a few lines of "Be a Clown" before he runs out of the studio, throwing his cane and clown's hat to the floor. He is in full clownface at his father's bedside and still wears the dog nose and exaggerated eye makeup when he sings in the synagogue.

Why Joey would not bother to remove all his makeup or why no one in the congregation would tell him to wash his face is never addressed. Were it not for the music that swells up in support of Joey Robin's return to the temple, we could speculate that he has suffered a breakdown with classic symptoms of schizophrenia. The lack of a finale back in the television studio—or even a speech such as Mary Dale's reassurances in the original screenplay that "He *has* to come back to us"— profoundly destabilizes the protagonist's character. Likewise, in many of the films that Lewis directed in the years just after his "Jazz Singer," he seemed to relish dramatizing the fragmented nature of his persona. In the "curtain call" that concludes *The Nutty Professor* (1963), for example, Lewis appears in Buddy Love's clothes but with the teeth of Julius Kelp. At the end of "The Jazz Singer," Lewis wears Yoselle Rabinowitz's clothes and Joey Robin's face.

## LIFE WITH FATHER

The narrative of father-son tension was undoubtedly what attracted Lewis to the original *Jazz Singer*. As in all versions, Lewis's rendering of the story does not confront anti-Semitism. The only problem remaining to face a Jewish entertainer is opposition from his father, thus placing even more weight on the oedipal narrative. But in Lewis's version, little else remains from the original or even from the various remakes. There is no appropriation of African American performance or sexuality, no prolonged flirtation with Mother, no boffo musical numbers, and no triumphant return to show business at the end. The closing moments, however, first when Joey visits his ailing father and then when the cantor hears his son singing across the street in the synagogue, are extremely similar to scenes at the end of the 1927 film. At least for men, these are the scenes in the original film that twenty-first-century Americans still find extremely moving, in spite of the archaic quality of the film. Looking for a dramatic situation that was close to home, Lewis may have found the story of a Jewish son coming back to his father an ideal vehicle for his aspirations as an actor. By giving his character the name with which he was born, Lewis registered his desire to make at least a portion of the jazz singer's story his own. (The casting of Alberghetti may reflect Lewis's marriage to an Italian American woman.) Although Jerry's father left home to pursue a career in show business and not the other way around as in the *Jazz Singer* narratives, Jerry surely had his father in mind when he remade the film that made a movie star out of Al Jolson, the entertainer on whom Lewis's father modeled his career. A few years earlier, in 1956, Jerry Lewis had recorded "Rock-a-Bye Your Baby," a song closely associated with Jolson, for a Decca LP (Krutnik 2000, 88). Like Jolson's Jack Robin, Jerry Lewis surpassed his father by becoming a star. And like the old cantor in the *Jazz Singer* narratives, Danny Lewis was quick to give his son advice, often with a degree of assertiveness that was too much for the son (Levy 1996, 242). Jerry Lewis himself told an interviewer that his parents had been so poor that they could not afford to give him a bar mitzvah. Shawn Levy has speculated that the 1959 "Jazz Singer" is "the bar mitzvah he never had" (242).

In spite of the high seriousness of what he was attempting, much in Lewis's "Jazz Singer" is typical of his work. The Lewis hero is constantly prevented access to conventional masculinity, and his attempts at controlling his career, his romantic aspirations, and his family life are consistently thwarted. His behavior vacillates between opposite extremes. With Ginny he is first overtly belligerent and then childishly contrite. He is just as capable of making a serious attempt at reconciliation when he arrives at his father's birthday party as he is capable of entertaining grandiose fantasies in his dressing room. Correspondingly, no song or dance number is ever presented in its entirety, either because the program cuts to them in progress or because they are interrupted—by editing or, most memorably, by a slap from the singer's father. Perhaps a song would have been performed in its entirety (as was usually the case in Lewis's films during the 1960s) if Lewis had been able to convince NBC to let the program run for ninety minutes. Nevertheless, the fragments we do see are often splendid. Jerry's version of "Makin' Whoopee," with which the program begins, is as engaging as the thirty seconds of his dancing later in the hour.

The program's surprise ending may reflect a profound ambivalence about show business in a performer who seems to live and die for his moments before an audience. One critic suggested that Raphaelson's "Day of Atonement" was an unlikely text to be based on the life of Al Jolson, since it is impossible to imagine Jolson giving up show business (Carringer 1979, 26). Much the same can be said for a script built around Jerry Lewis. But Joey Robin protests too much when he is given the opportunity to speak up for his career—enough to make us wonder what Jerry's real feelings about show business may have been at the time, and may yet be. Unlike almost all the other jazz singers, Lewis repeatedly makes speeches about the integrity of his profession. In what is surely intended as a highly ironic moment, Joey Robin applies clown makeup while earnestly explaining to his Uncle Nat why he cannot walk away from that evening's broadcast. He compares himself to a doctor who would not desert a patient, as well as to his own father who would not abandon his congregation. In none of the other versions of the story does the protagonist compare himself to a physician or a cleric, primarily because there is no need. Audiences went to those films because they loved the music of the jazz (and pop) musicians whose careers were being celebrated as unquestioned and unquestionable. The grandiosity of Joey's comparisons is even more obvious because they are spoken by a man in clownface. In a sense, the old cantor is thoroughly vindicated. The son's career carries none of the dignity he abandoned when he left home and the possibility of continuing the work of his father. Joey's return to the temple at the end suggests that the son finally agrees. Jerry's performance of the role at least raises the question of whether he agrees as well.

The final scenes also suggest that Lewis has long been conflicted about his work as an entertainer and his more lofty aspirations as a humanitarian. His on-again, off-again career as a director and actor, along with his Muscular Dystrophy Association Telethons, "in which an ultimate, and even ritualistic, confrontation with the pain of human suffering is staged in a continual and endless fashion" (Bukatman 1991, 193), surely reflect these same divided ambitions. The other side of Lewis's ambivalence—his reluctance to be anything other than a performer—is embodied in the spectacle of a man leading a Yom Kippur service in clownface. Although the moment is highly performative in a typically exaggerated Jerry fashion, both the comedian and the cantor are profoundly out of place.[1]

## NOTE

1. Many thanks to Chuck Hsuen, Scott Bukatman, David Hajdu, Robert G. Goldenberg, Harvey R. Greenberg, Eric Goldman, and, as always, Paula B. Gabbard. And if this essay has any value at all, it is because of the indefatigable persistence and support of Murray Pomerance.

# PART III

# JERRY LEWIS AND SOCIAL TRANSFORMATIONS

"We had that certain something that I wish I could say we planned." Larry Todd (Dean Martin, l.) with Myron Mertz (Jerry Lewis) in *Scared Stiff* (George Marshall, Paramount, 1953). Frame enlargement.

# 7

# Sex and Slapstick

## The Martin and Lewis Phenomenon

Frank Krutnik

We skyrocketed . . . like two blazing comets, the thrust taking us straight up to unbelievable stardom. And the ride was filled with a million laughs, guided by a special kind of love that I thought two guys had for each other.

—Jerry Lewis

THE BIG-SCREEN vehicles of Dean Martin and Jerry Lewis were among the most successful Hollywood films of the 1950s.[1] Film exhibitors in the United States routinely voted them among the top ten box-office attractions from 1951 to 1956, and eight of their films appeared in the annual lists of top twenty commercial attractions (three in 1953 alone). However, with the exception of *Artists and Models* (1955) and *Hollywood or Bust* (1956)—both directed by cult auteur Frank Tashlin—these films have received remarkably little critical attention. Designed to capitalize on the celebrity that Martin and Lewis were enjoying in other contexts as a star team and male couple, these films do not in themselves offer today's audiences a satisfactory insight into the astonishing impact that the team had during their glorious postwar decade.

Most commentators agreed that in and of themselves their Hollywood showcases generally gave a poor account of what Martin and Lewis did and of what made them so remarkably successful. The dynamic interaction that characterized their live work was often sacrificed onscreen by making the two men conform to a standard generic opposition between straight man and comic. As producer Hal Wallis put it, "A Martin and Lewis picture costs a half-million, and it's guaranteed to make three million with a simple formula: Jerry's an idiot, Dean is a straight leading man who sings a couple of songs and gets the girl. That's it, don't fuck with it" (Levy 1996, 104). By outliving other articulations of the Martin and Lewis partnership, their cinematic memorials offer today's audiences a skewed impression of what all the fuss was about. Rather than reading these films as self-contained texts, then, we need to approach them as part of a much broader cultural phenomenon that encompassed a range of media outlets. This chapter sketches a broader framework for understanding the cultural significance of the team, arguing that Martin and Lewis's success derived from their enactment of a special male friendship, which was most scintillatingly exhibited—even onscreen—through their very *liveness*.

In March 1946, twenty-nine-year-old crooner Dean Martin and twenty-year-old comic Jerry Lewis were booked as separate attractions on the same bill at New York's Havana-Madrid nightspot. They had already met some months earlier, but this time they got on so well that they began to intrude playfully into each other's stage business, an impromptu kibitzing that soon developed into more sustained afterpieces (Levy 1996, 64–65). On the evidence of these performances, *Billboard* reviewer Bill Smith predicted they had "the makings of a sock act. Boys play straight for each other, deliberately step on each other's lines, mug and raise general bedlam. . . . Lewis's double takes, throw-aways, mugging and deliberate over-acting are sensational. Martin's slow takes, ad-libs and under-acting make him an ideal fall guy" (Tosches 1992, 126–127). Meeting with even greater acclaim when they reprised their comic shtick at the 500 Club in Atlantic City, the two men decided they had best get together for real. Billed for the first time as Martin and Lewis, they opened at Philadelphia's Latin Casino in September 1946 (Levy 1996, 76).

By the early 1950s, Dean Martin and Jerry Lewis were just about the hottest stars of U.S. showbiz, their popularity fueled by appearances in movies, cabaret and theater, radio and television, phonographic recordings, and comic books. Their premier television appearance was on Ed Sullivan's variety show "The Toast of the Town" in June 1948, and they had similar guest shots on other shows before beginning their own showcase as one of several rotating hosts on "The Colgate Comedy Hour" in September 1950. They first gained exposure on radio by guesting on Bob Hope's show in October 1948, and within six months they were hosting their own series on NBC radio. *My Friend Irma*, the first of sixteen Martin and Lewis movie vehicles, was released by Paramount in August 1949. Capitol records signed them as both individual artists and as a team, but Martin's solo career proved the only fruitful result of this arrangement. (Lewis would not establish his own prowess as a vocalist until after the demise of the partnership.) The team also featured as the subject of a monthly DC comic book, which would subsequently continue as *The Adventures of Jerry Lewis* until the early 1970s.

While this kind of cross-media celebrity was by no means unknown in U.S. entertainment culture, the speed with which Martin and Lewis attained such prominence was quite remarkable. So, too, was the range of audiences they persuaded to embrace their wild, bewitching liveness—from the sophisticated urbanites who applauded them in the clubs, to the families who watched them on TV, to their ardent and occasionally hysterical young fans. Norman Taurog, director of five of the team's films, testifies to the excessive emotions they could inspire among their young enthusiasts. During their record-breaking two-week engagement at New York's Paramount Theater in July 1951, the streets were jammed with teenagers: "The response was almost orgiastic. Little girls were practically having orgasms every time Dean and Jerry opened their mouths" (Marx 1975, 142). The generation that ruled the entertainment scene when Martin and Lewis started had built their audiences over long and grueling decades. The familiar faces (and voices) of such performers as Bob Hope, Eddie Cantor, George Burns and Gracie Allen, Jack Benny, Bing Crosby, and Al Jolson provided a strong sense of continuity with prewar entertainment traditions of vaudeville, Broadway, and broadcast radio. Lewis spent his formative years in the shadow of his father Danny, a professional song-and-dance man who worked in burlesque, vaudeville, and the Jewish Borscht Belt resorts. Lewis says that when he came to devise his act with Martin, "I was stealing every burlesque notion that I remembered that I saw my dad perform" (JAS Productions 1992a). But things were changing, in show business as elsewhere—and Martin and Lewis's rapid rise to fame was itself a symptom of that change. They may have been influenced by prewar show business, but they also offered something completely different.

With Martin, Lewis could safely discard the act he'd been peddling onstage since he was sixteen, in which he performed outrageous mimes to the backing of phonograph recordings. The crooner's smooth and lazy baritone provided a real-life replacement for these canned voices. As Lewis puts it in his autobiography, the defining concept behind the Martin and Lewis experience was "Sex and Slapstick," as realized through the volatile communion of handsome man and monkey:

> I rented a typewriter and went to work shaping the act. After writing down the title, which I called "Sex and Slapstick," I laboriously typed out these words: *Since time immemorium, there has never been a two-act in show business that weren't two milkmen, two food operators, two electricians, two plumbers, and for the first time here we have a handsome man and a monkey. . . .*
> That was the premise.
> And that is precisely how we played it. Not only onstage, but whenever the mood struck. (Lewis, with Gluck 1982, 142–143)

Like Abbott and Costello, they joined together a straight man and a goofball, and like Hope and Crosby, they were another pairing of singer and comedian. But as an entertainment team, Martin and Lewis proved to be wilder, less predictable, more dangerous. Andrew Sarris remarks that comedy teams generally "have a certain internal cohesion that unites them against the world outside. That is to say that members of a comedy team have more in common with each other than with anyone else." Martin and Lewis, by contrast, managed at their best to sustain "a marvelous tension between them. The great thing about them was their incomparable incompatibility, the persistent sexual hostility" (Sarris 1968, 142–143). As Lewis points out, his bonding with Martin was premised upon their very difference—with the handsome crooner serving as a straight register against which he could launch his disorderly deformations. Martin was the legitimate facade, the easygoing front man who personified an idealized and self-possessed heterosexual masculinity. Yet he was yoked to this unruly, demanding, unrepressed, and uncoordinated misfit who served as an all-purpose conduit for otherness. The distinction between the two men is especially well emblematized by their voices. On one level, the contrast between Martin's smoothly dusky instrument of seduction and Lewis's needling adenoidal whine suggests oppositions between man and boy, Italian and

Jew, stud and queer. But there is another crucial dimension to Lewis's deviance: for while the grain of Martin's voice maintains a consistent identity, his disorderly partner perpetually shifts gear among diverse voices, registers, and identities. Lewis, in other words, encompasses not simply an alternative "voice" to Martin but an alternative mode of being, a splintering multiplicity that contends with the handsome man's singularity. In *Pardners* (1956), their rendition of Sammy Cahn and James Van Heusen's title song provides one of the duo's numerous partnership anthems—others include "What Would You Do Without Me" from *The Caddy* (1953) and "What Have You Done for Me Lately?" from *Scared Stiff* (1953). As they sing "Pardners" in the film of the same name, Dean and Jerry seem genuinely in love with each other, even though at the moment of recording they could hardly have been further apart: it proved to be their final screen duet. The number concludes with a Lewisian squeal that is utterly distinct not only from Dean's trademark crooning but also from Jerry's own vocalization in the rest of the song.

As I suggest below, however, the tension Sarris speaks of derives not solely from the differences between Martin and Lewis but from the fact that the two men coexist in such intimate proximity. In the process of colliding and colluding together—particularly good examples of which can be found in *The Stooge* (1953), *At War with the Army* (1950), *Scared Stiff*, and *Living It Up* (1954)—they share a conflictual harmony that encompasses closeness and distance, tenderness and hostility, euphoria and ambivalence.

Dean Martin and Jerry Lewis happened to find each other in the right place at just the right time. What they did together in the clubs and elsewhere connected with receptive audiences to a degree they could never have predicted—no matter what high-flying agents, publicists, and managers were on their case.[2] It is impossible to comprehend the phenomenal success of Martin and Lewis without taking into account the particularities of the context they sprang from. They joined forces only a short while after the end of World War II, for a career that would carry them and their audiences through the first decade of the cold war. Indeed, their debut at the Havana-Madrid occurred within a few days of Winston Churchill's famous "iron curtain" speech in Fulton, Missouri, which signaled the start of frigid relations between East and West. Martin and Lewis emerged, then, when the United States was being torn between jubilation at the war's end and anxiety at the less confident scenario that ensued. The team had such an impact, Nick Tosches suggests, because they provided "not laughter in the dark, but a denial of darkness itself, a regression, a transporting to the preternatural bliss of infantile senselessness. It was a catharsis, a celebration of ignorance, absurdity, and stupidity" (1992, 204).

But there was more than merely frivolous escapism to this catharsis and to what Martin and Lewis did and meant. Lewis himself made this plain when interviewed some five decades later for the television series "Martin & Lewis: Their Golden Age of Comedy":

> Remember, you just came out of World War II. And this country was hurting. And this country needed a binding of some kind. And to see two people care as much about one another as they did, and get you to laugh on top of it . . . I don't think that that act, or those two people, would have meant one tenth of what they were had it happened ten years before. (JAS Productions 1992a)

Their unpredictable and exuberant comedy doubtless seemed a welcome relief after the dutiful sacrifices of wartime, but as Lewis implies, his partnership with Martin went beyond simply refusing the claims of adulthood and responsibility. They celebrated instead an idealized alternative to postwar domestication by enacting a utopian vision of male friendship.

This was not something that Martin and Lewis simply performed but something they were perceived to *live*. Crucial to their image and to the cultural work they enacted as media signs was a conviction that though their act may have consisted of a relationship, that relationship itself was never simply an act because it was grounded in authentic affection. "One has the feeling," *Sight and Sound* critic Daniel Farson wrote in 1952, "that their success as a comedy team mirrors the success of an important personal relationship" (31). Nick Tosches notes, too, that their publicity aimed to portray Martin and Lewis as "freewheeling, fun-loving guys whose act was merely an extension of their everyday personalities and antics" (1992, 149)—an appraisal made especially credible by such cinematic routines as Dean and Jerry's trio with Carmen Miranda in *Scared Stiff* or the "Every Day's a Happy Day" number from *You're Never Too Young* (1955). Even when the team began to unravel, the very intensity of their deteriorating relations testified to the nakedly emotional as well as professional stakes the two men held in the partnership. The feelings may not have been especially nice toward the end, but at least they were real.

Martin and Lewis never seemed more "authentic" than when they were freely interacting before responsive audiences. Numerous witnesses testify to the scintillating *liveness* they unleashed in their cabaret work, a gloriously kinetic performance that revealed two men in the throes of ecstatic and transcendent interfusion. Describing what they had as "lightning in a bottle" (Soapbox Productions 1996), Lewis's nostalgic recollections of his time with Martin capture both the adoration he felt for his partner and his astonishment that they could share such intuitive rapport:

> See, all I had to do was tell Dean I was gonna do such and such; that during the numbers I was gonna be a busboy in the audience. That's all I had to tell him; he went with me. . . . If I started something, he'd pick up on it like a child goes after milk. . . . We had that certain something that I wish I could say we planned. We didn't plan it. It was innate within us that out of the blue he was doing six, seven, eight minutes of comedy and I was straight for him. (Tosches 1992, 139)

As is still evident from tapes of their television work, the material they worked with merely provided the spark for igniting an incandescent process of exchange and reversal as Martin and Lewis made live together. "It is difficult to record just exactly what their act is," Bill Davidson wrote in 1951, "for they rank among today's leading masters of the ad lib and the improvised business" (65).

Performing live, Martin and Lewis could be relied on to whip up a frenzied spectacle of abandonment in which they lost themselves both to each other and to the impulses of the moment. They were especially fond of overthrowing the regimentation of script and format. "Writers were never ever capable of really writing for Dino and I," Lewis says, "except giving us a frame, go . . . put them in that frame and then, bang! They're exploding" (JAS Productions 1992a). The "Comedy Hour" programs, their principal televisual forum, truly come alive not in the sketches but in more free-form contexts that allow space for the mutual riffing that characterized their nightclub act. Most often, the simple pretext is that Martin tries to sing his final song despite the persistent interruptions of his partner. One *Variety* reviewer noted that these finale sequences were "probably the highlight of all their shows . . . when lots of time is left open for them to do virtually as they wish" (*Variety* 1983–1997).[3]

Martin and Lewis's screen vehicles similarly attempt to evoke the live aesthetic of their cabaret act by means of showcasing performance routines that liberate the two men from their scripted identities. Examples include "The Donkey Serenade" sequence in *My Friend Irma*, the club performances in *At War with the Army* and *Scared Stiff*,[4] and the stage acts presented in *The Stooge* and *The Caddy*. A more fictionally coordinated example of such performativity characterizes a sequence in *Artists and Models* where Jerry runs down three flights of stairs to answer the phone while Dean is in the bathtub, then runs up to say there's a phone call, then runs down to see who is calling, then runs back up to report to Dean. The whole thing is played like a choreographic routine, right down to a finale that has Jerry, fully clothed, caught in the tub with Dean.

It was rare for Martin and Lewis to make it through the sketches on the "Comedy Hour" without some momentary derailing of the script. One sketch has Martin as a drugstore customer who requests a strawberry milkshake from Lewis's soda jerk.[5] Lewis is immediately transported into one of his distinctive needle-stuck-in-a-groove routines as he responds to Martin's command with excessive enthusiasm.[6] So carried away is he by excitement that Lewis repeats the words *strawberry milkshake* over and over again in different voices, until it becomes a kind of doodling mantra of disconnection from the world. Playing loose with the scenario staked out by his writers, Lewis seems to want to see just how far he can spin out this manic digression. While Martin watches haplessly from the other side of the counter, Lewis meanders into stratospheric realms of nonsense:

> *Strawberry milkshake,*
> *Put in the cream,*
> *Put in your ashtray,*
> *Turn out the light,*
> *Cos we're having a milkshake—*

At this, he breaks off and collapses into laughter—swiftly followed by both Dean Martin and the audience. As the two men try to fight off the merriment that has seized them, Lewis huddles closer to Martin on the counter. "Dean, I ad-libbed," he declares. "Don't you just love me?" He then reaches over the soda counter, clutches Martin's head in both hands, and kisses him full on the lips—pulling away with a femme gesture of delighted adoration.

Such joyous deviations from scripted business successfully underscore the liveness of performance in the face of mediation. What is especially interesting about this particular example, however, is how it presents a teasingly disavowed insight into the Martin-Lewis relationship. As Lewis told *The Hollywood Reporter* in 1948, the partnership works because of "the way we feel for each other that nobody can duplicate. . . . So there can never be another two-act like this because there's never going to be two guys who feel this way about each other. There couldn't be two men who are as close to each other as we are" (Marx 1975, 64). The soda-fountain sketch is but one of countless instances where the interaction between the two men opens a vein of guardedly explicit homoeroticism. The tub sketch and the imaginary dinner sketch from *Artists and Models* are others. In his fond reminiscences Lewis persistently describes the past he shared with Martin in terms of *love*, a slippery concept that encompasses a vast array of emotional resonances. Most frequently, Lewis means to suggest a mixture of admiration and fraternal intimacy, as when he informed one television interviewer, "The thing that Dean and I had was love for one another that we allowed an audience to see. Now, the love was my hero-worship for him; his love was me, the kid brother" (JAS Productions 1992b). However, the love Lewis expresses for his former partner often seems closer to infatuation. As his autobiography makes clear, the skinny Jewish kid was immediately enraptured by the assured manliness of the Italian crooner, who was ten years his senior. "Such an Adonis," Lewis sighed when the two were first introduced (Lewis, with Gluck 1982, 134).

Lewis frequently borrows from the conventions of heterosexual romance to convey the emotional intensity of his relationship with Martin. For example, a televised interview in the early 1990s explicitly compared the collapse of the partnership to a divorce:

> The love affair was so strong. And the break, though we wanted it, must have psychologically shattered us more than we knew. That's the only excuse I have for it. That's the only rational answer I can give you. We wanted to have nothing to do with one another. "How dare you spoil what I've created!"—is what both men are saying, to one another, who have agreed to part. (Tiger Television/BBC 1992)

The most magnificently perverse conceptualization of the partnership occurred in a 1993 interview, when Graham Fuller's question about the "formula" that made the team click elicited the following reply from Lewis: "It was the same chemistry, and this may sound weird—well, I don't know how it's going to sound—that happens when the sperm and egg make contact and can reproduce a magnificent miracle. That's what we had. I don't know of any other chemistry that's as godlike" (Fuller 1993, 93).

But Martin and Lewis's complexly nuanced relationship was as much a cultural myth as it was a personal friendship. As a myth it articulated and tried to make sense of the contradictory facets of masculinity in postwar America. Martin and Lewis's homocomic partnership helped articulate and defuse anxieties inspired by the intense intimacies between men that the conditions of wartime had encouraged. Steve Cohan makes a similar case for the appeal of Hope and Crosby, arguing that their hugely popular *Road* series provided a comic site for renegotiating the homosocial organization of masculinity during and immediately after World War II (1999, 23–45). But where Hope and Crosby first joined together onscreen in *Road to Singapore* (1940), before U.S. intervention in the war, Martin and Lewis were integrally a postwar phenomenon. They constituted a carnivalesque countercurrent to the heterodomestic affirmation that gripped the United States throughout the postwar decade. In his history of gay men and women during World War II, Allan Bérubé depicts this new civilian order as follows:

> As families were reunited and struggled to put their lives back together after the war, articles, books, advertisements, and the media promoted idealized versions of the nuclear family, heterosexuality, and traditional gender roles in home and the workplace. Accompanying this preoccupation with conformity was a fearful scapegoating of those who deviated from a narrowing ideal of the nuclear family and the American way of life. (1990, 258)

The special male friendship that Dean Martin and Jerry Lewis enacted came to define possibilities for imagining masculinity that deviated from heterosocial and heterosexual norms. Yet their relationship so mirrored the heterosexual ideal of the loving couple that Ed Sikov (1994, 186) could describe them as a same-sex variant of the screwball lovers of such films as *The Awful Truth* (1937) and *Bringing Up Baby* (1938). While women themselves play only marginal roles in Martin and Lewis's comedy, traditionally feminine functions tend to be distributed between the two men and expressed in a variety of configurations. Martin and Lewis's film vehicles may dispense with the regular heterosexual alibi that Dorothy Lamour provided for Hope and Crosby, but they routinely present Martin with a token love interest, while Lewis is often paired with an infantilized equivalent—as in *Jumping Jacks* (1952) and *The Caddy*. Such women tend to be dropped at the slightest provocation to leave the scene free for the two buddies, unencumbered by heterosexual ties. In such films as *Sailor Beware* (1951), *The Stooge*, and *Pardners*, the Lewis-figure's psychoneurotic deficiencies tend to be blamed on the indulgences of an overprotective mother—a strategy Robert Kass ascribes to the prevalent Momism of the postwar era (Kass 1953, 122–123). With Martin, Lewis's misfits can escape from maternal domination into the sheltering arms of a male buddy.

Besides locating Lewis as Martin's buddy or surrogate younger brother, the team's films also cast him in more eccentrically feminized roles as a doting lover or dutiful spouse—most explicitly, perhaps, in the sequence from *The Caddy* where Lewis is a paragon of wifely devotion to Martin's skirt-chasing gadabout (Krutnik 2000, 81–82). Contemporary critics protested about Lewis's persistent departures from the conventions of heterosexual masculinity. The entertainment trade journal *Variety* complained about his predilection for "nance stuff," while Bosley Crowther's *New York Times* review of *Money from Home* (1953) lamented that "Mr. Lewis runs too much to effeminacy, which is neither very funny nor very tasteful." In a more sustained and symptomatic discussion, Robert Kass similarly bemoaned the degrading spectacle of Lewis's "prancing imbeciles and mincing homosexuals" (1953, 122). Four decades later, Ed Sikov suggested that Lewis served postwar U.S. culture as "a jester in a court of sexual panic":

> By incarnating the kind of subversive homosexual desire that could not be overtly expressed let alone fulfilled (hence its sheer repetition), and by doubly subverting this desire by making it seem, as Lewis's character puts it in *Artists and Models*, "retarded," Lewis could express the (for want of a better word) homoeroticism that could no longer be denied on the screen but could scarcely be stated forthrightly in this era of officially-sanctioned gay-bashing. . . . He is

the hysterical manifestation of his culture's failed repressed—imminent sexual criticism incarnate. (1994, 190)

Sikov reads Lewis as "a gay icon from Hell," who both exercised and exorcised the specter of homosexuality (185). "Like the equally homophilic Laurel and Hardy," he remarks, "Martin and Lewis play the sexual side of buddyism for dangerous comic effect, turning a kind of vicarious homosexual panic on the part of audiences into pleasure by way of nervous laughter" (186–187). But it is crucial to emphasize that while Lewis may have offered a grotesque spectacle of homoerotic desire, the relationship he shared with Martin was itself far from grotesque. After all, so widely accepted were they as a "couple" that Martin and Lewis were even permitted to share a bed together in their television sketches, a liberty denied the heterosexual sitcom partnerships of Lucy and Desi or Ozzie and Harriet (Burke 2000, 3). The intense yet precarious intimacy of Martin and Lewis showcased a dizzying array of emotional and covertly erotic intensities between men. They entranced legions of loyal fans with their teasing masque of a special male friendship, a utopian bonding that allowed two such polarized men to sparkle and combine. Through the late 1940s and early 1950s, audiences were captivated as Martin and Lewis put on their show—competing playfully, having fun, being together, loving it. They inspired such affection among their diverse audiences that the dissolution of the partnership provoked a strong sense of public betrayal—for which Jerry Lewis ultimately bore much of the blame.

But that, as they say, is another story. . . .

## NOTES

1. The present chapter develops arguments about the career of Dean Martin and Jerry Lewis that are explored in more depth in my book *Inventing Jerry Lewis* (Krutnik 2000, 39, 84).

2. Broadway agent Abner J. Greshler signed Lewis when he was still a solo act and subsequently took over management of the partnership. When they began to hit it big, Greshler fed the team to publicist George B. Evans, who had coordinated the bobbysox hysteria that launched Frank Sinatra on the road to megastardom in 1943. Martin and Lewis later benefited from the support of such entertainment industry behemoths as Lew Wasserman's MCA talent agency (who snatched them from Greshler in 1950), Paramount Pictures, and NBC.

3. The one medium that Martin and Lewis failed to conquer was radio, not simply because it sacrificed the visual dimension of their interplay but also because by the late 1940s sponsor-driven network broadcasting was rigorously scripted and time plotted (Wertheim 1992, 263–269).

4. Including "Mamae Eu Quero" with Carmen Miranda, which had been part of Jerry's own stage "record act."

5. The sketch is included on the videotape *Young Jerry Lewis* (Passport Video 1990).

6. Such comic business recurs throughout Lewis's work and is frequently associated with his characters' inability to reconcile themselves to the requirements of service. His films frequently cast Lewis as some kind of servant—for example, *The Caddy* (1953), *Cinderfella* (1960), *The Bellboy* (1960), *The Errand Boy* (1961), and *The Patsy* (1964)—and rather than actively rebelling against the hierarchy that subordinates him, the Lewis figure often brings about the collapse of order through his unrestrained and overeager servitude. For further discussion of this issue, see Shaviro 1993, 110–111; and Krutnik 2000, 138–139.

A goofy and defensive half-wit lackey with the facial expressions of the mentally deficient. Polly Bergen (l.), Jerry Lewis, and Dean Martin (r.) in *The Stooge* (Norman Taurog, Paramount, 1953). Frame enlargement.

# 8

# The Imbecile Chic of Jerry Lewis

Mikita Brottman

MUCH HAS BEEN written about the rhetoric and behavior of Jerry Lewis in relation to physical disability, especially in regard to the way his comic routine appears to parody the symptoms of muscular dystrophy. The spastic twitches and gesticulations of Lewis's comic persona have been regarded by some commentators as making a mockery of disability, and as a result, his charity performances have sometimes been boycotted by the disabled (see, for example, Johnson 1992 and Haller 1994). Very little, however, has been written about the uneasy associations between Lewis's comic role as an imbecilic misfit and his enormous popularity with an audience struggling to come to terms with changing public perceptions of mental disability.[1]

In this chapter I examine the complex relationship between Lewis's Idiot persona and changing public perceptions of mental illness during the 1950s. I am particularly interested in how Lewis's aping of imbecility during a time when the mentally disabled were more publicly present than ever before reflected some pressing cultural anxieties about the proximity of mental illness. I want to show how, as a *faux* imbecile, Jerry Lewis functioned as a socially acceptable outlet for the public fear of mental illness, which manifested itself in the form of convulsive laughter.

Lewis invariably constructs his comic persona around a series of odd-looking misfits, grotesque in appearance and behavior. When he first began doing stand-up comedy in the late 1940s, he capitalized on his own stringy, funny-looking appearance, screeching voice, and emaciated body. As his film career took off in the 1950s during his collaboration with Dean Martin, he constructed his whole comic routine around the figure of a whining, cringing half-wit. This persona, sometimes referred to offscreen by Lewis as "The Idiot," was a seeming mental deficient characterized by frantic bodily twitches and a lack of physical and emotional control.

In essence, this Idiot persona mimics the "crazy" behavior of the mentally retarded—the kinds of tics, grimaces, and convulsive movements that once entertained working-class visitors to Bedlam, Charenton, and the Salpetrière. Today it seems retrogressive to think of mental dysfunction as amusing. Most people would agree that it is no longer acceptable to seek entertainment in mental deficiency. And yet an enormous number of jokes, cartoons, and comedies still revolve around and parody the behavior of the mentally disabled, suggesting that public perceptions of mental illness are still complicated, ambivalent, and confused.

In a prescient article published in *Films in Review* in 1953, critic Robert Kass provided a vivid description of Lewis's Idiot persona as it had appeared in the half dozen Martin and Lewis films the team had already made:

> In appearance, Lewis is a freak—a shockingly immature, stringy six-footer with a crew hair cut, wide and expressionless eyes, and a feeble-minded face capable of astonishing grimaces. He hides behind an idiotic laugh. His speaking voice is a squawk, and his singing voice is a shattering screech. . . . Despite unpredictable behavior, tantrums, fits of weeping, he is rather nice—because he is harmless. Men can look down with comfortable superiority upon his athletic and sexual failures; women feel a tender protectiveness as toward a retarded child; . . . he is the neighborhood freak, the affection-starved moron whom only a mother could love. (1953, 119)

Like a child suffering from an extreme form of hyperactivity, the Idiot is everywhere at once, grotesquely incompetent, chaotic, and unruly, crashing around, sometimes teetering on the edge of violence but never quite going over that edge, never quite becoming dangerous. Kass particularly objects to the anti-intellectual quality of Lewis's routine, his "supercharged lunacy" and "unconfined exhibitionism." He is especially repelled by how Lewis makes a comic shtick out of mental dysfunction, characterized by a complete lack of bodily coordination and a crazy, purposeless energy. Frank Krutnik explains how this disruptive behavior was notably emphasized in the Martin and Lewis comedies, where Lewis appears as Martin's "grotesquely deformed doppelganger." "Latching on to Martin as a straight man and a front man," explains Krutnik, "Lewis developed his comic persona as a hysterical inversion of the cool and self-possessed handsome man" (Krutnik 1995, 7).


## STOOGING

*The Stooge* (1953), one of Lewis and Martin's most popular Hal Wallis–produced comedies, directed by Norman Taurog, is a particularly useful example of Jerry Lewis's imbecile chic. The typically unsophisticated plot features Dean Martin as Bill Miller, an off-off-vaudeville circuit performer who has carved out a modest niche as a romantic balladeer. His act hits the big time when his agent persuades him to team up with stooge Ted Rogers, a manic moron played by Lewis. The film's epigraph concisely sums up the narrative: "New York—1930. This story is about some names in bright lights on the Great White Way . . . and a certain Dim Bulb."

In *The Stooge*, Lewis adopts his familiar Idiot persona, playing a fastidious, whiny man-child, overdressed in undersized suits that emphasize his flailing, simian limbs—the excuse for any number of broken windows, offended ladies, and flying hats. As Martin's oblivious halfwit lackey, Lewis is goofy and defensive, employing the facial expressions and physical gesticulations of the mentally deficient. He is a source of disorder not due to any inherent disobedience but more from lack of instruction—his mother is also something of a simpleton. As in similar Martin and Lewis comedies, the Lewis character lives at home. In one scene, we see him sitting in the kitchen in his overtight suit and tie, helping his mother bake a cake. When this scene of domestic harmony is interrupted by the arrival of Dean Martin, Lewis first attempts to disguise himself as an old codger by rubbing flour in his face and hair and, when this fails, leaps onto his mother's lap and clutches her in terror.

When Martin and Lewis go on the road, it is the suave Martin who takes the place of Jerry's mother in a series of similar domestic scenarios. In one vignette Jerry sits sewing a button on his shirt, asking Martin about his relationship with his wife, Mary (Polly Bergen). A scene set in the sleeping car of an overnight train shows Martin and Lewis preparing for bed, both dressed in pajamas—Martin in suave silks and Jerry in childish tightly buttoned flannels. This leads to an antic routine in which the nervous Lewis, who's "never been away from home be-fore," attempts to snuggle down in bed with Martin. The implications are less homoerotic than of a frightened retarded child seeking comfort from an adult.

Interestingly, *The Stooge* also includes a number of scenes in which it is Martin, "stewed to the gills," who turns into the retarded child, leaving it up to Lewis to slap him back into shape before the stage show begins. *The Stooge* also provides Lewis with his own love interest in the form of "Frecklehead" (Marion Marshall), a childlike, pigtail-wearing, lovestruck ditz, as prone to fits of lisping and pouting as Lewis is to whining and screeching. Frecklehead is Lewis's female equivalent, an Idiot girl, awkward and incompetent like Lewis but not unlovable in her own way. Similarly, however ridiculous and imbecilic Lewis ap-pears in *The Stooge*, he is always warm-hearted and affectionate, rather like a backward child who can be irritating at times but is never annoy-ing enough to become actively dislikable. Significantly, not only was the film a hit with audiences, but it is also remembered by Lewis with great fondness. He later claimed:

> Of all the films Dean and I made together, *The Stooge* is my favorite. We both felt that it was, in our early days, our best work because it trans-ferred two nightclub performers to the screen properly. It came closest to capturing what Dean and I had as a team. It was well written, and we just respected the work. (Neibaur and Okuda 1995, 61)

Despite all his attempts to distance himself personally from it, Lewis's Idiot act was hysterically popular; audiences loved his grotesque, mugging pantomimes of mental disability, granting him a kind of adulation rare in the world of comedy. Fans adored his whines, screeches, and panicked shrieks, his simian gesticulations, his moronic incompetence. Baffled by Lewis's enormous popularity, critics at-tempted to rationalize audiences' fascination with this bizarre aping of imbecility, complete with spastic gestures and emotional incompetence. It was hard to understand why the public proved so eager for the sight of someone publicly regressing to childhood and acting out the infan-tile fears and desires that more stable personalities manage to repress.

Most critics attributed the act's success to the combination of what Lewis once referred to as "the handsome man and his monkey." In other words, the appeal of Martin and Lewis was not a result of their closeness and cohesion but of the differences between them: Dino's suave savoir faire and Jerry's ridiculous incompetence. According to Andrew Sarris, "Martin and Lewis at their best . . . had a marvelous tension between them. The great thing about them was their incomparable incompatibility, the persistent sexual hostility" (1968, 142–143).

Robert Kass had a rather different explanation for the enormous appeal of Jerry Lewis, suggesting that his popularity was related to the fact that—unlike the work of more sophisticated comedians of the time—his humor had absolutely no relevance to contemporary social or political issues. And since Lewis was so much more popular than any other comedian, Kass, fearing that the Idiot was a kind of mirror that reflected the social and cultural tendencies of the times, concluded that audiences in the early 1950s were in the mood for facile slapstick, the lowest common denominator of comedy. "We have turned into what [George] Meredith termed 'hypergelasts,'" writes Kass, "excessive laughers or Bacchanalians, giddy spectators who roar at anything that takes our mind from the problems of our time" (1953, 121). Particularly disturbing, according to Kass, was the nihilism of Lewis's humor, its intellectual emptiness. "As for the emasculated, almost homosexual quality of some of Lewis's gags and inflections," he complained acerbically, "they are profoundly anti-human and anti-life, and the response to them is not unalarming. . . . Let us hope there is little of ourselves in the prancing imbeciles and mincing homosexuals he imitates" (122).

What Kass—clearly no fan of Lewis—seemed to find particularly disturbing about the intellectual vacancy of Lewis's comic routines was that they were, for some reason, exactly what the contemporary audience eagerly wanted to watch. "Lewis," concluded Kass, "is neither satirist nor parodist nor humorist. He is a Pied Piper of escapism, bleating an empty-headed tune which attracts millions" (122). The question that remains unanswered in Kass's somewhat precious and rather caricatured analysis of Lewis is why American audiences during the early 1950s were so eager to laugh at a whining, cringing, "prancing imbecile," openly making a public exhibition of his mental deficiency.

## THE ROOTS OF IMBECILE CHIC

To fully understand the roots of imbecile chic, we need to take a close look at the changes in public perceptions of mental illness during the

1950s. Before 1950, the only place to care for those who displayed behavior that relatives or the community saw as disturbing or anti-social was either a psychiatric hospital or a jail. Housed in such institutions were not only the obviously psychotic but also those addicted to drugs and drink, the mentally retarded, and the inordinately promiscuous. People with mental disabilities were seen in public far less frequently than they are today; as a result, the public tended to define mental illness in much narrower and more extreme terms than did psychiatry, and fearful and rejecting attitudes toward the mentally disabled were common.

Things began to change rapidly in the early 1950s, however, when the process began of reintegrating the mentally ill into the community. This was partly a response to the development of new psychotropic medications—the most significant of which was Thorazine, the first nonsedating tranquilizer—which reduced the frequency of lobotomies and eliminated the most violent symptoms associated with schizophrenia and other psychotic disorders (seizures, hallucinations, delusions, and so on). It was also partly the result of an evolving alliance between fiscal conservatives worried about the expense of large, state-run asylums and civil libertarians concerned that such institutions were much too restrictive. To countercultural activists, who rejected a political conservatism that preached division and secularization, the integration of the mentally ill into the community suggested a social sensibility that began to manifest itself in the radically democratic embrace of self-designated individuality and diversity. These developments were precursors of the more far-reaching phenomena that emerged in the next decade—a new articulation of heterogeneous, often undifferentiated social groups and a mixing of political and psychological demands for their dramatic visibility. The mentally ill thus became one group among many—beatniks, blacks, feminists—suggesting the radical potential of a united counterculture against the gigantic, normalizing hegemony of capitalist consensus.

As a result of these changes in public attitudes, the population at state hospitals began to decline. After falling from 23,560 in 1953 to lower than 20,000 in 1960, it continued to drop throughout the 1960s and 1970s, reaching 2,676 by 1980 (Tye 2001, 46). In 1880, 98 percent of people with severe mental disabilities were either in an institution or cared for at home; today, only 2 percent of the mentally ill are in hospitals, and 93 percent are in the community, in group homes, or in comparable settings. Massachusetts, for example, had eleven state mental hospitals in 1950; now it has only four. Had the number of asylum patients kept pace with the state population, there would have been more than thirty-two thousand patients in Massachusetts hospitals today. Instead, there are slightly fewer than one thousand, the majority of whom will spend less than a year in an institution (45).

This movement toward deinstitutionalization was both a result of and a reaction to a major change in public attitudes toward mental illness. The secularization of psychoanalysis, the development of group therapy and counseling programs, and the public visibility of the mentally ill meant that those with mental difficulties were gradually ceasing to be "them" and rapidly becoming "us." The development of new psychotropic medications often made mental illness virtually invisible; tics, twitches, and seizures were replaced by a sedated, zombie-like calm that allowed people to appear less peculiar and noticeable, if also less expressive, in public. In the past, as Michel Foucault explains, the madman's body had been regarded as the visible and solid presence of his disease, "whence those physical cures whose meaning was borrowed from a moral perception and a moral therapeutics of the body" (1998 [1965], 159). By the mid-1950s this was no longer the case: it was no longer necessary to see mental illness in terms of odd behavior, violence, and psychosis, indicating a movement toward increased acceptance of the fact that the mentally disabled were no longer separate from the public at large.

What is the connection, then, between the enormous appeal of Jerry Lewis's Idiot persona in the early 1950s—in *The Stooge*, his cross-eyed attempts to get drunk on champagne, his monkey business in the balcony while Dean croons smoothly on stage—and the new public exposure to former mental patients now living ordinary lives in the community? One might imagine that the new public presence of the mentally disabled would make audiences less, not more, predisposed to finding amusement in a comedian whose act involves what can be seen as an imitation of the grotesque appearance, behavior, and gestures of the mentally retarded as they had been imagined in an earlier age. To understand fully the appeal of Jerry Lewis, we must first understand how laughter functions as an index of repression, how the audience's warm reception of a comedian's routine can be seen as an indication of the audience's profound fear.

## LAUGHTER, CONSENSUS, AND CHAOS

Before the 1950s, the most popular comedians—such as Fred Allen, Sid Caesar, and Jack Benny—tended to be less physical in their routines, partly because their acts were developed with radio audiences in mind. The humor of early television comics such as George Burns and Gracie Allen (who had come from radio) also revolved less around physical escapades than around verbal banter on social and cultural themes—especially marriage, the family, the relationship between the sexes, and other areas of sexual and psychological anxiety. If their comic routines were chaotic, the chaos was external to the body, manifesting itself as the crazy, mixed-up world in which the comedians found themselves.

In the 1950s, however, physical shtick became much more fashionable, with madcap acts burgeoning in popularity—particularly those that mimicked imbecility, such as Abbott and Costello, the Three Stooges, and, especially, Jerry Lewis. These acts placed particular emphasis on the out-of-control physical body—Lewis's flailing arms crashing through glass windows and knocking Frecklehead in the face in *The Stooge*, for example. The world in which the protagonists live is stable and ordered; chaos manifests itself internally, in the form of a physical body in disarray. Significantly, the 1950s were famously a period of social consensus and conformity, and yet the decade was also, not coincidentally, a time that saw the emergence of subversive cultural productions, including beat writing and rock 'n' roll music. The appearance of radical cultural forms during an era notorious for its social conservatism indicates perceptible public doubts over whether this kind of mass consensus was really healthy.

The development of psychotropic medications and the new proximity of the mentally disabled meant that a source of spectacle had been taken away from a public with a significant appetite for challenges to social conformity and consensus. Even if this spectacle had been purely imaginary, its removal was critical; people were no longer able to enjoy the *frisson* produced by imagining the disorderly world of twitching, ticcing, violent mad people behind the bars of the local asylum. And yet, feeling a need for madness as entertainment is one thing; wishing to become mad oneself is quite another. Though no longer especially distinctive, these former mental patients had arrived in "our world" from the world of the irrational and still bore its stigmata. The fear of the possible contagious influence of mental illness continued to grow.

The increased presence of the mentally disabled led to an enormous increase in anxiety over the fact of mental illness and its proximity. This anxiety was enhanced partly by the frightening fact that mental disability was no longer distinctive enough to be visible, and partly by the fear that any moment a disease, accident, or sudden affliction could turn an intelligent man or woman into a drooling half-wit—Jerry, for instance, falling headfirst into the bathroom sink in *The Stooge*. One of the frightening things about the mentally retarded is that they remind us of the frail boundaries of our mental health and threaten us with the loss of the rational, adult relationship we've established with one another and with the everyday world. Once repressed, the fear of this threat—like all anxieties—returns to manifest itself in the socially "appropriate" guise of laughter at the *faux imbecile*.

Over the years, a number of perceptive philosophers and psychologists have conceived human laughter as fundamentally neurotic. It has been suggested that laughter is not, in fact, connected to humor at all but to a nexus of deep emotions related to fear, aggression, shame, anxiety, and neurosis. The lack of a sustained and coherent relationship between laughter and feelings of "mirth" has been well testified (see Thorson and Powell 1991). In his work on humor, Freud explains how unconscious material is held in repression by specific amounts of psychic energy; when some experience or observation stirs up this material, the psychic energy diverted to the task of holding the material in repression becomes destabilized for a second and is thereby transformed into laughter (see Freud 1960 [1928], 153).

Certain kinds of humor can be seen to function as a substitute response for frightening emotions that have no other means of expression. The ordinary substitute response is a common occurrence, as in the carpenter who accidentally hits his thumb and responds with groans, profanity, and facial grimaces. A less common form of substitute response is the "expression displacement"—a response intended to conceal from consciousness the real character of the emotional state, as in the case of laughter, which can come to serve as a displaced expression of hopelessness and despair. Psychoanalytic studies focus on how specific, if unconscious, motivations and satisfactions operate behind the screen of humor. According to psychoanalysis, only when the unconscious motives of the joker or comedian are recognized as paramount can humor be understood at all. In this light, certain displays of humor can be seen to function as a somatic displacement of invective and abuse, revealing bitter and hostile despair. The comic display constitutes a ritual form of protective cover—a socially sanctioned disguise—for hostility and aggression. Most frequently, the comedian is using the form of comedy to exteriorize or "get rid of" unpleasant truths and experiences, and humor is a means by which he can "pass on the blow" and, in the process, slough off some anxiety onto his listener-victims.

Consequently, humor is often used as an acceptable social outlet for those frustrations, tensions, and hostilities that have no other means of release in a society that seeks to exercise control over the aggressive drives of its members. To put it more simply, it isn't that we laugh "at" someone or "with" someone; it isn't that we laugh because we see ourselves as superior to somebody else or want to make them our victims. Rather, the object of our laughter is a proxy, an unconscious alibi concocted to outfox the judgmental function of the ego. What we are really laughing at, every single time, is ourselves. And so the cultural function of Jerry Lewis in the 1950s can be seen as that of a safety valve—a stooge, in fact—at whose madcap routines (swinging onto the stage from curtain ropes, falling asleep with a trash can on his head) the public can release their anxiety in the form of nervous and hysterical laughter.

The popularity of pathological tics and twitches among comedians of the 1950s found its echo in the convulsive laughter of the spectators, who may have been reminded that the human body cannot be kept under control and made to conform; our bodies betray us at every step. Laughter is a clear example of the body dominating reason, a vivid index of the loss of physical control. Jerry Lewis in particular seemed to stand for a challenge to bodily conformity, acting out upon his body national anxieties about whether or not this social and cultural consensus was really in our best interests. In the Lewis and Martin comedies, Lewis's desire to live up to the social and bodily standard that Martin set (trying to win the girls, for example, or to croon romantic melodies) and his conspicuous inability to overcome the nervous, convulsive movements of his body (spluttering on his martini, accidentally punching his girlfriend in the face) reflect a profound public anxiety about being able to "pull off" a normal presentation of self.

In this sense, what the relationship between Martin and Lewis seems to reveal is the enormous extent of repression that is necessary in our attempts to live up to our social ideals and all the frustrations, tensions, and anxieties that are produced in the construction and maintenance of social order. It might even be said that the Martin and Lewis comedies are radical works, in the sense that they reveal to us the irrationality of our social ideals and the impossibility of our ever conforming to them. Their humor allows an escape from the tensions and pressure involved in attempting to live up to an impossible social standard, as well as a release from all the surplus repression that this effort engenders.

In these comedies, in fact, Martin seems to represent the "higher faculties"—reason, judgment, choice, and will—and Lewis the lower faculties of sensation, motor response, automatism, and instinct. Significantly, Freud describes how the circus antics of clowns can produce great anxiety, particularly when a "dignified" clown (such as Martin) is pitted against a sillier one (such as Lewis). The crazy games of this mismatched pair can evoke in observers the traumatic split between childhood and adulthood, reminding us of the fears and conflicts of the latency period. Later Freudian and Lacanian analysts have discussed how, in such typical vignettes, the clown comes to represent the self, whose embodiment as mature adult (Martin) is mocked by the childhood personality (Lewis) and its fatuous monkey-shines. The adult is reduced, destabilized, and desexualized (castrated) by the child, a process that articulates fears of regression and disintegration. According to psychoanalysis, this presentation of self in two simultaneous modalities is typical of anxiety-evoking scenarios (see, for example, Soulé 1980; Chervet 1996).

In a marvelous article published in *Critical Inquiry* titled "From Charcot to Charlot" (2001b), Rae Beth Gordon charts the correspondence between a significant cultural and aesthetic style (physical comedy that involves ticcing, twitching, and spasmic movements) and the extraordinary upsurge of concern with and diagnosis of hysteria and epilepsy in nineteenth-century French medical practice and theory. She also charts a relationship between the ways in which movement was staged in early cinema and corporeal pathologies related to hysteria and epilepsy—contractures, tics, catalepsy, and convulsive movements—arguing that hysterical gesture and gait were an important inspiration and basis for the style of frenetic, anarchic movement that is so present in early French film comedy.

Gordon's description of the addictive appeal of angular tics and grimaces, especially in a culture characterized by sexual and political conservatism, is especially useful in helping explain the enormous appeal of Jerry Lewis to the American public of the 1950s. This interest in the relation between early French cinema and the corporeal unconscious—the study of automatic reflexes—provides the thesis of Gordon's recent book, titled, appropriately, *Why the French Love Jerry Lewis* (2001a).

## COMEDY, ANXIETY, AND NEUROSIS

In his discussion of the nature of clowning, psychoanalyst Joseph Levine regards the clown as expressing—in an appropriately controlled and yet uncontrolled form—the repressed aspects of a particular society (1961, 74). The public clown or comedian offers us an outlet for our anxieties about those events, situations, and taboos that we find most frightening and difficult to deal with in our culture. The comedian is thereby responsible for handling something "not proper" in society—something that Levine describes as "embarrassing, astonishing and shocking" (76). In the case of Jerry Lewis, this shameful taboo is the dread of mental illness.

Significantly, the more Jerry Lewis became identified with the ridiculous and familiar figure of the Idiot, the more eager he became, at interviews and press conferences, to promote himself as a thinker, a scholar, and a man of dignity. Offscreen, he went to great lengths to pass himself off as a serious intellectual, affecting a sober, sententious disposition as if to further distance himself from the Idiot. Lewis's arrogant and disdainful behavior toward the press has been well documented. In his biography *King of Comedy* (1996), Shawn Levy diagnoses many examples of Lewis's delusions of grandeur, most often characterized by intellectual and sexual boasting—obvious attempts to erase the impression of mindless, sexless prepubescence that his characters created.

In his book *No Laughing Matter*, Gershon Legman has some sobering thoughts about those who feel compelled to enter the world of comedy, especially when they have a "need to 'do their thing' aggressively and publicly," and have "found a protective cover for their neurosis" in forms of popular entertainment (1982, 49). According to Legman, the public comedian "is only attempting to reassure himself on the subject of his most desperate fears, whistling under his rictus-mask in the darkened parts of his own soul that nauseate and frighten him the most" (49). The comedian's act, according to Legman, is essentially both a compulsive confession and an evasion of the moral judgment that he deserves and yet so desperately fears:

The whole tragedy of the comedian or teller-of-jokes is this—that he can never really be shriven at all, since his true guilt is inevitably concealed from the audience by the very mechanism which excites the audience's laughter. The cycle of telling and listening, listening and telling, must therefore be endlessly and compulsively repeated for a lifetime, the teller visibly taking the least pleasure of all in the humor at which he struggles so hard, and in which, at the end, he stands like the hungry child he is, darkly famished at their feasting while the audience laughs. (49)

Over the years, critics have sometimes found Lewis's comic routines curiously disheartening, suggesting an implicit understanding of how humor can serve as a displacement for feelings that are more akin to hostility and despair. In his review of *The Stooge* for the *New York Times* in October 1953, Bosley Crowther described the film as not only "oddly depressing" but actually "perilous to one's simple faith in man." In 1961, in the *Los Angeles Mirror*, Al Capp described how he accidentally wandered into a movie theater showing *The Ladies Man* (1961) and could endure it for no more than twenty minutes. He couldn't stand the film any longer, he explained, not simply because he was bored. "It was something more painful: I felt it had been somehow indecent of me to peek at a grown man making an embarrassing, unentertaining fool of himself." "It may well leave you in a state of depression," read the *Newsweek* review of *Hardly Working* (Ansen 1981), while the critic for *Time* magazine wrote of Lewis's performance in the same film that "the only emotion he arouses is pity" (Schickel 1981). And of the disastrous Broadway show "Hellzapoppin'"—during whose production, according to backstagers, Lewis displayed symptoms of profound exhaustion and grief, weeping openly at least fifty times—Kevin Kelly wrote in the *Boston Globe*, "The evening's beckoning, wide open, gap tooth smile finally is revealed as a mock tic paralyzed in place" (1977). As Victor Hugo comments of Gwynplaine in his novel *The Man Who Laughs* (1889), "What a weight for the shoulders of a man,—an everlasting laugh!"

## NOTE

1. Many thanks to David Sterritt for his help and advice with this chapter.

Jerome Littlefield's (Jerry Lewis) "neurotic identification empathy" emerges most acutely in his dealings with Mrs. Fuzzyby, an inveterate hypochondriac (Alice Pearce), in *The Disorderly Orderly* (Frank Tashlin, Paramount, 1964). Frame enlargement.

# 9

# Sick Jokes

## Humor and Health in the Work of Jerry Lewis

Lucy Fischer

Comedy distances pain, but leaves signs of it everywhere.
—Mason Cooley

Medical students, especially men, learn to become agents of [emotional] disconnection.
—Ellen Singer More and Maureen Milligan

LET US CONSIDER two texts from the 1960s starring Jerry Lewis.
The first is a film, *The Disorderly Orderly* (1964), directed by Frank Tashlin. In it Lewis plays Jerome Littlefield, a hospital worker who toils in that capacity because he has failed in his attempts to become a doctor. As the title would indicate, though his job is to take "orders" and keep "order," his hiring throws the institution into outright chaos. The second text is a television episode from the dramatic series "Ben Casey." In "A Little Fun to Match the Sorrow" (1965), Lewis plays Dennis Green, a resident in neurosurgery who is under the supervision of the gruff and demanding Dr. Casey (Vince Edwards). Again, Lewis's character is frustrated in his pursuit of a medical career. As a perennial jokester, he fails to convince Dr. Casey that he can become a serious and sensitive physician.

Clearly, the two works are related by the fact that Lewis is cast in both as a struggling medical professional. It is also entirely possible that, given Lewis's role in *The Disorderly Orderly*, a later "tie-in" with "Ben Casey" was planned. For the purposes of this essay, however, I treat his casting in these "twin" works as less than arbitrary and more than a public relations stunt. Rather, I explore the relationship between his stance as a successful comic and his formulation as a failed doctor.

## THE DISORDERLY ORDERLY

Much of the writing about Lewis's comic style has focused on his compromised masculinity (see, for example, Bukatman 1991, 196). Supporting this notion, in *The Disorderly Orderly*, Jerome Littlefield's professional problems are part of his overall inadequacy as a man. The film begins with an abstract, extradiegetic sequence that announces to the viewer that the narrative will consider a hero manqué (obviously the favored protagonist of comedy). A disembodied male voice-over introduces us to three possible lead characters for the cinematic tale (all played by Lewis): a soldier who "dreams of being brave" but then cowardly screams, "MA!!!" when tested in battle; a mountain climber who dreams of "conquering the savage force of nature" but gets dizzy and tumbles when he reaches the mountaintop; and a medical worker who dreams of "scaling the heights of pure science" but who panics and calls for his mother when confronted by a sick patient. Mimicking the words of the host on the game show "To Tell the Truth" (1956), the male announcer asks for the "real" movie hero to "fall down." The one who obliges is the hospital orderly, the most pedestrian figure of the lot.

Already Jerome's problems are apparent to the viewer, and like those of the other two personages we have confronted in the prologue, his travails involve the impossibility of assuming an adult masculine pose. Clearly, Jerome's last name (*Little*field) tends to minimize his stature, and the fact that he cries for his parent when under pressure makes him even more childlike. Not surprisingly, throughout the narrative his comic ineffectuality is foregrounded specifically in encounters with maternal figures.

Primary among these is Nurse Higgins (Kathleen Freeman), who is his professional nemesis (in this and several other films). She constantly scolds and upbraids him, and she is often the one who suffers physically from the turmoil he unleashes. Once, for example, when Jerome has angered a patient, the man throws his breakfast across the room; unhappily, it lands on Nurse Higgins. Jerome also has problems with the matronly Mrs. Fuzzyby (Alice Pearce), a disagreeable patient whose wheelchair he must push around the grounds. In contradistinction to these "bad mother" figures is Dr. Howard (Glenda Farrell), the supervisor of the institution. We learn that she was once engaged to Jerome's father, a renowned physician, and that she sees herself as the mother Jerome might have had. Rather than be dismayed by Jerome's incompetence, Dr. Howard is understanding of it and encourages him in his hapless pursuit to become a doctor. That Lewis's characters often have "oedipal" problems has been noted by certain critics (Bukatman 1991, 198), a fact that jumps out at us in a comic line Jerome utters about his deceased father: "I loved his wife," he says, "she was like a mother to me." How seriously the film takes the oedipal complaints of its comic hero is clear from its casting him as a psychiatric patient—a circumstance made more credible by the fact that the Whitestone Sanitarium where Jerome works is a mental facility. In one psychiatric session, Dr. Davenport (Del Moore) makes reference to the fact that Jerome has had dreams of a "three-headed" mother.

That Jerry Lewis's farcical persona should be portrayed as an infantile subject should come as no surprise, for Sigmund Freud's seminal theory of the comic involved the notion that we find another person's behavior amusing when his activities remind us of those we performed as a youth. As Freud states, "The complete comparison which leads to the comic would run: 'This is how he does it—I do it in another way—he does it as I used to do it as a child'" (1960 [1928], 224–225). Thus critics have likened the humorous waddle of Chaplin's Tramp to the gait of a toddler, the inane giddiness of Pee Wee Herman to the silliness of a boy, and the mischievous bickering of Laurel and Hardy to the rivalry of youthful siblings. But the psychiatric thrust of *The Disorderly Orderly* goes beyond the standard representation of the comic as a child figure. In the first sequence of the movie, when a patient named Fat Jack (Jack E. Leonard) is admitted to the hospital, Jerome is dispensed to bring him a straitjacket (which Nurse Higgins calls a "lunatic suit").

Instead of Jerome outfitting Fat Jack with the apparatus, however, Fat Jack manages to dress him in it—establishing an equivalence between the two. As a result, Jerome misses a date with the beautiful Nurse Julie Blair (Karen Sharpe), spending the night "tied up" on the sanitarium lawn. As the narrative progresses, we realize that the real reason Jerome is in therapy is that he has failed at becoming a physician, a profession bequeathed to him by his dad. We learn that he was thrown out of medical school for having a condition called "neurotic identification empathy," which seems to be a form of "sympathy pains" or of "medical student disease." Whenever Jerome hears the details of someone else's illness, he is led to feel a physical distress similar to the symptoms of the syndrome described. As he tells Julie one day, "I'm oversensitive to someone who has pain . . . I feel what they feel and I'm sicker than they are." While Jerome thinks that his affliction makes him unsuitable for the medical profession, Dr. Howard believes that it displays a love of people that will serve him well, if and when he achieves his goal.

Jerome's "neurotic identification empathy" emerges most acutely in his dealings with Mrs. Fuzzyby, an inveterate hypochondriac. As he rolls her wheelchair around the sanitarium grounds, she talks to a variety of patients about her myriad maladies. To one person she describes pains in her gall bladder and how the bile and acid back up into her esophagus. As she does this, we see Jerome standing behind her, grimacing, retching, and looking queasy. To another person she recounts the aches in her leg and how her bone marrow is defective. Again, Jerome appears highly distressed and begins to limp around. Finally, she tells a third person about the problems with her weak, undersized kidneys—at which point Jerome (who is standing beside a running fountain) bolts to the bathroom to relieve himself. Obviously, in each case, he has felt the condition that Mrs. Fuzzyby has delineated, a habit that would prevent him from attaining the distanced stance required of a physician. With the boundaries between self and other continually perforated and permeable, he could not achieve the stable and healthy identity of "doctor."

While, on the one hand, Jerome has theoretical empathy for his patients, his behavior unwittingly hurts them. It is here that the tomfoolery of the film truly resides. Howard Thompson, for example, calls the world of Jerry Lewis "mad antics in a house of pain" (1964, 8). In the opening sequence of *The Disorderly Orderly*, Jerome is wheeling a man with a bandaged foot down the hall. Because the patient is puffing on a cigar whose smoke obscures Jerome's vision, he rams the man's leg into the wall. When Jerome enters a woman's room to fix her television set, he causes her mechanical hospital bed to collapse with her in its clutches. After harshly swabbing a toothbrush over a patient's mouth, Jerome discovers the man's set of full dentures in a glass by his bed. When Jerome brings a patient in a body cast to the hospital lawn, he accidentally knocks him over and watches in paralysis as he rolls down the hill. When Jerome rummages through the medicine closet, he accidentally knocks over a huge bottle of pills, spilling them all over the floor. For the next few moments, people slip in zany contortions in the hospital's main hallway. When Jerome mounts a scaffold to paint the hospital exterior, he lets a can of blood red paint fall off and land square on the head of the institution's chief executive, Mr. Tuffington (Everett Sloane). On a more abstract level, when Jerome mistakenly double-exposes two X rays, one man's liver winds up in another woman's ear.

What these burlesque events reveal to us is that comedy often entails *pain*. Whether it is at the man who slips on a banana peel, the fat woman whose skin gets caught in her zipper, or the blind man who walks into a wall, laughter is often harvested at someone else's discomfort and expense. Not only must the audience of comedy be numb to suffering, but so must the comic who makes light of his own or of others' afflictions. As Charlie Chaplin once stated, "Life is a tragedy when seen in close-up, but a comedy in long-shot."[1] It is for this reason that Jerome Littlefield's psychic malady is so interesting in terms of the star text of Jerry Lewis (whose initials and first name are nearly identical to that of his protagonist). Not only would Jerome's excessive identification with people make him unsuitable as a doctor (who must temper empathy with a heavy dose of objectivity)—it would make him unsuitable as a comic (who must temper sympathy with a heavy dose of cruelty).

Not all the humor in the film is based on bodily violence. Some is of the conceptual kind that made Lewis's comic style so popular with the French intellectuals, especially when he turned to directing his own films. At one point Jerome walks into an area that bears a sign that reads "Absolute Quiet." Julie finds him there and reprimands him for standing her up on a date. Rather than let the audience hear this argument, the filmmaker renders it to us silently in subtitles, as though the sign for absolute quiet could actually cut off sound absolutely. The next time Jerome passes the "Absolute Quiet" sign our expectations are confounded. He chooses that moment to take an illicit bite from an apple that he takes from a gift basket he is delivering. Rather than being silent, however, the noise of his chewing is cartoonishly loud. In another conceptual gag in the film, we view and hear a series of different wind chimes ringing across the hospital grounds. The apparent last in the series is a human skeleton that rattles ghoulishly outside a medical office. At still another moment, Jerome primes a pump that is labeled "Mineral Water." Instead of hearing liquid collect in a pitcher, however, we hear the sound of solid metal hitting the vessel. Perhaps the most abstract gag of all, however, takes place when Jerome fixes a patient's television set. She complains that all she can see on the screen is "snow" (meaning the static interference that blocks the picture). When Jerome loosens the cover on the front of the set, however, real snow pours into the room in a horrendous blizzard.

Interestingly, the relation of comedy to medicine in *The Disorderly Orderly* bears parallels to a much later work in the melodramatic mode, Randa Haines's *The Doctor* (1991). In that film, Dr. Jack McKee (William Hurt) is portrayed as a droll and acerbic surgeon who uses humor to distance himself from the tragedy of his patients' lives. Whenever McKee performs surgery, he blasts an irreverent song over the operating room sound system: "Why Don't We Get Drunk and Screw?" When he is asked to consult on a surgery patient about to be sedated, he jokes with him about the "dubious" qualifications of his anesthesiologist. When a female heart surgery patient comes to him for a postoperative visit and expresses distress about the scars on her chest, he tells her that she looks like a *Playboy* centerfold "and has the staples to prove it." When, over the course of the narrative, McKee becomes seriously ill himself, he suddenly understands the inappropriateness of his "gallows humor" from a patient's point of view. As his sardonic irony wanes, his sense of empathy grows, as though the two were inversely related. No longer a wry comic, he becomes a compassionate doctor.

All the gags in the Lewis film revolve around Jerome's physical "labor," which is extensive given his job as a hospital orderly. As Steven

Shaviro has noted, Lewis often plays such unskilled workers in his films—figures who are under the authority of others. Furthermore, Shaviro sees this role as tied to another aspect of Lewis's comic persona—his tendency to suffer endless "abjection and humiliation," perhaps a variation on the pain he inflicts on others (1993, 119). For example, not only does Jerome end up imprisoned in a straitjacket on one occasion; on another he finds himself sliding down a laundry chute after trying to deposit bed linen into it. Similarly, when the ambulance arrives at the sanitarium carrying Fat Jack, it runs directly into Jerome's body. While Buster Keaton's comic humor is based on his agile way of avoiding physical trouble (as when the facade of a house falls on him so that an open doorway, aligned with his body, protects him from harm), Lewis's burlesque style emphasizes his awkwardness and wallows in the agony that results from it. As Shaviro notes, "The painful, negative emotions that surprisingly proliferate in Lewis's movies . . . are the direct consequences of subordination: of being assigned a low position in the social hierarchy and being compelled to take orders" (108). Hence the orderly who must take orders creates such a disorder that it punishes both himself and others. Shaviro also makes an interesting point about the way in which Lewis's "labor" is articulated in his films:

> At one extreme, physical labor gets done in an impossibly brief amount of time . . . at the other extreme, many of Lewis's gags are built around an excruciating slowness of unfulfilled anticipation. Simple physical actions (carrying a heavy suitcase, balancing a heterogeneous group of objects, shutting a door without slamming it, climbing up and down a ladder . . . ) are not only occasions for the display of Lewis's brilliantly choreographed clumsiness, but take painfully long to accomplish. The ultimate tendency of such routines is toward the elimination of any sort of culmination or payoff. . . . There is no resolution, positive or negative; Lewis labors on, in a state of perpetual, unresolved disequilibrium. (119–120)

What seems implied here is that Lewis's comedy is not only based on acts of represented labor but that, in its extreme extendedness and lack of climax, it is also *belabored*—a fact that perhaps accounts for the pain (versus pleasure) many viewers experience in apprehending Lewis's style.

Whether from an excess of sympathy pains or a tendency toward "abjection and humiliation," Jerome is clearly conceived as a "sick" individual in the film—a classic hysteric (Bukatman 1991, 196; Krutnik 2000, 8). Reflecting this, Shaviro uses the term *contagion* to allude to how the embarrassment of Lewis's protagonist infects even his uncomfortable audience (1993, 108). Toward the end of *The Disorderly Orderly*, however, Jerome seems suddenly "cured" (at least of his alleged neurotic identification empathy) when he wins the affection of a female patient—Susan (Susan Oliver)—a suicidal ex-cheerleader whom he once secretly adored in high school. Unbeknownst to her, he has been working overtime at the sanitarium to pay her hospital bills—this despite the fact that she rejects him. Again, Jerome's problem seems an excess of empathy: he feels so sorry for her (despite her rudeness) that he disrupts his life to put hers in order. In so doing, he assumes the masochistic position. That his "cure" should come from romance seems not inexplicable when we recall that Dr. Davenport diagnosed his problems as arising from "love frustration." In fact, his trouble seems to date back to the time of an adolescent "primal scene," when he witnessed Susan kissing her football-hero boyfriend.

In informing Susan about Jerome's saintly sacrifice and dedication, Dr. Davenport states something strange but significant. He says to her that if Jerome "could have had children, he would have made some man a perfect wife." Clearly, the gender-bending aspect of this statement is intriguing, placing Jerome in the female position. But the real role that Jerome might have played "could he have had children" would not simply have been that of wife but that of mother. Hence his excess of empathy seems entirely to "feminize" him (as does his masochism)—not an illogical consequence, since, on a cultural level, it is women who are traditionally linked with both caregiving and martyred suffering. As Ellen Singer More states, "In popular culture the term 'empathy' is associated with a set of traits frequently connoted as 'feminine,' especially emotional attunement and identification with the feelings of others" (More and Milligan 1994, 19). Given the psychoanalytic discourse of *The Disorderly Orderly* (in which our comic hero is actually in therapy), Jerome's illness attempts to replace the nightmarish "three-headed" mother of his dreams with another version of her: a feminized nurturing self. Hence his "cure" and his growth to the distanced role of doctor is represented as a triumph of masculinity over femininity in him.

It is after kissing Susan (and becoming a "Man") that Jerome seeks to test his newfound objectivity. For that purpose, he asks Mrs. Fuzzyby to recount her afflictions. Miraculously, he finds that he is now immune to the effects of her litany. It is after this event that one of the most violent and extended comic sequences of the film takes place—as though Jerome's "immunity" to the hypochondriacal woes of Mrs. Fuzzyby extends to the comical woes of his burlesque "patsies." Thinking his medical career finished, Jerome drives off in a hospital ambulance without realizing that Mr. Tuffington is on a gurney inside (placed there because of his unfortunate encounter with Jerome's paint can). As an extended car chase ensues (in which Jerome is pursued by Nurse Higgins and Dr. Howard), Mr. Tuffington's gurney rolls down hills and through intersections (narrowly evading oncoming vehicles), eventually careening off a pier into the ocean. Beyond this, countless pedestrians are startled as the ambulance crashes into cars and garbage cans. Finally, on a gurney himself, Jerome rams into a supermarket, knocking over hundreds of stacked food cans, which shoot out into the street—like ammunition balls from a cannon.

It is within this scene of carnage that a distanced (and more "masculine") Jerome asks Nurse Julie to marry him. It is significant in this respect that when Jerome's gurney topples the grocery store's pyramid of aluminum cans, it reveals a couple kissing inside it. At this moment of new heterosexual potency, Jerome realizes he can become a doctor and transcend his assignment as a lowly orderly. Adult manhood (sexual, medical, and comical) has been achieved in the name of emotional distance—and at the expense of feminine empathy.

### "A LITTLE FUN TO MATCH THE SORROW"

At one point in *The Disorderly Orderly*, Dr. Howard compares herself to fictional television doctors and mentions the name of actor Sam Jaffe. As we well know, Jaffe was the performer who played Dr. Zorba in the "Ben Casey" series, which aired from 1961 to 1966 (the period in which *Orderly* was made). This reference, as well as Lewis's presence as an actor, ties *The Disorderly Orderly* to "A Little Fun to Match the Sorrow." In the latter, Lewis appears as Dr. Dennis Green, a neurosurgery resident under the tutelage of Dr. Ben Casey. (Interestingly, a review of *The Disorderly Orderly* in the London *Times* called Jerome Littlefield a "would-be Doctor Kildare"—thus comparing him to the other major fictional doctor of the era and Dr. Ben Casey's major competitor.)

As the drama begins we see Green and a fellow resident, Dr. Sullivan, alone together in a hospital room. Green is fooling around: speaking in Lewis's trademark high-pitched adolescent voice and placing a glass slide before his eye like a monocle. When Ben Casey comes into the room, he is obviously displeased with Green's shenanigans and hints that he might be "moving on" from the hospital "sooner than he thinks." Later, Green entertains a child patient by eating gummy candy that sticks to his mouth, making it look as though he were missing a tooth. When Dr. Casey encounters Green in this posture, he again upbraids him. Still another time, Green puns on the words *patients* and *patience* when Casey tries to make a serious point to him about doctoring. For all these reasons, Casey deems Green an immature "clown." In Green's characterization as a physician-comic in this 1960s television episode, we have a preview of the real-life figure of "Patch" Adams, brought to the screen in 1998 in a movie starring Robin Williams. While the narrative of *Patch Adams* ultimately validates an unconventional doctor's approach, this "Ben Casey" drama does not.

Clearly, Green's stance as a jokester has also had a negative effect on his social life. One of the patients in the hospital is an elderly man whose daughter, Karen, Green previously dated. When he asks her why she dropped him years ago, she states that she "could never take him seriously," that they "never had a single serious moment together." When Karen's son says that Green is "funny," she comments sardonically, "Yes, hysterical" (a word with clear double meaning). Green asks her out to dinner and there seems to be a temporary rapprochement between them. When Dr. Casey appears at the restaurant, Green asks him to join them but then announces abruptly that the couple was "just leaving." After Casey storms off, insulted, Green informs Karen that he was "just joking"; but she rejects his explanation. He becomes more and more sardonic, claiming that he will bill himself as a "neurological comic" who can work with "no anesthesia, just laughs"—a phrase that prefigures the kind of sentiment that might be expressed by Jack McKee in *The Doctor*. Green brags that he will pack crowds into his "operating gallery" (which we know is sometimes called a "theater").

Dr. Casey is so concerned with Green's flippant attitude that he goes to his supervisor, Dr. Zorba, to ask that the young physician be dismissed. He tells his mentor that he is not sure that Green can ever be trusted "under pressure." Zorba, however, wants to give Green another chance. So Casey decides to put Green to the test by requiring him to inform a woman that her husband (who has been shot in a hunting mishap) is about to die. As soon as Green learns of this assignment, he is overwrought and begins to make several medical mistakes. He instructs a nurse to give a patient the wrong drug; luckily, she catches the error. Next, he tries unsuccessfully to pawn off the job of informing the woman to another doctor. When he finally confronts the woman, he embroiders the truth, refusing to give her the bad news. Dr. Zorba observes Green's conversation and accuses him of deceit, ordering him to remedy the problem immediately. "Oh God, why can't I do these things?" Green exclaims. Again under stress, he explodes at a number of hospital workers who ask him for help as he moves through the corridors. To make matters worse, he learns from Dr. Casey that he will also have to assist in an operation on a young boy with a brain tumor, who is not expected to live. When Green meets Karen in a waiting room, she asks how her father is doing. Again he embellishes the truth, claiming that her dad needs additional tests before his prognosis can be determined. When Green tries to be funny, she angrily calls him a "clown," at which point he blurts out cruelly, "Your father . . . will never leave this hospital!"

When Green learns that the man with the accidental gunshot wound has expired, he panics—running through the halls, knocking over an orderly with a tray (as though in ironic reference to his own former cinematic self, Jerome Littlefield). Green escapes into a dark stairwell and pathetically hugs the wall; Karen finds him there and comforts him. "I worked so hard to be good," he proclaims "but something was missing. . . . They didn't tell me that I would have to face people, be near them, comfort them. They didn't teach me *how not to die* when telling someone he would." After Green's remark, Karen uses the term *clown* affectionately on him, characterizing him as "sweet" and "gentle." Interestingly, when a stand-up comic gets no laughs from his audience, he also speaks of having "died."

In a later scene, Dr. Casey (who has unaccountably become more sympathetic to Green) finds him packing to leave—having given up on his pursuit to become a physician (just as Jerome did in *The Disorderly Orderly*). Casey encourages Green to perform the operation on the child and accuses him of merely "acting." Green replies that without his humor and wit he is defenseless, "naked, stripped bare." Ultimately, Green gains the courage to assist in the surgery. He appears in the operating room with a clownish hand puppet that jokes with the boy before he is given anesthesia. The operation is a great success. In the episode's coda (which seems to take place some time in the future), Green is married to Karen and his fellow physician, Dr. Sullivan, makes hopeless attempts at being as funny as his friend once was.

Clearly, there are aspects of "A Little Fun to Match the Sorrow" that resonate with associations to *The Disorderly Orderly*. In both works, Lewis plays not only a medical professional but a highly troubled one with serious psychological problems. Interestingly, however, the ailments his two characters experience seem diametrically opposed. In *The Disorderly Orderly*, Jerome suffers an *excess* of empathy that prevents him from attaining the objectivity required for medical practice. In "A Little Fun," however, Dennis (like McKee in *The Doctor*) suffers from a *dearth* of empathy, which prevents him from feeling the emotion that should tie him to his patients. What connects the two characters, however, is that in both texts the question of empathy is linked not only to health care but to humor. When Jerome learns how to be distant from patients' woes, he has not only the qualifications to be a doctor but also the credentials to be a comic (witness his brutal *tour de force* car chase in *Orderly*). When Dennis relinquishes his comic defenses to be an empathetic doctor, he also gives up his jokester role, which seems appropriated by his hand puppet and his physician colleague. Although the conclusion of each work is quite different, both highlight what we might term "sick humor," the relationship between empathy, comedy, and the "medical gaze."


## EPILOGUE: CELEBRITY AND CHARITY

It is interesting that, in *The Disorderly Orderly*, the sanitarium at which Jerome works is supposed to be one that caters to people in show business. As noted, the first patient to arrive on the scene is Fat Jack, a man who is supposedly the host of a comic television program. Later on in the film, when Mr. Tuffington explains his philosophy for making the sanitarium profitable, he claims to seek an appeal to entertainers and agents because statistics show them to be "22 percent crazier" than the general public. This discourse on celebrity makes us aware of the stars in the film—most notably of Jerry Lewis. Furthermore, it conceptually links them to a medical institution.

Given that both *The Disorderly Orderly* and "A Little Fun" were made in the mid-1960s, it is interesting to note that 1966 was when Lewis began to "star" in the annual Muscular Dystrophy Association Telethon—a role that has gained him more fame than those of his movies (which declined in popularity at around the same time). In the version of the event that ran some twenty-one and a half hours on September 2, 2001, two hundred television stations were linked in a "Love Network" to broadcast the star-studded variety show. Not only is Lewis the host of the telethon, but he serves as the national chairman of the Muscular Dystrophy Association, an agency that works to defeat neuromuscular diseases. While the organization seeks to cure these afflictions in both children and adults, Lewis's work has been most associated with the disorder's younger victims, whom he refers to as "my kids." Interestingly, his comic persona (when not designated "The Idiot") has often been called "The Kid" (Krutnik 1994, 14). What this third star text tends to do is add a level of "reality" to the conjunction of Jerry Lewis, comedy, and medicine—since the performer has come to be associated (for a contemporary generation) with his charity work in a medical context. Furthermore, this event (which a Web site describes as a "labor of love" for Lewis) takes place on Labor Day, reminding us of the fact that his persona was so often a menial worker.

While Lewis's incarnation of Jerome Littlefield in *The Disorderly Orderly* associates the actor with an excess of empathy that would make him an ideal host for a disease-related telethon, his reputed real-life persona would not; for the performer is thought to be "difficult" and often less than compassionate. Frank Krutnik (who has written a study of Lewis's *oeuvre*) relates the time in 1997 that he contacted Lewis while the star was appearing in "Damn Yankees" in London. When Krutnik received a call back from Lewis, he was encouraged that the comic might grant him an interview—until he realized that Lewis had telephoned solely to make clear how much he disliked Krutnik's work (Krutnik 2000, 6). Similarly, Shawn Levy relates the star's inexplicable bipolar response to him.

Lewis's Muscular Dystrophy Telethons also raise questions about the relationship between humor and empathy. While the September 2001 show boasted the presence of such comic figures as Lewis, Kermit the Frog, and Ray Romano, it also implied upsetting details about the tragedy of muscular dystrophy (including footage of its unfortunate victims). Hence the viewer's desire for light entertainment (spurred on by such comic Las Vegas acts as Penn and Teller) would have come up against her sense of sorrow and empathy. Clearly, the yin and yang of the telethon dynamic is just this uneasy balance between capricious fun and maudlin sentiment—between uproarious laughter and cloying tears ("a little fun to match the sorrow").

Adding to the complexity of this paradigm is the fact that Lewis's particular form of physical comedy has often been deemed "spastic" (Krutnik 1994, 12). By this critics mean that, in embodying individuals who are outrageously awkward, Lewis often makes his protagonists appear quite literally to be "suffering from chronic muscular spasms" (*American Heritage Dictionary*, New Second College Edition, S.V. *spastic*, 655). Hence he has been criticized for engaging in "sick jokes," as it were. In *The Disorderly Orderly*, for example, there is a moment when Jerome is assigned to bandage a patient's leg. He has such poor control of his small and large motor skills that he unwittingly gets the man's entire body (as well as a nurse's) tied up in the dressing. Thus, on some level, Lewis could be conceived as the least likely and most inappropriate comic to host a telethon for neuromuscular disease (as opposed, say, to Charlie Chaplin, whose style of bodily humor was based on grace). It is clear how much Lewis dislikes the term *spastic* as a reference to his style of physical comedy. When Levy used it in an interview question posed to Lewis, the star responded with the following tirade: "The word 'spastic' is terrible. Some fucking writer who didn't take the time to watch the work titled my work" in that fashion (Levy 1996, 486).

Ultimately, the same unresolvable tension between comic distance and empathetic intimacy that characterizes *The Disorderly Orderly* and "A Little Fun to Match the Sorrow" marks Lewis's Muscular Dystrophy Telethon. His humor, at home in the medical arena, probes productively comedy's relation to both physical and mental "health." Whether Lewis is charity host, Jerome Littlefield, or Dennis Green, his comic work is "sick" in a fascinating and positive respect, since it continually invokes the tenuous balance between pain, empathy, and the dispassionate ability to effect a cure.

## NOTE

1. Quoted in Charlie Chaplin's obituary, *Guardian* (London), Dec. 28, 1977.

Jerry (l.) as Japanese "mother" in *The Geisha Boy* (Frank Tashlin, Paramount, 1958). Trudging up the steps and carrying Mitsuo, he stops to mop his brow, thus giving us an unimpeded view of a strictly maternal action. Frame enlargement.

# 10

# The Geisha Boy

## Orientalizing the Jewish Man

David Desser

ALTHOUGH DIRECTED BY Frank Tashlin, *The Geisha Boy* (1958) was produced by Jerry Lewis and represented his continuing maturation as a solo star performer after the 1956 termination of the enormously popular and successful Martin-Lewis pairing. In fact, in only his second film since the Martin-Lewis breakup, Lewis went a long way toward creating what would become his signature persona: the sad sack, the bumbler, the schlemiel with a soft heart who manages, against all odds, to get the girl in the end. This persona was in some ways a carryover from the Martin-Lewis pairing, but it shows significant growth and development as Lewis had now to handle both the comic and romantic duties previously split by the duo. The developing Lewis persona, sometimes called by Lewis himself "The Idiot," would achieve its apotheosis later under his own direction, but *The Geisha Boy* certainly set the tone for the more mature films to follow.

While Lewis's artistic maturation is certainly one important context in which to situate *The Geisha Boy*, there are two other, interrelated contexts on which this essay concentrates. The first is Hollywood's developing and ongoing fascination with "the Orient," particularly Japan, as seen in previous films such as *The Teahouse of the August Moon* (1956), *The Bridge on the River Kwai* (1957), and *Sayonara* (1957). The second is a context far less often acknowledged, let alone explored, and that is what we might call an emerging sense of "Jewish masculinity."

*The Geisha Boy* has perhaps fallen into a black hole of critical neglect (though arguably, Lewis's entire career, save for *The Nutty Professor*

[1963], has been largely and until lately ignored). By being situated in its historical moment through recourse to what I am calling the "Orientalist context," and by linking this context to the issue of Jewish masculinity, *The Geisha Boy* emerges as a significant film not only for a more thorough appreciation of Lewis's oeuvre but also in terms of postwar American values revolving around feminism and masculinity. Moreover, by approaching the film by way of these linked contexts, we may see Lewis as very much the precursor to—and thus as consonant with—contemporary issues of masculinity. It is especially interesting to think of *The Geisha Boy* in terms of how images of Jewish men help negotiate masculinity.

It has long been noted how postwar cinema struggled to redefine and refeminize American women while revealing profound anxieties about postwar masculinity. It has not been so often noted how *The Geisha Boy* and Lewis's persona participate in this contestation and anticipate later developments. What I am calling the Orientalist context is central to the manner in which the film functions in light of the 1950s penchant for anti-feminist hysteria and to how the exoticized "Asian" woman came to be seen as a counterpoint to the (allegedly) increasingly strident, unfeminine American woman. This is particularly evident in the films of Frank Tashlin. But Tashlin was also conscious of the "feminized" American man. Thus his teaming with Jerry Lewis is a happy one for the productive tension between anti-feminist hysteria and a newly and acceptably feminized man. In specific, the Orientalist mode enables the creation of a more masculine persona for Lewis, "the feminized Jewish man." Drawing on the work of Jewish cultural critic Daniel Boyarin, this chapter demonstrates how Lewis creates a kind of "sissy" figure, unmasculine by traditional standards, often overtly feminized and maternal. The feminized Jewish man who is "The Geisha Boy" is conflated with the image of the Asian woman to both participate in the feminization of American women in the 1950s and create an alternative image of masculinity that later generations of Jewish men, and the culture at large, would come to embrace.

## LEWIS AS SISSY-BOY/WOMAN

If Jerry Lewis intended to create a solo career that could stand alone after the hugely successful Martin-Lewis pairings (sixteen films in the eight years from 1948 to 1956, as well as a television series, "The Colgate Comedy Hour" [1950–1955]), it would seem he went about it in the wrongest way possible. Having already created the persona of an asexual, weak, feminized juvenile boy-man, with both *The Delicate Delinquent* (1957) and *The Geisha Boy*, his first two solo films, he hardly took any leap forward in maturity, physical ability, or confidence. Indeed, a strange pattern established in the Martin-Lewis films—in which the pair would remake classical Hollywood films originally starring a woman and in which Lewis would assume the woman's role in the remake—would continue in his post-Martin films, in which Lewis would similarly assume a female role. In *Living It Up* (1954), a remake of the classical comedy *Nothing Sacred* (1937), starring Fredric March and Carole Lombard, Lewis assumed the Lombard role; in *You're Never Too Young* (1955), a remake of *The Major and the Minor* (1942), Lewis assumed the role originally played by Ginger Rogers. In his early post-Martin films, Lewis played a baby-sitter in *Rock-a-Bye Baby* (1958) and two years later assumed the role of "Cinderfella."

Further denying Lewis a kind of separation from the Martin-Lewis pairings is the fact that the duo were often featured in service comedies, such as *At War with the Army* (1950), *Sailor Beware* (1951), and *Jumping Jacks* (1952). In his immediate post-Martin films, Lewis appeared as an entertainer for servicemen in *The Geisha Boy* and a former naval officer in *Don't Give Up the Ship* (1959). I would argue, too, that in films such as *The Delicate Delinquent* (in which he tries to become a policeman), *The Bellboy* (1960), and even the relatively late *The Disorderly Orderly* (1964) we find Lewis in something like service roles. This lack of differentiation in setting from the Martin-Lewis teamings impacted on Lewis's persona, in which there seems to have been little change after he separated himself from Dean Martin. The service comedies render both figures as somewhat juvenile, men subject to the rules and discipline of authority, while within the Martin-Lewis pairing itself we find Jerry always the inferior, always the juvenile to Martin's adult. Thus, within the Martin-Lewis teaming and afterward, what I have in mind is the image of Lewis as a "boy."

*The Geisha Boy*, *The Bellboy*, *The Errand Boy* (1961): all are titles in Lewis's post-Martin career. Yet by the time of *The Geisha Boy*, Jerry Lewis was thirty-two years old; by the time of *The Errand Boy*, he was thirty-five. This willingness to conceptualize his persona as an adolescent would eventually wear thin. He tried for a more adult role in *The*

*Nutty Professor*: as Julius Kelp he may have been a nerd, but as least he was a "professor"; and he was notoriously convincing as the Dean Martin–like Buddy Love. By 1965, *Boeing Boeing*, while juvenile in its attitudes toward women and sex, found Lewis a bit more adult, if not mature. Not until *Three on a Couch* (1966), when Lewis was forty years old, did he make a film in which he was both a grownup and a mature man.

Simulating women's roles—as in *Living It Up* or *You're Never Too Young* and then, after Martin, with *Rock-a-Bye Baby* and *Cinderfella* (1960)—Lewis's persona can be understood as juvenile or immature, specifically feminized especially in relation to Dean Martin's suave, romantic figure. *The Geisha Boy* continues to both juvenilize and feminize Lewis's image, while it also brings forth an image of homosexuality, of queerness, since the geisha began as male prostitutes before the role became strictly for women. It was precisely by means of "the geisha" that Japan had itself become well known and feminized in the postwar era.

## JAPAN-AS-WOMAN, OR LOVE AMERICAN STYLE

The concept of Orientalism in which the Orient (the Middle East, Asia) is exoticized and feminized is too well known to be repeated here. But it is worth noting that both before the Second World War and after, American associations with Asia followed a particularly masculinist tack that did not require the brilliant insights of Edward Said to reveal. For instance, American ideology, scripted into the Hollywood cinema, always allowed a certain white, male privilege in which "Other" women were available to white men (though obviously not the reverse). Silent-era and pre-Code Hollywood were replete with love affairs between white men and "South Sea Island Beauties." Nor did this cinematic prerogative for miscegenation extend to Asian women, although Native American women, Latinas, and Jewish women had their chances at interracial harmony with white men. Asian men in particular, however, were continually feminized, even when, on certain levels, they were admirable, as in *Broken Blossoms* (1919) or *The Bitter Tea of General Yen* (1933). The early films of Sessue Hayakawa (most notoriously *The Cheat* [1915]) show clearly the feminization of the Asian man, while later films allow Hayakawa a bit more dignity and masculinity—a glowing exception, to be sure.

The films of the postwar era concentrate on feminizing Asia with a particular venom and with a strong sense of urgency, through the mechanism of white male–Asian female romance. Gina Marchetti documented this well in *Romance and the "Yellow Peril"* (1993), with particular emphasis on films such as *Love Is a Many-Splendored Thing* (1955) and *The World of Suzie Wong* (1960). She also notes that this pattern is repeated in *Teahouse of the August Moon, Sayonara,* and *The Barbarian and the Geisha* (1958), all set specifically in Japan. (*Teahouse* is set in Okinawa, but the film does not particularly distinguish between native Okinawans and the Japanese; moreover, the male lead is played by Marlon Brando in yellowface, and the female lead is Kyo Machiko, one of Japan's leading actresses of the period.) The Glenn Ford–Kyo Machiko pairing in *Teahouse,* the Marlon Brando–Miiko Taka duo in *Sayonara,* and the John Wayne–Ando Eiko coupling in *Barbarian* not only repeat the white male (i.e., masculinist) privilege of the prewar era but also specifically highlight the militarist context in which these pairings occur. *Teahouse* is set during the American Occupation of Japan; *Sayonara* focuses on American soldiers in Japan for the Korean War; and, most interestingly, *The Barbarian and the Geisha* concerns the Black Ships of Commodore Perry, who forced the opening of Japan to the West (a revealing sexual metaphor). The opening up of Japan in the nineteenth century and the Occupation of Japan after World War II, followed by the use of Japan as a staging area for Korea and for R&R for American soldiers, not to mention the overall presence of American military bases on Japan then as now, allow for—indeed, call for—the Occupation of Asian women.

But it isn't enough to have feminized Asia entirely: to have defeated Japan's (male) military, to have occupied its territory, to have colonized its consciousness, and to have forced its women to cede themselves to American servicemen. The women also become hyperfeminized: exoticized through costume and sexualized through images of passivity, servility, and availability, most spectacularly seen through the image of the geisha. With her elaborate costume and hairdo, her *samisen* and *koto,* her politeness, and her demureness, the geisha became the predominant image of Japan after World War II. For the perceptive Gina Marchetti, geisha became "Hollywood's chief emblem of postwar reconciliation. . . . Metaphorically, a bellicose Japan, through the figure of the geisha, became a yielding and dependent nation" (1993, 178–179). Similarly, while Hollywood films used the geisha to exoticize and feminize Japan,

American audiences, newly exposed to Japanese films in the wake of the success of *Rashomon* (1950), either preferred or were continually given Japanese period films featuring precisely the costumes, the color, and the spectacle embodied in the image of the geisha.

Although they did not all necessarily return to the war-mongering of the war years, not all Hollywood films of the postwar era involved images of Japanese passivity and reconciliation. The same year that brought us *Sayonara*, with Americans making love, not war, in Japan, also brought us *The Bridge on the River Kwai*, where war, though seen as folly, nevertheless involved implacable and dangerous enemies, the most memorable of whom was portrayed by the unforgettable Sessue Hayakawa. An Academy Award nomination greeted Hayakawa for his portrayal of Colonel Saito, while the film itself won Best Picture along with other awards, including, perhaps most memorably, Best Score. The "Colonel Bogey March" could be, and often was, whistled by every schoolboy who had been—as boys will be boys—swept up by the film's vision of heroic warfare. Hayakawa himself achieved the stardom that he had enjoyed fully forty years earlier.

## OF GEISHA BOYS AND ROSIE THE RIVETERS

Released in 1958, *The Geisha Boy* enters the fray of Hollywood's imaging of Japan and the Japanese woman with its own story of interracial coupling, its own look at the white male–Asian female symbolic duo. Instead of a romantic star such as Glenn Ford or Marlon Brando or the hypermasculine if less romantic John Wayne, here we have Jerry Lewis. Opposite him as the female romantic lead is Nobu McCarthy, a Japanese American actress making her film debut, a woman every bit as feminine and chaste as her Japanese geisha-like sisters. Also significantly appearing in the film, and in her film debut, is Suzanne Pleshette. Thus, like *Sayonara*, the film offers the possibility of a romantic triangle with Lewis at the apex. As in the militarist context of the other films, American servicemen and a certain "war" footing are employed here: Lewis portrays Gilbert Wooley, a second-rate comedian/magician who arrives in Japan on a U.S. military plane as part of a USO tour. The military context is further emphasized by a deliberate referencing of *Bridge on the River Kwai* through the appearance of Sessue Hayakawa overtly invoking his Colonel Saito role—though tamed, of course, as befits a comedy. Footage of Alec Guinness taken from *Bridge on the River Kwai* and the recurrent use of the whistled "Colonel Bogey March" ensure that the reference is known by the audience. Military imagery is further enforced when Wooley is stripped of his USO "uniform" to the accompaniment of a military drumbeat on the soundtrack. Finally, Wooley is sent to Korea to entertain battle-weary troops stationed along the Thirty-eighth Parallel, apparently subject to enemy bombardment and intense loneliness.

The overt reference to *Bridge on the River Kwai* is also accompanied by an overt reference to *Sayonara*, when Wooley comments to Kimi Sikita (McCarthy), remarking on her beauty and charm, that he knows why "Marlon Brando dug this place." But if Lewis is less a traditional romantic star than Brando and less a traditional hero than William Holden, he is also far less militaristic than either. Wooley is not in the service but part of the USO. His so-called court-martial emphasizes that fact, as does his claim that he is "too yellow" to go to the front. When he helicopters to the front lines, he winds up in a flooded ditch; when shelling begins, he abandons his act and heads for cover; as entertainment, his rabbit proves more attractive to the soldiers than he does. Even a Japanese youngster is better able to handle the target pistol in Wooley's act than he is. Thus Lewis is doubly disgraced as a suitable figure for an Orientalist fantasy—neither romantic nor heroic. And yet his bumbling ways and gentle heart endear him to the Japanese woman, Kimi. But even here, the way to her heart is through a child.

*The Geisha Boy* is a kind of woolly text, befitting Lewis's character's name. It is a shaggy-dog story, lacking only the dog but substituting a rabbit, whose main point is to get Jerry-the-boy-man to Japan, to have him involved in an interracial romance, to spoof *Bridge on the River Kwai*, and to take potshots at emerging American feminism. The film's plot is minimal, a series of gags, set pieces, and locations put to comic use. What is most interesting throughout all these things, however, is how Lewis is less a romantic figure and more a sort of father or friend figure; for the film's most compelling relationship is not that between Gilbert Wooley and Kimi Sikita but that between Wooley and Mitsuo Watanabe (Robert Hirano), Kimi's orphaned six-year-old nephew. For this relationship to proceed, Wooley must first be established as a kind of asexualized being, infantilized, juvenilized, and feminized, in order for his relationship with Mitsuo to seem honest and true and to compare him, favorably, with a hypermasculinized Japanese counterpart.

To do this, the film first introduces a figure of hypersexuality, a monstrously aggressive woman, to play as comic foil to Wooley and to introduce the twin themes of anti-feminism and feminized masculinity.

The first character introduced into the film is Lola Livingston (Marie McDonald), seen in an overhead shot as she exits a limousine. Framed by a high angle shot that emphasizes her ample cleavage, Lola exudes the oversexuality characteristic by this point in the 1950s of Marilyn Monroe and, especially, Jayne Mansfield. A peroxide blonde, Lola is mean, vindictive, nasty, and selfish. She takes an immediate dislike to Wooley and will be the willing instrument of his disgrace and the unwilling instrument of his redemption. Most of all, however, she is the *vagina dentata* to Wooley's pre-oedipal sexuality. Their three major encounters are characterized by a cloying sexuality, one that toys with Lola's overt sexualization and Wooley's lack thereof. In the first sexualized encounter, Wooley's rabbit, Harry, crawls into bed with the hypersexualized starlet. Reaching over to grab the rabbit, Wooley comes face to sleeping face with Lola in an uncomfortable near-kiss. Harry then crawls under the covers and undulates his way down Lola's body, finally emerging at her feet. The rabbit has gone where no Wooley has gone before!

The second encounter involves an unintended undressing as a result of Lola's attempts to rid herself of Wooley's presence as she deplanes in Japan. At the top of the staircase she attempts to pose for the gathered cameramen, only to find Wooley accosting her with an apology. As she pushes him away and even strikes him, her dress comes loose and eventually falls off. She bounces down the stairs in a state of déshabillé that Wooley tries to correct by rolling her up in the red carpet at the foot of the stairs. This sequence of events manages to draw a laugh from young Mitsuo, the first time he has laughed in many years, thus winning his love and Aunt Kimi's gratitude. But it is precisely the innocence of these actions, the complete lack of anything sexual, that permits Mitsuo to enjoy the sight of an aggressive woman's deserved comeuppance.

The third and final encounter (Lola's last appearance in the film, in fact, though she is mentioned once later) again involves nudity, as Wooley unknowingly enters the women's side of a public bath. (Interestingly, the Chinese characters—*kanji*—for "woman" and "man" are clearly visible on the curtains by the entranceway, but surely few, if any, American audience members would know how to read them any better than Wooley does. If one can read them, then there is that momentary sense of comic anticipation as we see Wooley push aside the curtain marked "Women.") Sure enough, there sits Lola bathing (alone) in the steam. Only this time Wooley is not simply embarrassed but endangered, for he is seeking refuge from "The Great Ichiyama" (Ryuzo Demura)—the overmasculine counterpart to Lola's hypersexualized woman. For if Wooley is physically intimidated by the hypersexualized Lola, he is no less overmatched by the monstrous Ichiyama (whose name means "one mountain"). At over seven feet tall, the Great Ichiyama is a rather freakish figure, an unlikely baseball pitcher and an even more unlikely romantic hero. Instead, he functions to continue to unman Wooley, to provide the model of (over)masculinity against which Wooley is juxtaposed, just as Kimi is the properly feminine woman in contrast to the mammarian Lola.

Of course, the properly feminine woman may have already been introduced in the form of Suzanne Pleshette's sensitive, attractive WAC sergeant. Her introduction, in fact, comes even before we meet Wooley. She seems all too aware of Lola's petulance and hyperkinetic sexuality. Yet it is precisely she who twice complains about the attraction "Oriental" women have for American men. She speaks of having lost her fiancé to a Japanese girl and, seeing Wooley's (apparent) attraction to Kimi, angrily sends him to the Korean front. It is she who speaks the film's clearest condemnation of emerging American feminism. "Believe me," she vows, "the next man I meet, I'm going to forget the so-called American emancipated-woman type of independence and treat him just the way the girls in Japan do!" Wooley, however, when he seemingly agrees with the sergeant that the Japanese are a wonderful people, is actually speaking about Mitsuo: "Especially when they're about six years old going on seven." That is, Wooley has not specifically indicated that he prefers Japanese women to American women, that he prefers Kimi to the sergeant. Instead, it is his feelings for Mitsuo that have won him over. Thus it is not the Orientalized woman who has triumphed but the feminized man.

## TAMING JAPAN, FEMINIZING THE MAN

The postwar, neomilitaristic treatment of Japan in films such as *Teahouse of the August Moon*, *Sayonara*, and *The Barbarian and the Geisha* served to tame Japan, to feminize it through the strategy of interracial relationships featuring American men and Japanese women. Exoticizing Japan was another way of taming the principal content of its image, from fearsome militarism to benign tourism. Thus the films focused on a Japan even the Japanese may barely have recognized—teahouses, geisha, small gardens, *tatami* rooms, *kimono*. *The Geisha Boy* participates in this tendency. Kimi, Mitsuo, and grandfather (Hayakawa) live in a very traditional manner in a home replete with a small stream, garden, and tatami room where they gather to eat dinner. Wooley and Mitsuo take a touristic trip through the countryside, visiting the exotic and the traditional: the giant Buddha at Kamakura, Mount Fuji, a Buddhist temple, a hot springs resort. The film also serves to tame Japan by making it quaint and cute, a meeting of the traditional and the modern: posing for photographs at tourist sites and taking in a baseball game featuring the Los Angeles Dodgers (a brief, almost inexplicable sequence unless we understand this desire to tame and domesticate the Japanese for American consumption).

At the same time the film tames the Japanese, it seeks similarly to tame, to unman, Lewis's Gilbert Wooley. His ineptness with women, as seen in the sequences with Lola, translates into his barely mastered magician's act. Outsmarted even by his pet rabbit, Harry, Wooley is an unlikely romantic figure, an unlikely man, and thus more appropriately a geisha boy. It is his ineptness, after all, combined with his basic good nature, that attracts Mitsuo to him. Although Mitsuo almost immediately asks if Wooley will be his father, Wooley is more like Mitsuo himself than he is a father figure: both were orphaned at a young age; both were raised by an unmarried aunt. Much of the childlike behavior Lewis exhibits serves further to link him to the actual child. But if his childlike persona is obvious though noteworthy, less obvious but even more noteworthy is his feminization; specifically, far from behaving like Mitsuo's father, Wooley often acts like his mother.

Twice on the touristic trip Wooley takes with Mitsuo, he performs a role and function specifically associated with women in Japan. In the first instance, which is quite subtle and thus easy to overlook, we see Wooley paddling a small boat on a lake and hear a screechy singing voice on the soundtrack. I take this to be Lewis's attempt to speak a kind of *faux*-Japanese (as he will do later at the baseball game), except that he is singing in a feminized voice and rowing a boat: rowing such small boats and singing while doing so is strictly the province of women in

Japan. The second maternal image given to Wooley is made much clearer. From a side angle, we first see two Japanese women trudging up a flight of steps, babies held to their backs by blankets or long scarves. Next comes Wooley, similarly trudging up the steps and carrying Mitsuo; he stops to mop his brow, thus giving us an unimpeded view of a strictly maternal action.

Of course, Wooley is not completely unmanned; he is allowed to overcome both his juvenilization and his feminization in one, and only one, romantic encounter between him and Kimi. This kiss comes significantly after the lengthy touristic interlude. After their long day(s) of touring, Wooley and Mitsuo enter a restaurant and are entertained by geisha. Significantly, the links between Wooley and Mitsuo continue here: as Wooley is entertained by a geisha playing a *samisen*, Mitsuo also is entertained by two young girls dressed as geisha. We may take this as a kind of male bonding around the hyperfeminized image of the geisha. This is the moment when the geisha boy is allowed to act like a man. Returning to Kimi's home, Wooley puts the boy to bed and is rewarded by a sultry kiss from Kimi. Although she is clearly the one who initiates the kiss, Wooley is finally the capable and romantic man, as he returns the favor in fine Hollywood fashion. This masculine triumph remains a singular instance in the film, however. Even the ending is ambiguous. A successful magician by film's end, thus making him something more of a grownup, Wooley has integrated both Kimi and Mitsuo into his act. We take it there is a marriage here between Wooley and Kimi, perhaps signified by the revelation that Harry the Hare is really a Harriet, as dozens of bunnies appear out of the magic hat. This substitution of show-business success for romantic success and the displacement of sexual potency onto Harry/Harriet leaves the film curiously circumspect about Wooley's attainment of adulthood and masculinity. Lewis is thus perhaps not entirely ready to take on the demands of the militarist-masculinist role in the Orientalizing feminization of Asia. But he is ready to demonstrate the attractive appeal of the Orientalized, feminized man—the Jewish man.

## LEWIS THE MENSCH

Despite his being juvenilized, demasculinized, and outright feminized, Gilbert Wooley nevertheless presents an attractive image of manhood to two attractive women: Sergeant Pearson and Kimi Sikita. That Kimi easily (and offscreen) breaks off her engagement to the Great Ichiyama is understandable in the context of the Americanization of Japan; that Sergeant Pearson is obviously attracted to Wooley is less understandable except in terms of Lewis's ongoing efforts to bring a certain maturity and romantic appeal to his persona. But what attracts the sergeant and Kimi to him is precisely his boyishness, awkwardness, and earnest unselfconsciousness. His lack of the overtly militarist masculinity characteristic of Glenn Ford, Marlon Brando, and John Wayne makes him an attractive figure to women of less hypersexuality, less aggressiveness than that of Lola Livingston, whose instant dislike of Wooley is thus revealing. In Tashlin's comic condemnation of 1950s liberated womanhood we may also see no less a condemnation of the hypermasculinity offered in rebuttal to this harsh vision of feminism.

Jerry Lewis's persona in *The Geisha Boy* has not been especially identified as "Jewish." This would be the work of the next generation of Jewish filmmakers—Woody Allen, Mel Brooks, Sidney Lumet, and Paul Mazursky, in particular. Lewis's persona was masked as Jewish, as was typical in the 1950s film and television stardom of the likes of Milton Berle, Jack Benny, and Sid Caesar. The masking meant sometimes a physical inadequacy or feminization (shown in Berle's crossdressing or Benny's legendary cowardice or cheapness, though not in the performing of Sid Caesar, who was notoriously strong and tough); the use of popular-culture parodies; show business as a primary milieu; a comic stance toward life; and self-deprecating humor. These aspects became part of the fundamental construction of later Jewish stars who would add more overtly Jewish dimensions to their personae. I want to recover Lewis's persona as Jewish, albeit only briefly here.

Little is overtly Jewish in Jerry's role in *The Geisha Boy*. Yet there is one aspect of some note, a double entendre that reveals Jerry's Jewishness but also speaks to the film's plot and theme: misunderstanding Mitsuo's name, or unable to pronounce it, Lewis calls him not Mitsuo but "Mitzvah." This Hebrew word betrays his Jewishness but also speaks to the *mitzvah*, the good deed, he is performing in bringing friendship to a little boy. Lewis's unthreatening sexuality, his physical ineptitude, his feminization all speak to the cultural image generally associated with Jewishness. Daniel Boyarin, perhaps one of the most interesting cultural critics writing on and working in and through a Jewish perspective, writes the following: "As I reflect on my coming of age in New Jersey, I realize that I had always been in some sense more of a 'girl' than a 'boy.' A sissy who did not like sports, whose mother used to urge me, stop reading and go out and play" (1997, xiii). But instead of subscribing to the masculinist fantasy of mainstream culture as his mother wished, he rejected that approach: "Rather than producing in me a desire to 'pass' and to become a 'man,' this sensibility resulted in my desire to remain a Jew, where being a sissy was all right." Two important rhetorical advances are made via this stance: the first is that the Jewish man, Boyarin, does not deny the image widespread throughout the culture, that being Jewish renders a boy effeminate; the second is that being "Jewish" provides an alternative image of masculinity. That is, the effeminate Jewish man of antisemitic rhetoric is, in fact, a sissy, but a sissy is, in turn, the "real man":

> He whom a past dominant culture . . . considers contemptible, the feminized Jewish . . . male, may be useful today, for "he" may help us precisely today in our attempts to construct an alternative masculine subjectivity, one that will not have to rediscover such cultural archetypes as Iron John, knights, hairy men, and warriors within. (Boyarin 1997, xiv)

Working in the 1950s and 1960s, Lewis's persona was at once in touch with a newly feminized, sensitive male evident in the personae of Montgomery Clift and James Dean but at odds with emerging postwar reassertions of masculinity in the apotheosis of John Wayne and the stardom of Marlon Brando, Steve McQueen, and Clint Eastwood. Following the death of Dean and, later, Clift, where would we find this sissified, sensitive character again?

Lewis's film career was essentially over by the late 1960s, when he was too old to play the sissy-boy, the idiot, the feminized hysteric. But his legacy would recur in interesting ways, and perhaps not until the rise of Jim Carrey and Adam Sandler would we be able to come to appreciate how much he changed the possibilities of stardom and the image of masculinity. By way of Woody Allen, Mel Brooks, and Albert Brooks, Jerry Lewis made being Jewish—a Jewish man—okay and allowed both the WASPish Carrey and the Jewish Sandler to achieve the sort of stardom that, while now almost forgotten, Lewis himself enjoyed.

Now he can disappear; there is no longer a place for the real, only the simulacrum. Jerry Langford (Jerry Lewis) evaluating the stand-up comedy of Rupert Pupkin (Robert De Niro) in *The King of Comedy* (Martin Scorsese, Twentieth Century Fox, 1983). Frame enlargement.

# 11

# Jerry in the City

## The Topology of *The King of Comedy*

J. P. Telotte

> A strange topology is hidden in the obviousness of televised images.
>
> —Paul Virilio

IN EXAMINING THE impact of modern mass media on our culture, Paul Virilio (1991) describes one of the key effects of media's general "derealization," the way it suggests there are no boundaries, that we have immediate access to all that we see. But there always remains, as he notes, something "hidden" amid this "obviousness," a "lost dimension" or "strange topology"—a depth—that we might little expect and that can prove disturbing, even provoke a shock of recognition. Martin Scorsese's *The King of Comedy* (1983) models that shock for us right from its start, as it shows a group of autograph seekers, some of them quite violent, descending on comedian Jerry Langford (in a tellingly reflexive turn, played by Jerry Lewis) as he emerges from a midtown Manhattan studio and heads to a waiting limousine. Assaulted by one crazed fan named Masha (Sandra Bernhard), Jerry is pulled free by another, erstwhile comedian Rupert Pupkin (Robert De Niro), leaving Masha trapped in Jerry's limousine. This prologue to the opening credits ends with a point-of-view shot from within, a freeze-frame as Masha looks at Jerry and presses her hands to the window, just as if she were pressing on the television screen that has always mediated her relationship to her idol and kept her at a frustrating distance. As Masha sits trapped in the limousine, her look of outrage suggests her surprise at the sudden, added boundary that separates her from the person she has thought to catch backstage, apart from his pervasive presence as a televised image. For here, even in living flesh, practically by her side, he still exists for her only at a mediated distance. It is a surprise, the film implies, that is commonly shared in the postmodern world where, as Virilio offers, "the screen abruptly became the city square, the crossroads of all mass media" (1991, 25)—for many, the very locus of reality.

The King of Comedy traces out the consequences of this surprise by exploring on several levels the human topology that has resulted from the derealizing effects of the media. One of those levels shows up in its dissection of the autograph seekers and celebrity stalkers who have become all too enthralled with that "obviousness" Virilio mentions as being offered up by the media culture for our entertainment and our seeming possession. That culture has produced a widespread sense that everything is accessible to us and that there is no depth or elusiveness to anything in modern life. Starting from the pack of autograph seekers and celebrity hounds that the prologue sketches in the broadest strokes, the film traces the trajectory of one particularly obsessive fan, Rupert, as he tries to become first Jerry's equal and then his successor as the self-proclaimed "King of Comedy." Although we do not see the initial creation process, Rupert is, quite literally, a media creation, the ultimate product of the derealizing effect Virilio describes, and a type with which we have become quite familiar thanks to numerous headline stories of such celebrity groupies, stalkers, and murderers in recent times. (John Lennon's murder in 1980 by Mark Chapman seems one inspiration for the film.) Yet another, ultimately more significant strategy for investigating this derealization is the film's use of Jerry Lewis. Drawing on his status as a movie and television star, as someone who, like the narrative's Jerry Langford, exists for many simply as a mediated figure, The King of Comedy manages to comment on a world where boundaries are increasingly hard to define and on the function of celebrities such as Lewis when reality itself seems to have been transformed into a kind of "crossroads" between the imagination and everyday experience.

We can begin to trace the human effects of this derealization in the character of Rupert, a figure drawn by the lure of celebrity because, as he admits, it seems to give "meaning" to "our lives"—a meaning that has so far eluded him. In her study of Scorsese, Mary Pat Kelly points up this dimension in many of the director's characters, figures who all

seem driven by a desire "to go beyond the narrow role that a material-
ist society assigns them" (1991, 12). Probably the most obvious example
is Travis Bickle's doomed pursuit of the upper-class Betsy in *Taxi Driver*
(1976). Rupert Pupkin seems taken from a similar mold, although Scorsese has acknowledged that he "hadn't really understood" this character
too well (Kelly 1991, 153). While Rupert is someone who wants to transcend his limited lot, the derealizing effect Virilio describes has so conditioned his own grasp on reality—and thus his sense of what that goal
entails—that he seems unlikely to ever move beyond his "narrow role"
as groupie and comic wannabe. Much of his time, we gather, is spent
obsessively constructing the superficial elements of such celebrity: rehearsing to be a talk-show host like Jerry, pretending to play to an audience, practicing trading quips as if on such a show, and trying to shut
out reminders of the real world, particularly his mom and her repeated
questions about what he is doing in his room. And that imagined position, as someone just like Jerry Langford, is matched by scenes from Rupert's imagination, in which he interacts with various celebrities (Dr.
Joyce Brothers, Victor Borge), does a stand-up comedy routine that we
never really get to hear, acknowledges the applause of a studio audience and other stars, even weds on television the former cheerleader
who snubbed him throughout high school (Diahnne Abbott). The implication is that, like many others in our culture, Rupert lives much of
his life in an imagined world or, more accurately, a world that has
largely been imagined for him by television, and one that holds out the
promise of validating his life, locating its own "lost dimension."

Much like Masha in the opening scene, Rupert seems to live behind
a kind of invisible barrier, symbolized by the television screen but really
the functional result of a pervasive media context. As Virilio explains,
the "constructed space" of the modern technological environment, of
the modern city, "is more than simply the concrete and material substance of constructed structures"; it is also, and perhaps more significantly, "an imperceptible order, which is invisible but just as practical as
masonry" (1991, 21). On the one hand, that space is simply the set of
physical and class structures reified by the media and designed to
maintain a certain order. These structures are embodied in, for instance,
the security forces at the studio and at Jerry's offices; the elaborate series of intermediaries and assistants that one must go through in order
to reach Jerry; the tapes Rupert submits as a kind of audition; even the
servants at Jerry's house, who quickly recognize that Rupert and his

girlfriend, Rita, are not the sort with whom a celebrity like Jerry typically associates. On the other hand, it is the complex process of mediation itself that produces this sort of "invisible" but equally effective organization and barrier. Rupert's constant fantasizing of himself on television, with Jerry or even *as* Jerry, follows from his obsession with both Jerry's televised image and, more generally, mediated celebrity, with a felt need for media affirmation of his own life and personality. That need suggests his own inability to recognize that such an "affirmation" also serves to derealize his life.

This complex pattern of affirmation and derealization shows up particularly when we see Rupert imagining various scenarios of success, such as Jerry confessing, "You've got it"; "We were wrong and you, Rupert, you were right"; and "I envy you." When Rupert admits to Jerry on their first meeting, "I studied everything you ever did," he admits to more than just admiration; he points to an obsessiveness that has become his life, as we see in the world he inhabits: the dark basement room with television, tape recorder, a cardboard image of Jerry and various other television and film celebrities, cutouts of audience members. He has simply tried to "construct" a familiar media realm for himself by way of bridging those many barriers the media world imposes on or represents to his life. The media world has come to represent a kind of city, a real environment for someone like Rupert, and it prods him to fashion his own place in that world, to locate himself within that city.

Jerry Lewis, though, simultaneously the goal of Rupert's mediated desires and, as the reigning "King of Comedy," a barrier to their fulfillment, is the real key to the film's vision of a cinematically derealized world. While initial production discussions mentioned using Dick Cavett in the Jerry Langford role and then settled on Johnny Carson, Scorsese eventually realized "that Carson wasn't right because the phenomenon of his talk show wasn't that well known outside America" (Thompson and Christie 1989, 90). He simply did not adequately embody the "mediatization" on which the film was coming to focus. So, after considering and rejecting a number of other possibilities—Frank Sinatra, Orson Welles, even Dean Martin—he decided to cast Lewis precisely because he so effectively linked to the landscape of contemporary media culture in a variety of ways. As Shawn Levy offers, Scorsese saw Lewis as "the embodiment of High American Show Business of the Late Twentieth Century" (1996, 420). Lewis's lengthy movie career as both

actor and director; his stage work, especially in Las Vegas; his many television appearances (some will recall Lewis's two-week stint as guest
host of NBC's "The Tonight Show" in June of 1962); his comic book figure; and especially his annual Muscular Dystrophy Association
Telethon had assured his place in both the media landscape and the
popular imagination. Scorsese capitalized on that reflexive potential,
using Lewis's own dog for Langford's, having Lewis wear his own
wardrobe, placing a picture of the young Lewis on Langford's mantel,
and employing Lewis's own caricature trademark as Langford's. In
short, he deployed a variety of what Levy terms "naturalistic strategies" (1996, 421), effects that, on the one hand, were designed to help
Lewis feel at home with his character but that, on the other, also
prompted viewers to conflate the two, to recognize how much of Lewis
was in Langford's character and Langford in Lewis.

A further—and ultimately more important—dimension of this
identification is Scorsese's mining of Lewis's long-established media
persona to further his thematic concerns. Much as in the case of a prior
Scorsese character, such as Jake La Motta of *Raging Bull* (1980), Lewis
provided the director with an opportunity for exploring the disturbing
effects of celebrity produced by that media existence while also reflecting on the nature of a "life lived on the margins" of everyday reality
(Kakutani 1999, 102). As we have already noted, Rupert's character represents one such marginal existence, and one with particularly deep
roots in Travis Bickle of *Taxi Driver*, Jimmy Doyle of *New York, New York*
(1977), and Jake La Motta. They are all types with which Scorsese was
quite familiar, denizens of the modern city, at home in that mass media
"crossroads" even if never quite able to figure out how to push through
the television screen, to become something more than, as Rupert fears,
"schmuck for a lifetime."

But through Jerry Lewis and the various media touchstones he
brought to the film project Scorsese could also examine another sort of
life on the edge, another sort of existence on the margins of the city of
mediated reality: for Lewis, as Jerry Langford, represents the sort of figure who exists for many people only as an "obvious" and superficial
image, a type that occupies the various "screens" that mark our world,
a persona with whom we have developed, on a cultural level, a (perhaps too) comfortably mediated relationship, as the film's opening encounter with Masha illustrates. It is when he is found to retain a certain
human depth, or what Virilio terms a "strange topology," that the film

achieves its assault on that pervasive derealizing effect, on the consequences of what Mark Crispin Miller has described as our life in a "boxed-in" world, that is, a world where television has become not just an "imposition on some preexistent cultural environment," but also the very "environment" we inhabit (1988, 8).

Compared to the initial choice of Johnny Carson, then, Lewis brought to the role not only a figure equally familiar to television audiences but also one who, unlike Carson, had over the course of many years developed a well-defined persona both in and beyond TV. From the time of his early stage and screen partnership with Dean Martin, through the long series of films that he both starred in and directed, and even in the course of his annual telethon, Lewis had established a character with interesting parallels to that of Rupert Pupkin. As we have seen, Pupkin is a figure who lives a precarious—and potentially dangerous—existence. A loner who lives with his mother and easily slips into a dream reality in which he is Langford's protégé and eventual successor, he imagines himself something else; as screenwriter Paul Zimmerman offers, he is ultimately "someone who would rather die than live anonymously" (Kelly 1991, 153). And if we are to accept the film's ending as reality rather than one more of Rupert's many imagined scenarios for his life, he eventually manages to become that something else, a new "King of Comedy." In effect, he enacts a media myth of such transformation.

Of course, this sort of character transformation was always central to the Lewis persona as well. Frank Krutnik notes, for example, how throughout his films Lewis initially projects a character who seems "a locus of deviance, a clown prince of disorder, a monster from the id" (2000, 2)—a description that could just as well apply to most of the characters De Niro has fleshed out for Scorsese's films. And the Lewis persona is similarly prone to dreaming about another sort of life for himself, even to having reveries like Rupert's. Yet this characterization is crucial for establishing a context or base from which his potentially subversive character can eventually metamorphose into a socially acceptable figure, can find an identity that can be integrated into society. The change was essential if Lewis's recurrent "Kid" figure was ever to grow up and assume the adult responsibilities—of love, marriage, parenthood—that were so often the happy end of his comic trajectories and that ultimately reassured audiences rather than challenged them.

Of course, in his early pairings with Dean Martin, Jerry Lewis—and the movie audience—always had the advantage of a normative model for comparison, a figure who easily fit into his world, almost effortlessly met its demands. Lewis's "grotesque body comedy," as Krutnik describes his act (2000, 16), could readily be measured off against Martin's suave and controlled manner. In *At War with the Army* (1950), for example, Lewis's PFC Alvin Corwin is constantly having to measure up to the standards of his sergeant, Martin's Vic Puccinelli; and in *Pardners* (1956), Martin's Slim Mosely Jr. makes Lewis's sheltered character, Wade Kingsley Jr., into a cowboy so that he can survive in the West. In a number of Lewis's later, self-directed films, he varies the same narrative model by subsuming Martin's character into his own. Thus in *Cinderfella* (1960) he plays the inept and homely Fella as well as his magically transformed self, the suave, princely type who manages, just as Martin typically did, to win the hand of a charming lady, in this case Princess Charmein. Perhaps the best example, though, is *The Nutty Professor* (1963), in which the lonely and nerdish college professor Julius Kelp, with the aid of a potion he develops, turns into the smooth and outgoing Buddy Love, a near parody of Martin as the "Rat Pack" stalwart. In this instance, though, the transformation is rather too close to the model and makes the pattern so transparent that he must change further. Still, the implication is that, for good or ill, Lewis always had a certain element of the Martin character in him—an element that might be coaxed out by Martin's deft model or repeated hectoring or that might simply be liberated by Lewis's own desire or persistence. If in his films Lewis constantly enacted, as Krutnik puts it, "a spectacular dissolution of identity" (2000, 8), then it was to prepare us for a necessary transformation, one that would enable his character to function successfully in society—in any case to get the girl, find general affirmation, and perhaps even perform much like Dean Martin.

With *The King of Comedy* that potential for transformation is crucial, first, because it suggests a trajectory that Rupert's character too might follow, and indeed seems set on following—from misfit outsider to beloved celebrity. The film could, very simply, become a Lewis-type comedy. Secondly, it points toward the expectations that attach to Jerry Langford as a figure who might be anticipated to function in the fashion of his/Lewis's mediated persona, and indeed to be little else. The extent to which Rupert, Masha, and the various other celebrity followers here buy into both possibilities attests to the power of that derealizing effect Virilio describes, while it also allows the film to challenge its audience's relationship to contemporary mediated culture, to warn about how much we have "denatured direct observation and common sense" (Virilio 1991, 111), in great part by confusing the media world with the real, by failing to see how easily one begins to seem like or substitute for the other.

The problem is that the broad narrative of Jerry Lewis/Langford, the narrative of the likable yet anarchic persona who can suddenly become acceptable, has come to replace the reality of Lewis/Langford, at least in the minds of those who inhabit this new media city. As an example we might consider the elderly woman whom Jerry meets on a New York street. She recognizes him, tells him what a great fan she is, and then demands that he talk to her nephew on the phone and say something funny for him. Uninterested in Langford the man, she wants him to be his persona for her, and when he demurs, her attitude immediately changes. As Mary Pat Kelly describes it, she "descends into invective" (1991, 152), screaming at him, "You should only get cancer! I hope you get cancer!" The unrealistic belief that he essentially is his comic persona and that any other life has no claims of priority takes on added weight when we consider that this scene was not in the film's original script but was drawn from Lewis's own life and testifies to the same level of claims his fans typically make, the same denial of depth that characterizes their relationship to him.

The film, however, carefully underscores Jerry's reality, the fact that he lives not just in the screen as "city square" that Virilio describes but in a very real world. Thus the narrative shows us Jerry's in-town apartment, a drab and spartan accommodation in which the television is constantly running as company, and his office, where his associates plan his show; and when Rupert convinces himself that Jerry has extended an open invitation to get together, we view Jerry's suburban home, a large and apparently lonely place run by his servants—a place, in any case, that seems pointedly different and something of a refuge from his city/media life. These various locales sketch a figure who is not glamorous or even especially happy with his life, and one for whom celebrity is hard work, even a burden. As Scorsese himself explains, such scenes worked to build a sense of "the isolating consequences of fame" (Kakutani 1999, 102).

Just as important for fashioning this sense of depth and difference are the scenes that repeatedly show Jerry walking the streets of New York, for they gradually develop how ill at ease he feels in this world that is simultaneously real and disconcertingly false.[1] While a number of Lewis's earlier films drew on an urban setting and tried to play off of that environment—most notably *Living It Up* (1954), *Artists and Models* (1955), and *The Delicate Delinquent* (1957)—none has the feel or look of a real city; all seem highly stylized, as is particularly evident in the gang fight depicted early in *The Delicate Delinquent*. In fact, while *The King of Comedy* was the forty-sixth film in Lewis's career, it was the first he had ever shot in New York City and one of the few actually done on location (Levy 1996, 420). Lewis seems uncomfortable, even wary as he walks through the city, in part because his persona was always a denizen of a highly stylized environment, because he needed such a malleable world to accommodate his potential for change, but also because the city, especially as Scorsese sees it, has become something quite new, something to be wary of. No longer the center of habitation of 1950s America, it had turned into a temporary place from which Americans fled for the safety of the suburbs, just as Jerry Langford does in this film. In effect, the city had become an unstable environment, increasingly saturated with the fallout of mediatization and derealization.

It is appropriate, then, that the film emphasizes the threatening nature of this derealization through a series of scenes that place Jerry on the streets of New York, braving "the crossroads of all mass media." The first, already described, is when he emerges from his studio at the film's opening to be greeted first by well-wishers and autograph seekers but then by obsessives such as Masha, whom he sees as a real physical threat. This scene ends on that threatening note with Jerry—questionably aided by Rupert, who is, after all, another of those celebrity chasers—fleeing as if for his life. In the second scene, Jerry again emerges from a safe haven, in this case his apartment building, and walks through the crowded city streets, exchanging jokes with a cab driver, waving to construction workers, and exchanging greetings with various passersby. Here the tone shifts more gradually yet dramatically as he encounters the old lady who first tells him what a big fan she is and then hopes he gets cancer. Immediately after, Jerry realizes Masha is stalking him, and he sprints to his office building to escape—in his panic even resorting to the familiar Jerry Lewis spastic run. The third scene completes this threatening pattern. It shows Jerry leaving his apartment building and greeting people on the streets, but these actions are observed from the point of view of Rupert and Masha as together they stalk and prepare to kidnap him. And in this case there is no escape, as Jerry is forced into Masha's car at gunpoint and taken away while, in a familiar symptom of the modern metamorphosis of the city, no one on the street either notices or is disturbed by the event. Masha and Rupert earlier remark that Jerry seems afraid "to be alone" on those city streets; rightly so, since apparently every time he emerges from the relative safety of work or residence, he risks this unpredictable behavior of the city's residents, an instability that has come to characterize the people at this "crossroads."

The final scene in which Jerry moves through the city sheds an even more revealing light on this relationship. In this instance Jerry leaves not a safe haven such as his apartment but Masha's house, where he has been held prisoner, as he tricks her, takes her gun—a fake, a movie prop as it were, something that, as Masha notes, "*looks* real"—and runs through the dark city streets looking for help. In the night, with the streets deserted and a nearly nude and screaming Masha chasing Jerry, the city certainly looks threatening, if also rather unreal. The effect is a nightmarish combination of menace and absurdity much like that which Scorsese fashioned in his later urban comedy *After Hours* (1985). Certainly no haven, the postmodern derealized city, a world with its own "strange topology," populated by those who both worship and stalk celebrity, and marked by unpredictable change, here becomes a distinctly disturbing place.

The further point to this "escape" into a near nightmare world becomes clearer after Jerry eludes his pursuer but is suddenly brought up short by a store window displaying rows of televisions all tuned to his own show, on which he watches Rupert doing a comic monologue, one in which he brazenly boasts that "the only way I could break into show business" was "by hijacking Jerry Langford"—by literally *taking* his place. What Jerry confronts, I suggest, is the real face of this new city, the face of Rupert and his like, ultimately the face of the derealizing power he has helped generate. At this point we might begin to understand the true reason why, as Rupert and Masha sensed, Jerry seems afraid in the city. His fear is not simply of being alone in this world—although loneliness, as lack of any real human connection, is part of it—but of being just one more reproducible image, one "King of Comedy" readily supplanted by another, one more figure whose identity, even his reality, hinges on the electronic image. Fittingly, the close-up of him staring at this mediated reality—and in a look of outward regard, at us as well—is the final shot of Jerry in the film. It suggests a kind of shock of recognition of his own fragile position in this world, as well as of our own complicity in this effect. In what could well have served as a suitable coda for the film, this scene simply makes the media's power both to realize and to derealize most obvious.

It is a moment of recognition, though, that does point toward the film's problematic epilogue, wherein we learn of Rupert's subsequent history. Imprisoned for more than two years for kidnapping Jerry, he apparently becomes a media celebrity: for in the wake of his appearance on Jerry's show, watched, we are told, by "a record 87 million households," Rupert's face appears on the covers of *Life*, *Newsweek*, *Time*, *People*, and even *Rolling Stone*, thus demonstrating how easily one can become part of the written or mediated record of contemporary culture. Subsequently, his autobiography, *King for a Night*, written during his prison term, becomes a best-seller and is optioned for a movie. Moreover, the media reconstructs him as a figure quite different from the manic kidnapper we have seen; he becomes almost the sort of comic type we find in various Jerry Lewis films of an earlier time. Upon his release, he appears on television where we hear an announcer describe him as "legendary," "inspirational," and, of course, the new "King of Comedy." It is as if his most desperate human action had been translated by the media as simply an elaborate joke—again as a form of "obviousness" without any depth or significance. This television appearance that ends the film begs the question of his accomplishment—and fittingly, for a film that has emphasized the derealizing effects of the media, the question of the very reality of its own conclusion. For Rupert does nothing; he simply stands there receiving applause, as if celebrity were, after all, nothing more than being known, no more than what he originally wanted, which is to appear on television, to be acknowledged by the media. The slow track-in to a close-up, though, points up the uncertainty, even fear in his face at having gotten exactly what he asked for, at what the film suggests is becoming a general cultural desire—being quite literally reduced to nothing more than an image.

Of course, that final image of anxiety does not quite sort out the conclusion for us, does not give us a satisfactory clue as to whether this last sequence is reality or simply another of Rupert's reveries, such as we have seen throughout the film. It could well be that he has, thanks to a kind of nightmarish bargain between the public and the media, gained precisely the sort of fame he longed for, although not through any show of talent. In fact, when Scorsese, after teasing us several times, finally lets us hear Rupert's stand-up performance, it becomes clear that he has no real comic ability; his jokes are unoriginal and not really funny. So if he is, as the television announcer offers, "the man we've all been waiting for," then this conclusion is a further indictment of that public desire and public taste. The film suggests that we shall get precisely what we want and deserve in this thoroughly mediated world.

And if this final scene is simply another of his imaginings, then we are left with the cold comfort of his arrest and imprisonment, of the temporary—although, as contemporary events have shown, ultimately unavailing—protection this new world offers against such types. More to the point, though, it suggests how, through our media-bound imaginings, we all contribute to that derealizing effect, extend the unreality our culture has already generated, and all too readily opt to inhabit that "city," as Rupert in his imagination apparently does.

The transformation from person to icon—the voyage to the mediated city—exemplified by both Langford and Pupkin does involve a kind of growth. Traditionally, the Jerry Lewis persona undergoes growth or transformation as he moves from an infantile to a more adult, and even adept, nature. However, he does so within a rather abstract world, a derealized realm that lacks depth and complexity, and thus one that makes such growth seem quite easy, simply an act of will or, as Rupert illustrates in *The King of Comedy*, of obsession. Indeed, Rupert learns the lessons of the Jerry image quite well; so well, in fact, that the image effectively manages to replace him. He certainly knows how to "act" like a person who is a celebrity; he rehearses it in his room, practices it out on the streets. And he has learned some of the complexities of modern urban life, at least as those lessons are repeatedly spelled out for us in the media: how to deal effectively with the difficulties of kidnapping, extortion, and media representation. Yet Jerry Langford's initial failure to recognize in Rupert this very pattern, indeed his own model, is telling. He assumes that Rupert, like himself, has a life apart from his performing persona, that he is something more than the "obviousness" of a televisual image. But after his escape, as he encounters Rupert's multiple media images in the shop window, he sees his own image as both victim and contributor to this derealizing impulse. Jerry can disappear then because there may no longer be a place for the real, only the simulacrum; his "strange topology," the human depth that lingers beneath his own televised image, no longer has a place in this "crossroads of all mass media."

Perhaps using Jerry Lewis to indicate, even to gauge, the increasing derealization of a hypermediated world is too heavy a burden to place on a figure who had long specialized in portraying, as Shawn Levy offers, "the world's most abject misfits" (1996, 423). Yet as Krutnik observes, Lewis had become at the same time "a complexly mediated subject" (2000, 5), a figure who, in real life and as cultural persona, had evolved into a media icon.[2] Jerry clearly represents such an icon to the other characters in *The King of Comedy*. His eventual disappearance from the narrative and replacement—whether real or imaginary—by "the man we've all been waiting for" testifies to the power of that iconicity, to how such figures and the media context in which they exist wield a transforming power. As Krutnik further offers about *The King of Comedy*, "All meaning stops at the image in the media-saturated world" (2000, 199). But for exactly that reason, the simple image may also be enough. The problematic conclusion of the film extends the problem of the real into our own world, implicates our own cinematic experience, and in that implication forces us to consider the empty end toward which the derealizing impulse might lead. Jerry thus serves a warning function, becomes another sort of yardstick—a cultural one. For through Jerry the film positions us all at a crucial "crossroads" and asks what sort of city we want to inhabit.

### NOTES

1. In this context we might recall Frank McConnell's description of the modern city in film in his book *The Spoken Seen*. There he talks about how film has captured the emergence of "the modern, depersonalizing city"; through its ability to image in an immediate way "the solidity and the clutter" of that world, it also manages to convey the city's "peculiar danger and triumph" (1975, 47–48).

2. Dana Polan traces how "the Lewis sort of film" gradually developed into a kind of youth genre in itself and "the Lewis case," as the French have termed it, became a yardstick for gauging critical tastes in cinematic comedy (1984, 43, 46).

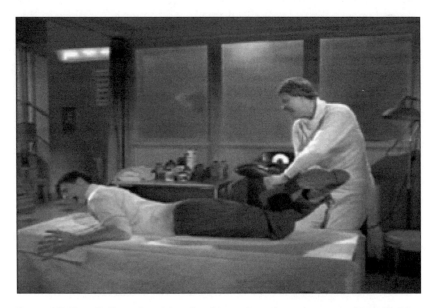

Eugene Fullstack (Jerry Lewis) twisted into shape by a masseuse (Patti Ross) in *Artists and Models* (Frank Tashlin, Paramount, 1955). "His shrieking somnambulocutions turn him into a receiver, or perhaps a transmitter." Frame enlargement.

# 12

# Terminal Idiocy

*(The comedian is the message)*

Scott Bukatman

IN 1964, MARSHALL MCLUHAN published *Understanding Media: The Extensions of Man* and changed the face of pop culture forever. *Understanding Media*, poised between the academicism of McLuhan's earlier writing and the utopian typographical "happenings" of *The Medium Is the Massage* (McLuhan and Fiore 1967) and *War and Peace in the Global Village* (McLuhan and Fiore 1968), resonated with a culture in technological and generational transition, and especially loudly for a United States only beginning to recognize the quagmire of its "living-room war."

In *Understanding Media*, McLuhan operated as a kind of global positioning satellite for the rest of North American society, becoming as a result the most conspicuous theorist of technological shock since Walter Benjamin. Shock, for both Benjamin and McLuhan, was the only conceivable relation to a technology that seemed to subjugate and liberate in equal doses, even in the same instants. McLuhan, however, and most unlike Benjamin, embraced the role of prophet, preaching a gospel of electric acceptance, a condition that would follow automatically (as opposed to automatonically) from an understanding of the dynamic interconnectedness of electronic systems and especially from a vision of "remote" technologies as literal extensions of the human nervous and perceptual systems.

McLuhan's work would increasingly enact the synesthesia he held as concomitant with life in that "global village" in which we indisputably dwelt. But in *Understanding Media* the emphasis is on a culture in transition, and McLuhan traces the complex ambivalences produced by a series of media—*media* as understood in both traditional terms (radio, telephone, film, television) and in McLuhan's new expanded definition (electricity, typewriters, advertising).

He might go unmentioned by McLuhan, but in films from the late 1950s to the mid-1960s the body of Jerry Lewis channeled anxieties surrounding the pervading, perverting, invasive aspects (the pervasion) of electronic technology. In describing Jerry as an automaton trapped in a twitchifying feedback loop of an electronic circuit, Gilles Deleuze proposed something similar, but his brief observations can be effectively nuanced with reference to *Understanding Media*. Against the ground of McLuhan's argument, Jerry appears as a more problematic figure of the electronic age than Deleuze suggests: one caught in the moment of transition between mechanico-industrial and electronic paradigms of technological being, a body trapped in the "critical pressures of the new electric environment" (McLuhan 1964, xi). At the same moment that McLuhan theorizes a transition from industrial age to electronic culture, Jerry is performing a body racked between these two paradigms. His subjectivity, played out upon the surface of his body (a surface that includes his voice), is no longer capable of being defined against the unitary concentration of the Machine but is not yet comfortable with its dispersal into global circuitry and information circulation. He spins, tilts, and stammers, but he keeps on talking and ticking (and ticcing). His is a sustained, unrelenting synesthesia without the relief offered by the state of shock—he is jolted (shocked) but never numbed (state of shock); the "amputation" of the senses that McLuhan describes is denied. No one, I suggest, embodied the trauma of what I once called *terminal identity* as effectively as Jerry Lewis.[1]

## LOYALTY TO THE SPONSOR: THE MISE-EN-SCÈNE OF MASS MEDIA CULTURE

The same year that saw the publication of *Understanding Media* also saw the release of *Who's Minding the Store?* (1963), a Jerry Lewis vehicle directed by Frank Tashlin. In the late 1950s, Tashlin's work enshrined an exemplary ambivalence regarding American popular culture (*whose* ambivalence—Tashlin's, his American audience's, or his French critics'—was not entirely clear, although time has tended to point toward those crazy *auteurists*). Tashlin's films featured an eye-popping embrace of Technicolor and CinemaScope, grotesque visual and performative cartoonishness, and a *faux*-sophisticated mockery of Hollywood, Madison Avenue, and the female form. With his often inspired blend of slapstick, satire, and calendar art, Tashlin was kitsch with a vengeance.

McLuhan never took on Tashlin, but he did consider another, analogous piece of self-referential popular culture: "*MAD* magazine," he noted, "simply [!] transferred the world of ads into the world of the comic book" (1964, 152). I wonder whether McLuhan knew that Harvey Kurtzman, *MAD's* creator, had come to comics by way of the hierarchical, organization-man-in-the-gray-flannel-suit world of advertising,[2] as had one of the magazine's earliest contributors, the humorist Stan Freberg. *MAD* played with the content of mass media, presenting savvy parodies of the content, structures, and aesthetics of movies, television, comic books, and advertising. Its style was also the stuff of mass media: picture stories, caricature, brevity.

Tashlin's visual language was one of outsized billboards and bright, flat color—the same language that Pop would soon appropriate. *Artists and Models* (1955) condenses a range of popular culture icons in its opening scene: Jerry in a malfunctioning smoking billboard, voraciously reading *Bat Lady* comic books. The credits for *Will Success Spoil Rock Hunter?* (1957) were a series of parodied commercials.

The public recognized the absurdity of advertising, but that awareness did nothing to short-circuit the ads' impact (McLuhan 1964, 202). McLuhan suggested that we listen to the kids: "Today our ten year olds, in voting for *MAD*, are telling us in their own way that the TV image has ended the consumer phase of American culture" (152–153). Advertising had become a self-referential iconic system, the lingua franca for a media-saturated populace. Meanwhile, the weakened link between media representation and consumer object served as a harbinger of what Guy Debord around 1964 would label "the society of the spectacle."

In *Rock-a-Bye Baby* (1958), Jerry's landlady watches a TV commercial extolling a brand of chicory coffee: *No coffee, just flavor*, announces the announcer. *Drink some! NOW!* And so she does. Right away. McLuhan writes that "the advertising industry is a crude attempt to extend the principles of automation to every aspect of society" (1964, 202). Miss Bessie (Ida Moore) watches another ad, this one for Superbo cigarettes, and Jerry, unbidden, lights one and passes it to her. "Ads push the principle of noise all the way to the plateau of persuasion. They are

quite in accord with principles of brainwashing" (202). Once all prod-
ucts have been consumed and the "Late Late Early Late Show" is back
on, Miss Bessie can finally direct her attention toward Jerry. "You know
I believe in loyalty to the sponsor," she reminds him. "That's the trouble with the world today—not enough loyalty." For McLuhan, loyalty
to the sponsor (but not necessarily the product) was a last, dwindling
refuge for "fragmented, literate individualism" within a postnational
and increasingly secular globalism. What once we rendered to God or
Caesar now (tenuously) belonged to Madison Avenue, but even that
loyalty seemed atavistic: "So great is the change in American lives resulting from the loss of loyalty to the consumer package in entertainment and commerce, that every enterprise, from Madison Avenue and
General Motors to Hollywood and General Foods, has been shaken
thoroughly and forced to seek new strategies of action" (280). The more
pervasive advertising becomes, especially when abetted by the power
of television, the more it generates its own set of conditions: the *best*
must always be *NEW and IMPROVED*. "What possible *immunity*," he
asked, "can there be from the subliminal operation of a new medium
like television?" (286)—a question eloquently embalmed in the elderly
Miss Bessie's simultaneous construction as TV zombie and moral
guidepost.

## THE JERKING AND THE TWITCHING:
## IMPERFECT AUTOMATION AND THE NEW ELECTRIC MAN

Jerry's films are filled with that staple of film comedy, a give-and-take
tug-of-war between comedian and machine, a topic of no little interest
to McLuhan. It's a kind of generational marker that McLuhan's dominant point of reference within cinematic comedy should be Chaplin: the
rediscovery of Buster Keaton's comedy of automatism and adaptability
would not occur until about a decade later, while Lewis and Tashlin
were surely *too* contemporary, *too* vulgar. Jerry embodies the end of the
modernism that is exemplified through Chaplin's comedy. In *Modern
Times* (1936), Charlie cannot control the spasmodic, repetitive movements endlessly required on his assembly-line job: on a break or outside
the factory "he repeats his compulsive twitchings with an imaginary
wrench" (McLuhan 1964, 253).

Charlie is defined through a division of labor and the crudest kind of use-value, but the pathos of his performance and the clarity of the visual metaphors (e.g., Charlie swallowed by the factory machine) reinstate the character as an embattled soul in jeopardy. As McLuhan writes, "The clown reminds us of our fragmented state by tackling acrobatic or special jobs in the spirit of the whole or integral man" (253). (This idea is superbly illustrated by the animated, cut-out Charlot figure that opens and closes Leger and Murphy's *Ballet mécanique* [1924].) This was as true of such solo film comedians as Keaton and Lloyd as it was of Chaplin.[3] Noël Carroll (1998) argues something similar of Keaton's work, finding the diminished role of the craftsman in American culture to be effectively recalled not only by Buster's symbiotic, solitary relationship to a locomotive engine in *The General* (1927) but by Keaton-the-filmmaker's always evident craftsmanship as well.

Which brings us to Jerry's "compulsive twitchings." Unlike Chaplin and Keaton, both of whom subjugated technology through their display of balletic or athletic mastery, every spastic movement of Jerry's takes him toward his own oblivion (and this extends to the lack of control that Lewis reveals as a director—even in the period when he bills himself as "the total filmmaker").[4]

American modernity of the 1920s figured the machine as somewhat more discreet from the organic and human than did its European counterpart. While fusion with the machine was a source of anxiety (hence the protection offered within Benjamin's state of shock), separation was nevertheless imaginable: Keaton's engineer *must* leave his engine to effect his girl's rescue; Chaplin's Tramp *will* kick his feet and walk off down the road. There is the possibility of world and self existing unencumbered by the prosthetics of industrial technology. The mass media, by contrast, as McLuhan theorized the phenomenon in the mid-1960s, presented itself as an all-pervading, self-referential, and totalizing experiential "reality." We could fail to acknowledge this condition of being, but in doing so, McLuhan argued, we would amputate what was in effect part of our selves, our very nervous systems, thereby leaving us blind, deaf, dumb, and stupid. The global village, by definition, offered no hiding place.

Under these conditions, Jerry becomes something other than an updated version of Chaplin's "mechanical doll, whose deep pathos is precisely to approximate so closely to the condition of human life" (McLuhan 1964, 253). While Keaton adapts and Chaplin transforms the world, Jerry is assimilated to the machine, becoming, in effect (and almost literally), a machine himself. "He's a human Dispos-All," Agnes Moorehead acidly observes in *Who's Minding the Store?* "All he needs is a switch!" Later, Ray Walston's character notes, "This boy is a dynamo!" When not actually being defined as a machine, Jerry is often cast as the mere servo-mechanism of the machines that seem to work *him* (over): the exercise equipment in *The Nutty Professor* (1963), for example, or the exercycle in *Who's Minding the Store?* And how about that team of masseuses who turn him into a rag doll (the medium is the massage) in *Artists and Models?* The mise-en-scène of *Store* is dominated by stem-to-stern product placements, and the resulting designer clutter manages to enervate any anarchic impulses. The consumerist environment of the department store becomes autonomous, self-defining—so different from the space of Chaplin's oneiric transformation in *Modern Times*—despite one *Weekend* (1967)–like multiple-car pileup and a truly apocalyptic encounter with an overinflated vacuum cleaner. The film becomes an unbecoming reflection on Jerry's impotence before a series of misapplied appliances whose real function, seemingly, is the emasculation of the American male (who is no longer "the boss in his own ranch-style house"). In a film so insistent upon its fear of powerful women, that hovering Hoover anticipates nothing so much as the giant breast terrorizing the countryside in Woody Allen's *Everything You Always Wanted to Know About Sex* (1972).

Keaton's characters are marked by an automatism that must be replaced by active human adaptability; his characters are machines that fail because they can't respond to changing information or circumstances. Jerry is more frequently cast as a machine that just plain doesn't work—hence the "jerking and the twitching" and the falling and the spilling and the stuttering and the spluttering and the "Laaaadyyyy!" and the "Whoa, Dean!" and the dangling and the spinning and the breaking and the whole thing with the lack of bodily control.[5] Jerry called it *Hardly Working* (1980).

But note further that while Jerry is constantly at war with the Mechanical, stuttering to a screeching, spastic halt in a constant enactment of techno-physical breakdown, he is also always (and at the same time) effortlessly becoming Media. He "becomes" a typewriter in *Who's Minding the Store?* and a television in *Rock-a-Bye Baby*. In *Artists and Models*, Jerry is "a little retarded" example of comic books' nefarious influence, dreaming of Vincent the Vulture and spewing out superhero narration and secret rocket formulas. His shrieking somnambulocutions turn him into a receiver, or perhaps a transmitter, or perhaps a receiver of the transmissions of his own unconscious.[6] Or, as *he* explains to a psychiatrist on TV in a panel discussion, "My subconscious was battling against my conscious and the basic intelligence of my mind wouldn't allow myself to comprehend some of the problems that were forethought prior to sleeping and at the same time not having any rest because of no sedation whatsoever to make my rest and dreams any brighter or smarter than they were when I was much younger!" This is automatic speech: a breathless chain of free association in which the operation of generating words supercedes its semantic function; syntactic hopping and skipping in which Jerry the talking machine moves beyond be-bop to the comedic equivalent of free jazz.

In *Who's Minding the Store?* Jerry challenges the power of the transcriber and the psychoanalyst when speaking to the department-store president: "Your brain must be very busy to be a president with a CLICK-CLACK BIH-SHTOOM SHTOOBIDOOM—Like an IBM machine!!" "This is no longer the age of the tool or machine," Deleuze wrote. "This is a new age of electronics, and the remote-controlled object" (1989, 65). And Jerry, that servo-mechanism for every mechanism, becomes *the* comedian for the information age. Citing Jerry's dismaying jerking when he gets "that lucky feeling" in *Hollywood or Bust* (1956), Deleuze troped Jerry as a primitive cyborg—a slapstick Stelarc twitching in desperate response to constant and conflicting commands. Like a malfunctioning IBM machine! But how could he *not* malfunction, our Jerry, with one foot lodged in the machine age and the other sinking into the new electronic swamp? Whoa, Dean!

## THE DUMMY ACT: TECHNOLOGICAL DETERMINISM AND IMPROVISATION

One of Jerry's earliest forays into professional entertainment was with something known in the biz as a "dummy act," in which he performed "outrageous mimes to phonographic records" (Krutnik 2000, 39). McLuhan cites John Philip Sousa on the medium of the phonograph— "With the phonograph vocal exercises will be out of vogue! Then what of the national throat? Will it not weaken? What of the national chest?

Will it not shrink?"[7]—and extends Sousa's argument: "The phonograph is an extension and amplification of the voice that may well have diminished individual vocal activity" (1964, 241).[8] Jerry's dummy act looks like a significant example of the Sousa doctrine: the chicken-chested performer appears as an automaton whose movements and behavior are entirely determined by the prerecorded, precedent status of the phonograph record. In *You're Never Too Young* (1955), Jerry lip-synchs to a record by Dean: in this ventriloquist act, an act of condensation, Dean is the voice, Jerry the dummy.

This determinism is nowhere clearer than in the inevitable breakdown of phonographic technology as the record player winds down or the record skips or the wrong record is played. In *The Patsy* (1964), the staff of a dead comedian decide that they should use their combined talents to create a new star; their new "patsy" (Jerry) will be, in other words, programmed. Perhaps they should have beta-tested—Frank Krutnik describes the scene when their big-hearted ex-bellboy patsy performs their material: "Stumbling onto the stage, he knocks the microphone off its stand and then proceeds to decimate the polished routines that have been taught to him. . . . Stanley presents a spectacle of maladjustment" (2000, 159). Even the dummy act, perhaps a metaphor for this entire performance of middle-management ventriloquism, goes awry, awfully.

These scenes have earlier analogues in the 1932 film *Horse Feathers*, as the Marx Brothers—including Harpo—use a phonograph recording to masquerade as Maurice Chevalier, and in *Shall We Dance* (1937), where Ginger steals the balancing weight from Fred's turntable, causing his responsive tap dances to skip and wind down accordingly. Fred, however, is always more comparable to Chaplin, as we cannot help but marvel at the inventiveness of his routines, the grace with which he "collapses" into a sullen sitting position. How different a figure Jerry presents in these moments, dumb and dumbfounded, raging against the machine that was meant to compensate for his own disability.

But we should also see the skillfully disastrous performance in *The Patsy*—a performance of performance as a disaster—as a chaotic and inchoate resistance to programming and control: Jerry's Stanley Belt will ultimately emerge triumphant by performing in his own way.[9] Even within the more independent parameters of the dummy act, removed from the overdetermined narrative of humiliation that marks *The Patsy*, the dummy-automaton theory doesn't really stand up. Dean, defined as the preexistent voice, the unified self fixed (by definition) in his ability to repeat (but also sentenced to it), might become less attractive when measured against a Jerry defined as the ephemeral, performative self whose every moment is new.

McLuhan writes that without the "hot" medium of the phonograph, especially when entwined with radio, "the twentieth century as the era of tango, ragtime, and jazz would have had a different rhythm" (1964, 241). From serving initially as a "talking machine" whose primary function was neutral transcription, the phonograph imposed new rhythms of mechanical reproduction and influenced the emergence of ragtime's syncopations. Early 78 rpm records, in McLuhan's view, were similar to early narrative film before sound: they "produced a brisk and raucous experience not unlike that of a Mack Sennett movie" (243). In contradistinction to Theodor Adorno, who regarded commercial recording as antithetical to the performative improvisation that quickly came to define jazz as a musical form, McLuhan labors mightily to regard recording as crucial to any dialectical understanding of popular music in the twentieth century—not only as something popular but as music. Without the recording there is no song. Wayne Koestenbaum has written of the experience of listening to soundtrack albums in the private space of the family rec room. The diva's voice exists here as pure voice, a voice without a literal bodily presence, and this absence is precisely what permits the listener to emerge as a listening subject, a diva of aurality: "Her voice enters me, makes me a 'me,' an interior, by virtue of the fact that I have been entered" (1993, 11). Marni Nixon, doubly disembodied in dubbing for the visible bodies of Audrey Hepburn, Natalie Wood, and Deborah Kerr onscreen, does her own dummy act and is Koestenbaum's privileged example of the disembodied diva, but Jerry's channeling of Dean's voice through the medium of his own body demands its own kind of attention. Imperfectly Dean, perfectly Jerry—perhaps the performer of this dummy act is no dummy but a dialogic subject possessed of a new kind of self.

McLuhan finds something similarly performative in the speech acts of the 1960s disc jockey; the voice of the DJ "alternately soars, groans, swings, sings, solos, intones, and scampers, always reacting to his own actions." Further, it moves "entirely in the spoken rather than the written area of experience" (1964, 81). For McLuhan, the spoken word "does not afford the extension and amplification of the visual power needed for habits of individualism and privacy" (82). It implies a public space (of speaking and hearing) and fully occupies only the present moment of its utterance. Speech is responsive to nuance and capable of modulation and encourages a performed response in a way that the written word does not. It always allows the possibility of improvisation.

Of course, Jerry's own speech is characterized by its free association, syncopated rhythms, and more than slightly Tourettic set of neologistically nasal stutters, stops, and extended lines—a speech both smoothly improvised and stutteringly stuck. *Ba-ba Ba-ba Ba-ba Ba-ba Bat-Lady!!!* And so, actually, what the dummy act presents is what we should now recognize as the characteristic Jerry dialectic between an obliteration of subjectivity through its subservience to the determinism of the playback and an assertion of self *against* that automatonistic determinism through the real-time responsiveness of performed improvisation. "Riffing against the machine," let's call it.

## CONCLUSION

Using criminals, cripples, and children as examples of "nonconformists ... unable to meet the demand of technology that we behave in uniform and continuous patterns," McLuhan writes that "literate man is inclined to see others who cannot conform as somewhat pathetic" (1964, 31). Because by their nature "they are not expected to fit into some uniform and repeatable niche that is not their size anyway," these subalterns are permitted to "create their own spaces" (31). The spaces created by the films and body and status of Jerry Lewis (*The Delicate Delinquent* [1957], "The Kid," the chairman of the Muscular Dystrophy Association), are indeed "pathetic" spaces of failed conformism, articulations incapable of repetition, devoid of uniformity, unsusceptible to control. And yet the pathetic spaces of such "nonconformists" are not as irrelevant as they might first appear.

What one constantly witnesses in the films of Jerry Lewis is not a simple automatism but a full-bodied resistance to the unnatural stimuli of technologies in transition—his body spasms rather than glides, crashes rather than operates. In McLuhan's terms, Jerry represents a failed autoamputation for the audience: his body is too evidently the servo-mechanism of machinic and electronic forces. The agony of Jerry Lewis lies in his proximate intimacy to these "extensions of man"—a pathetic proximity that precludes the consolations of satire (as found in

Chaplin, Tati, and even Tashlin), the comfortable illusions of self-sustaining selfhood, or any coherence at all.

## NOTES

1. As I used it in my 1993 book, "terminal identity," a phrase borrowed from William Burroughs (McLuhan's evil twin), referred to both the demise of traditional notions of the subject and the rise of new subjectivities around the pervasion of electronic technology. While many of the examples that I used in the first chapter, "Terminal Image," dated from the mid-1960s, Lewis had temporarily fallen off my radar screen.

2. See Kurtzman's quasi-autobiographical "Goodman Brown" stories from the mid-1960s, reprinted by Kitchen Sink Publishing in 1984.

3. Comedy teams were always another story.

4. See my earlier essay "Paralysis in Motion: Jerry Lewis's Life as a Man" (1991). Any comments about Jerry's lack of physical control must always except the moment of dance, when a glorious, temporary reconciliation between body and stimulus is effected.

5. To paraphrase Martin Short's brilliant late-Jerry parody on SCTV, even if it was the same it would be entirely different because of the earlier thing.

6. Thanks to Daniel Hoffman-Schwartz for this suggestion.

7. The phrase "the national chest" fairly begs for some Tashlinesque response.

8. This is, we must understand, written *avant la karaoke.*

9. Which, unfortunately, looks to the nondiegetic spectator a lot like Charlie Chaplin's or Red Skelton's "own way."

PART IV

# JERRY-BUILT

The old black magic: Stella (Stella Stevens, l.) entranced by the "something" of Buddy Love (Jerry Lewis) in *The Nutty Professor* (Jerry Lewis, Paramount, 1963). Frame enlargement.

# 13

# "The Inner Man"

## Mind, Body, and Transformations of Masculinity in *The Nutty Professor*

Peter Lehman and Susan Hunt

*THE DISORDERLY ORDERLY* (1964), *The Delicate Delinquent* (1957), *The Ladies Man* (1961), *The Geisha Boy* (1958), *Cinderfella* (1960), *The Nutty Professor* (1963)—these titles of films starring Jerry Lewis (with most produced and/or directed by Lewis as well) suggest that wavering opposition and oxymoron may be principal concerns, particularly regarding gender. Our interest is in the cultural assumptions about masculinity that are revealed by the varying masculinities represented in Lewis's *The Nutty Professor*. A primary dichotomy in the film is between the mind and body, through which two opposing masculinities are represented: a bumbling, incompetent, nerdy college professor transforms into a suave, sharp-dressing, sexy lounge singer. The film is thus situated within a long-standing literary and cinematic tradition in which a nonintellectual, "earthy" male (the "body guy") is depicted as a good lover and placed in opposition to an intellectual, well-to-do or even upper-class male (the "mind guy") who is not a good lover. In these narratives a beautiful, intelligent woman is attached to the intellectual male in some way, but her sexuality is awakened by the "earthy" man.

The most salient example of twentieth-century narratives of this type may be D. H. Lawrence's 1928 novel, *Lady Chatterley's Lover*. *Red Dust* (1932), *Duel in the Sun* (1946), and *The Man Who Shot Liberty Valance* (1962) are examples of films from earlier decades that contain various aspects of this pattern. The 1990s, however, saw a proliferation of these mind/body narratives (and derivatives of them) with films such as *Legends of the Fall* (1994), *Titanic* (1997), *The Piano* (1993), *Sirens* (1994), *The Horse Whisperer* (1998), *Moonlight and Valentino* (1995), and *I.Q.* (1994), among many others. In most of the mind/body narratives, the "body guy" is literally a figure with a conventionally attractive physique—a displayed "buffness" that suggests strength and conforms to the 1990s aesthetic for male beauty, such as Brad Pitt's character, Tristan, in *Legends of the Fall*; Jon Bon Jovi in *Moonlight and Valentino*; and the handyman, Mark Gerber, in *Sirens*. Actors such as Robert Redford in *The Horse Whisperer* and Harvey Keitel in *The Piano* are older but still depicted as having some kind of physical prowess or mastery of their bodies. The "mind guys" are often conventionally handsome, as necessitated by the dictates of cinematic casting (Sam Neill in *The Piano* and *The Horse Whisperer*, Hugh Grant in *Sirens*, and Billy Zane in *Titanic*), but their lack of physical mastery is often demonstrated or they are depicted as flawed in some way. Grant is excessively clumsy; Zane and Neill are controlling and violent.

It is not without interest that Lewis's *The Nutty Professor* was remade in the 1990s along with its sequel, to which we return below, thus contributing to the ongoing cultural fascination with the mind guy/body guy dichotomy. Although the original *Nutty Professor* and the recent mind/body films are more than thirty years apart, both narrative structures support the enduring American cultural myths that intellectual men are poor lovers who develop their minds at the expense of their bodies and that body-oriented men (especially earthy, athletic, working-class men) are inherently good lovers. The duality in representation taps into and reinforces other persistent cultural discourses about intelligence that circulated in the 1960s as well as the present: it's sissy to be smart; brainy people are anti-social nerds; and it's not normal to be too intelligent.

*The Nutty Professor* invokes a second narrative tradition in which the mind and body men are located in the same character, a pattern epitomized by Robert Louis Stevenson's *The Strange Case of Dr. Jekyll and Mr. Hyde* and its many film adaptations. *The Nutty Professor* makes several explicit references to the Jekyll-and-Hyde cinematic tradition, the most obvious being a shot of Professor Julius Kelp's hairy hand the first time he transforms into his counterpart, Buddy Love. Others include Kelp keeping a diary and being unable to regulate his potion's effect, leading to catastrophic reversals back into his original persona. Jekyll-and-Hyde narratives typically involve sexuality and class issues, but in a fundamentally different manner than the other mind/body tradition we have identified. These narratives, as William Luhr (1978) has shown, vary widely in their representation of sexual concerns and themes such as repression and the sexual "nature" of humankind, but none of them is centrally concerned with the body guy as a good lover in the Lawrence tradition. Rather, the body guy becomes a manifestation of varying uncontrollable urges, such as rebelling against society's norms by giving free rein to elements of human behavior normally controlled by proper social etiquette. Lewis has brought two quite different literary traditions together in *The Nutty Professor*, wedding Stevenson's *The Strange Case of Dr. Jekyll and Mr. Hyde* with *Lady Chatterley's Lover*.

In *The Nutty Professor*, Professor Kelp's transformation into Buddy Love turns on the issue of acquiring "proper" masculinity and becoming a good lover. As such, the film replicates another central feature of mind/body films that is lacking in the Jekyll-and-Hyde tradition: a beautiful, intelligent woman positioned between the mind guy and a body guy. Insofar as Jekyll-and-Hyde narratives (but not Stevenson's original) involve a woman, it would be more accurate to say the woman is trapped between the mind guy and the body guy, the latter of whom harrasses and threatens her. The central cultural message in the Lawrence tradition—female sexual satisfaction can be awakened and fulfilled only by a body guy—is not operative in the Jekyll-and-Hyde tradition, where, far from being reified, the body guy is a monster to be eliminated.

In Lewis's tale, Kelp, a college chemistry professor, seeks a more culturally ideal body through chemistry after conventional body-building techniques fail. He desires a bigger body after one of his football-player students publicly bullies him and a female student to whom he is attracted refers to him as a "small man." A chemical he creates causes Kelp to change into singing swinger Buddy Love, to whom the female student, Stella (Stella Stevens), is attracted. Stella is also later drawn to Kelp in his professorial persona and proposes to him after his dual identity is revealed.

Kelp conforms to other intellectuals in the pattern in that he is depicted as clumsy, childish, and definitively unsexy (like Hugh Grant's Rev. Anthony "Pooh" Campion in *Sirens*). The opening credit sequence is structured around Kelp's inability to handle his own chemicals. A series of spills culminates with an explosion that destroys the classroom and sends his students fleeing. In contrast, sexy Buddy Love finesses the tools of his trade—his voice and the piano—and many of the same students magnetically encircle him as he sings and plays "That Old Black Magic," a song that appropriately refers to his "magic" touch with women. Kelp's voice is whiny and nasal, like a child with a cold; Love croons. Kelp's style of dress also suggests childhood, with his too-short pants, white socks, and bow tie; Love swings with "hip" clothing. Kelp has buck teeth and a little-boy hairstyle, and he slouches, while Love swaggers with a self-assured demeanor, complete with trendy hairdo and poised cigarette. Given the pronounced opposition between the masculinities that Kelp and Love represent, Kelp's characterization as a chemistry professor is of interest in that his occupation speaks to our culture's belief that success in romance and sex are a matter of a couple having "the right chemistry." In the film business itself, one hears the common complaint that in some films there is "no chemistry" between the romantic leads. This reliance on the chemistry metaphor to describe good sex and romance itself suggests the cultural belief that these are primarily matters of the body, not the mind. Ironically, even where acting is involved, no matter how good the acting may be, it comes to naught without the right "chemistry."

Although sexiness—"the chemistry"—is decidedly on the side of Buddy's body, Lewis's version deviates significantly from the paradigmatic mind/body pattern. Lewis's Buddy Love is urbane and middle-class, not a man of nature or a member of the working class, and his appeal is from dress, style, and demeanor, not an exposed, muscled, athletic body. Indeed, in an extended gag, after we see the hairy hand during the first transformation scene, we see a long, point-of-view, moving camera shot (itself reminiscent of the opening of Rouben Mamoulian's *Dr. Jekyll and Mr. Hyde* [1931]) of people staring at Buddy Love. We think they are staring at his "hairy" apelike body, only later to learn that they are staring at the striking manner in which Love dresses and behaves. The 1990s body guys nearly all display athleticism or a toned body suggesting athleticism (Brad Pitt's Tristan in *Legends of the Fall*). They are comfortable in nature and the outdoors and adept at manual labor (Harvey Keitel's Baines in *The Piano*), and these traits are unequivocally seen as positive, intrinsically connected to sexual prowess. Lewis, in contrast, depicts the muscled athlete in a negative way—as the proverbial dumb jock whose only talent is bullying others. Stella, the beautiful woman, rebuffs the athletes and overtly refers to them as dull. Buddy insults them at the nightclub he calls "Dullsville," where he performs and entrances the patrons.

Buddy embodies the antithesis of dullness. He arrogantly says, "Okay, kids, you can all relax. Now that your desperate attempt at having a good time's flunked, have no fear, Buddy's here. Let the good times roll." His exciting persona is contrasted with both the world of the muscle men and that of the college intellectuals, who are all portrayed as boring. The lugubriousness of the college faculty is succinctly depicted when a camera tracks them on a greeting line at the senior prom, largely oblivious to the toe-tapping big-band music that floods the hall. Their sedateness is contrasted with Kelp's newly acquired, if awkward, animation as he moves to the music at the end of the line—ostensibly liberated by Buddy's unconscious influence on him. The exciting/dull polarity is operable also in the 1990s mind/body narratives, but in the latter films the earthy, athletic, working-class male (not the urbane entertainer) represents vivacity. In *Titanic*, for example, Jack (Leonardo DiCaprio) takes Rose (Kate Winslet) to steerage for a "real party," in contrast to the staid formal dinner on the upper deck. In the narratives of both eras, intellectuals and the well-to-do, whose success depends on the use of their minds and not their bodies, retain the dubious distinction of being dull and boring.

Although the locus of excitement differs from Lewis's representation to the 1990s pattern, Buddy Love is still positioned on the side of the body in that he is firmly dissociated from the world of the mind. Stella says of him, "If Buddy has any real intelligence he has a fantastic way of hiding it." He humiliates the dean of Kelp's college, Dr. Warfield (Del Moore), in a protracted and nasty manner: he gets him to stand on a table to perform "To be or not to be," then costumes him in a ridiculous way between frequent interruptions. The scene culminates with Buddy pulling the dean's pants down before leaving. The camera lingers on the clueless dean giddily reveling in the attention he's just received from Buddy. In Kelp's chemistry classroom, Buddy denigrates the notion of intellectual pursuit when he tells Stella, who is taking a makeup exam, to proceed with her "little test" after he kisses her. In the 1990s mind/body films, beautiful women are frequently shown gazing upon the exhibitionistic bodies of earthy men performing athletic feats or deliberately displaying their bodies in other ways for the women. Buddy's appearance and demeanor also provide the forceful spectacle that captures and paralyzes the gaze, even before he displays his musical talent. The power of his appeal is the site and sight of his body. Buddy may tacitly acknowledge that his power does not lie in a muscled physique, but he still has a body orientation in that he sees himself as getting what he wants from the way he presents and uses his body— in this case, how he dresses and postures it—not from how he develops his mind.

However, in a manner that profoundly draws on the Jekyll-and-Hyde tradition, Lewis complicates a simple privileging of "body guy" Buddy by representing his disposition as repulsive. As we expand upon below, Buddy is both the desirable "dick" and the offensive "prick." In a protracted scene, Buddy humiliates a bartender (Buddy Lester) in a manner similar to Kelp's humiliation by a student athlete earlier in the film. Also, Buddy's behavior and treatment of Stella are not very different from Hyde's (Fredric March) behavior and treatment of Ivy (Claire Trevor) in Mamoulian's film. As Stella says of him, he's "rude, disrespectful, self-centered and discourteous"—at the very least an egomaniac. His talent is formidable, but his personality is reprehensible. In contrast, the gamekeeper in Lawrence's *Lady Chatterley's Lover* and the body men of the 1990s narratives are beyond reproach. Their masculinity is privileged, if not glorified. These men reshape women's sexuality by awakening new desires that only they can fulfill. In current parlance, they possess the desired "dick" without a trace of the offensive "prick" in sight, an oversimplification and denial of the ugly side of that form of masculinity. Typically, body men of the 1990s are attracted to beautiful women and sexually desire them; with that attraction, they see in an instant that the women are missing something—something they know they can satisfy (consider DiCaprio's first sighting of Winslet in *Titanic* and Tim Robbins's first encounter with Meg Ryan in *I.Q.*). Some Hollywood films, however, such as Sam Raimi's *The Gift* (2000), present a complex variation on the mind guy/body guy opposition and acknowledge the brutal, monstrous side of the body guy. Here the body guy, played by Keanu Reeves cast against type to emphasize the point, is a "ladies man" who brutally beats his wife and mistresses. He seems more like Hyde than like the attractive Robert Redford character in *The Horse Whisperer*.

Thus, in representing Buddy as a Hydelike, unappealing figure in many ways, Lewis's *Nutty Professor* complicates the simplistic dichotomy of the other mind/body narratives, including those of 1990s cinema. No male in Lewis's paradigm-splitting trichotomous notion of masculinity represents an ideal—not muscled athlete, not talented entertainer, not intelligent professor. *The Nutty Professor* signals a difficulty in representing any secure, positive, or ideal masculinity. Lewis also raises the issue of masculinity functioning as a masquerade, in that both the mind guy and a version of the body guy are manifested in the same character/actor/body, demonstrating that one just has to learn how to perform a certain kind of masculinity. This notion is essentially absent from 1990s films, where the polarity between the mind guys and body guys is generally maintained through casting as well as narrative structure (consider body guy Brad Pitt and mind guy Henry Thomas in *Legends of the Fall;* Harvey Keitel and Sam Neill in *The Piano*). With the same actor's body representing both characters in the polarity, anybody (literally any body) can embody both extremes. Yet, as we shall see, *The Nutty Professor* gets mired in contradictions in its effort to resolve the mind/body dichotomy.

After six months of trying to become a muscular body guy at the gym, Kelp visits a doctor (Milton Frome), in despair that his efforts have failed. The doctor says to him, "Only some men respond to bodybuilding exercise whereas others just don't." Such an essentialist view of masculinity reaffirms the mind guy/body guy dichotomy to the extreme by asserting that only some men possess the capacity to develop their bodies. But the doctor also remarks, "A man's mind from childhood right through old age never stops growing, not in size or measure but by constant learning and knowledge. On the other hand, man's body does stop at a precise point." This emphasis on the lifelong growth of the mind is unusual, to say the least, in mind guy/body guy films, where the emphasis is normally on the mind being a restrictive prison from which one seeks liberation, as opposed to a growing, vital thing.

The doctor's reference to the growth of the mind not being an issue of "size or measure" foregrounds a normative notion of masculinity. In that view, masculinity is thought of precisely as a quantifiable and measurable commodity, including the body in general (e.g., height, musculature) and sexually (e.g., penis size). The body and penis are indeed often thought of primarily in terms of size and measure, and the male body in *The Nutty Professor* metaphorically represents the body as a penis. Scott Bukatman perceptively observes of the film, "It represents only the smallest act of will to recognize *The Nutty Professor* for what it is: a phallic allegory in which Love represents Kelp in an erect, active and threatening state" (1991, 201). It would be equally accurate to call the film's representations of the male body a penile metaphor rather than a phallic allegory. When Kelp sees an ad for Vic Tanny gyms in a magazine, he decides to join the gym and take up body building. The ad sets the stage for later representations of both Kelp's body and his father's in a crucial flashback. In the ad we see drawings of two men in classic "before-and-after" poses. The difference, of course, is startling. The stereotypical "ninety-nine-pound weakling" on the left is drawn as scrawny, with no muscles, and for that matter little of anything else. His shorts hang loosely, implying that there is nothing to fill them. Of most importance to us, however, is the manner in which the man's arms hang straight down, against his body; they are totally limp. Next to him stands a well-developed, highly muscled man with his arms prominently placed on his hips, his tight shorts stuffed to the limit. If the weakling's limp arms signify the flaccid penis, the strong man's pose clearly demonstrates what Richard Dyer identified in 1982 as the hard muscles that signify the erect penis.

The weakling's pitiably dangling arms appear on Kelp's body in a crucial scene later in the film. As Buddy Love performs "That Old Black Magic" at the prom, the transformative potion wears off. Kelp's voice begins to oscillate with Love's until it fully takes over. Love stops singing and stands by the microphone, explaining the situation to a hushed crowd (there are always onlookers to assess and admire or pity the spectacle of masculinity in this film). As he talks, his body turns in stages from Love's to Kelp's. As he becomes Kelp, his arms hang straight down by his side in an exact replication of those of the weak man in the Vic Tanny ad. Earlier, an outrageous gag (reminiscent of Frank Tashlin's cartoon humor) shows Kelp trying to lift weights in the gym. His arms, however, are not strong enough; instead of him lifting the weights up, the weights pull his arms down, all the way to the floor! We see Kelp with his long, weak arms dangling uselessly. Later when he lies in bed, they are so long that he uses them to scratch his toes. These images invoke the cultural connection between weakness and

flaccidity, and the extraordinary length of the arms, far from being impressive, merely draws attention to their uselessness as hanging ap-
pendages. Indeed, the gag underscores this, since it was an effort to
strengthen those arms and make them hard that led to the ludicrous
spectacle of their exaggerated limpness. "Real men" get harder at the
gym; in contrast, Kelp's limpness becomes a spectacle.

If one aspect of the pitiable penis is limpness, another is smallness,
and it is this that emerges in the flashback with Kelp's father. Kelp's father, played by an actor small in stature to begin with (Howard Morris),
is introduced from a high angle as he cowers and shrinks from his commanding, powerful wife (Elvia Allman). As she orders him to the dinner table, he shrivels further, as if he might altogether retract from sight.
His body impersonates a penis suffering from a simultaneous attack of
extreme fear and blast of frigid cold. The image of retraction recapitu-
lates an earlier scene, when Julius shrinks into a padded easy chair to
the point of disappearance as the dean berates him for blowing up his
classroom. Indeed, these images of shrinkage are nearly as exaggerated
as Kelp's distended arms in the earlier gym scene. Between father and
son, then, we see the body figured in the form of the two most embarrassing and humiliating images our culture offers of the penis: impotent, hanging uselessly for all to see, and retracted, threatening to disappear from sight and taking the alleged dramatic spectacle of masculinity with it.

Interestingly, Peter Segal's *The Nutty Professor II: The Klumps* (2000),
on which Jerry Lewis served as executive producer (along with its star,
Eddie Murphy), makes the connection between Buddy Love and the
penis explicit. The film begins with what appears to be Professor Sher-
man Klump's wedding. During the ceremony he develops a huge erection that transforms into Buddy Love literally bursting out of his pants
zipper and disrupting the event. We then learn that we have been wit-
nessing a nightmare that Klump is relating to his psychiatrist. Love's
persona, however, takes over from Klump and insults the psychiatrist's
analysis of the dream by blurting out, "All the diplomas on the wall
don't make up for the little Vienna sausage in your pants. Is that why
they call you shrink?"

The sequence is remarkable for the explicit manner in which it con-
flates Buddy Love with a huge erection and equates the mind guy and
his analytical intelligence with a shrunken, little penis. Buddy Love's

exit from the film is as relevant in this context as his entrance. After being tricked into swallowing some youth formula in the midst of a board meeting with a pharmaceutical company, Love transforms into a naked baby. As the attractive woman who heads the company stares at his groin, the baby responds by asking what she's staring at, declaring that he has an "impressive package for a toddler." Even as a baby, Love is marked by his large penis, which stops the executive dead in her tracks.

The film is full of various other penis references, one of which is of particular interest in the above context. Klump's father is portrayed as a man grown impotent with age, and his mother as a woman consequently frustrated with unfulfilled sexual desire. In the final scene at the party, the husband and wife gleefully celebrate the appearance of his large erection, an event of monumental importance. From infancy to old age, the big penis is apparently central to the male life cycle. Indeed, *The Nutty Professor II* goes so far as to imply that the power of the penis is so important that a man who lacks it, even a genius, will degenerate into an idiot. When Professor Klump discovers how to rid his body of all traces of Buddy Love, his brain begins to degenerate in an irreversible process that destroys more than half of his mental abilities, including the use of language. It is only by reintroducing Love into his body that he is saved and his mental powers are restored. What good is a mind guy without a large penis—without his "buddy"? Klump's ultimate problem comes down to a matter of the body. He needs the big penis for his power; his intelligence is not enough. The original *Nutty Professor* seems to resist an essentialist notion of masculinity in that Kelp's problem is traced to a matter of family psychodynamics: the father is unable to defend himself (or Julius) from the mother's aggressions. An essentialist notion of masculinity is ultimately, if contradictorily, supported, however, in that the dysfunctional family is linked in a demonstrative way to the father's diminutive, shrunken penis of a body.

For all its brilliance in delineating and representing various bodily spectacles of masculinity both won and lost, Lewis's *Nutty Professor* ends up curiously incoherent about the mind/body dichotomy and the manner in which male sexuality is located therein. Again, Bukatman perceptively notes, "The spectator awaiting the promised resolution of this narrative will finally be presented with three endings in succession. The surfeit of resolutions of the Kelp/Love dichotomy unsuccessfully masks the fact that there is no resolution at all" (1991,

201). We inflect this in a somewhat different manner. Bukatman reads *The Nutty Professor* entirely from within a psychoanalytic perspective. For him, the lack of resolution reveals that "the passive male and the hyper-male cannot find a stable balance within a single subject" (201). Our interest in the film is primarily from a cultural perspective; it is part of a much larger project in which we are trying to understand various historical and cultural traditions for representing, talking, and writing about the mind, the body, and sexuality and the ideological impact of such representations and discourses. These projects are not at odds with each other; they are simply different, and what is for us one of the most fundamental aspects of this film Bukatman does not even remark on.

Unlike *The Nutty Professor II*, which clearly resolves the mind/body polarity (albeit in an ideologically offensive manner), Lewis's original film contains an odd lack of narrative resolution that stems precisely from his inability to resolve the mind/body dichotomy in relationship to sexuality within the culture. Only one aspect is clearly resolved: the body-builder version of the sexy body guy is clearly rejected as being undesirable, boring, and as sexless as the mind guy. Buddy Love's swinger persona, however, presents a problem that illuminates, for us, the film's unresolved and also contradictory character. This surfaces most directly in the scene where Stella dances with Kelp at the prom. When he asks her about Love's expected appearance at the dance, she replies, "I guess I'm looking forward to seeing him but I can't for the life of me figure out why." Kelp then proceeds to probe her feelings about Love's looks and personality, and much to his surprise Stella rejects them as unattractive. And when Kelp mentions Love's talent, Stella acknowledges that he is talented but quickly adds that intelligence is also a talent. Although Buddy is far from ideal, it is he who manifests the notion that the masculinity of certain men gives them a *je ne sais quoi* quality. Stella repeatedly tells Buddy off but continually agrees to meet him, saying, "He's got something." After he treats her arrogantly in Kelp's classroom, where she is taking an exam, he aggressively kisses her without her permission or without any suggestion that she wants it, then leaves. She inexplicably has a romantic gaze in her eyes in the scene's closing shot. What, then, is that "something" Buddy Love has? What is his appeal, and what exactly does he represent?

Kelp says to Stella, "Whatever you see [in Buddy] is very well buried. Perhaps he chooses to keep the inner man locked up so no one steps on him." Since Julius and Buddy are the same person, Buddy's inner man is the gentle, kind, and intelligent but dull and unassertive Julius. Julius's inner man is the direct and poised but obnoxiously aggressive Buddy. While most novels and films centered on the mind/body paradigm depict the mind guy as lacking some essential masculinity that the body guy has, *The Nutty Professor* depicts the mind and body guys as needing each other's masculinity—masculinities that are buried deep within each persona. The notion of the locked-up inner man echoes a motif in the film: Kelp is stuck or locked in a cabinet after a bullying athlete puts him there; he is locked in his playpen in his childhood flashback; his mynah bird, Jennifer, is caged; and, metaphorically, the "inner man" is locked within Kelp. Since Julius is the principal subject, what he "needs," according to the logic of a narrative informed by pop psychology, is confidence, assertiveness, and a more exciting demeanor.

The notion of the buried "inner man" is the film's foremost theme, and Lewis invokes psychoanalysis in an attempt to explain it. He traces the cause of Julius's (and Buddy's) problems as an adult to a matter of family dynamics: baby Julius was virtually ignored by a domineering mother and a cowering father. The dysfunctional family causes Julius to suppress certain personality traits so he won't be "stepped on." The family scenario presents a second dichotomy—dominance and submission—that intersects with the excitement/dullness polarity of the central plot scenario. Kelp's lack of assertiveness and consequent dullness are attributed to his father's cowardice in the face of his mother's dynamic but domineering aggression. Like the athletes and Buddy, Kelp's mother is a bully; she yells at and actually hits his father, who shrinks in response, reversing the stereotypical male-dominant/female-submissive order. As an adult, Julius ostensibly expresses a disdain for his mother's dynamic dominance in that every time he mentions her, he coughs in a choking manner before saying her name, and this is explicitly linked to his memory of her controlling behavior. In the film's closing sequence we see that the father, after marketing Julius's formula, has achieved aggressiveness, dominance, and an exciting demeanor, while the mother has become silent and dully submissive. It may seem that the "proper" gender roles as culturally defined have been established, but Julius takes no pleasure in this inversion. Now he chokes before saying his father's name. Kelp apparently has an aversion to the dominant person regardless of who it is. Every dominant person in the film hurts or humiliates others: Buddy humiliates the bartender and the dean; Kelp's mother humiliates his father and vice versa; the student athlete humiliates Kelp.

A principal concern in the film, then, is the disentangling of the appealing, positive excitement but also the hurtful dominance that Buddy represents. One logic dictates that Kelp would learn positive excitement, confidence, and assertiveness from the "unleashing" of the Buddy Love within him, while retaining his gentle, kind demeanor to counter the hurtful dominance. But the film contradicts its own narrative trajectory. In the scene where Love transforms into Kelp in front of the college faculty and students, he says that the lesson he learned was to be himself—his insecure, submissive, but gentle self. Indeed, in the end we see Stella making all key decisions for the befuddled Kelp, who calls her "dearest" in a manner reminiscent of his father in the flashback. Furthermore, he's shown at the end to be the same boring classroom lecturer that he was at the beginning. However, Stella's choice of mind guy Julius (over body guy Buddy) deviates from the paradigmatic mind/body pattern in that the figure of the professor opens a space for her actively to direct the course of her sexuality. She flirts with Kelp in a sexual manner, initiates their first kiss, proposes marriage to him, and, as we shall see, decides the terms of their sexual practice.

Stella's preference for the mind guy, however, is ultimately undermined. In one of the film's closing scenes, Kelp's father disrupts Julius's class lecture to hawk the sexiness-inducing potion Julius invented. The students run to Kelp's father in the same manner that they ran away from Kelp's classroom in the beginning. Stella rushes with everyone else to buy the potion that turned Kelp into Buddy Love, and as she walks off with Kelp to get married, we see two bottles of the potion hidden in her jeans. Behind Kelp's back, Stella turns toward the camera and winks at us, the spectators, underscoring the good time she's about to have with the aid of the potion. In addition, Kelp is already transforming into Love with a new hairstyle and braces on his teeth. The film, therefore, suggests a fundamental impossibility of representing an intellectual as sexy and self-possessed, a notion perhaps most demonstratively presented at the film's "first conclusion," when Kelp performs the long-anticipated kiss with Stella in a grotesque manner, grabbing his glasses instead of the woman.

Kelp's awkward kiss is the culmination of the prom sequence, a sequence that perhaps best elaborates the *je ne sais quoi*—the "something"—that Buddy Love has. As discussed above, when Love reverts to Kelp his body changes from one that is coordinated and rhythmic—capable of responding to musical rhythm—to one that appears uncoordinated and clumsy. Even when Kelp begins to get rhythm as he "dances" to the music at the end of the prom reception line, he looks comically ridiculous. The assumption is that a man couldn't know what to do with a woman's body if he does not appear to have control of his own. This underlies the notion that the body guy—including Buddy—is naturally a good lover. One just has to look and know that the body guy is coordinated and can respond to the rhythms of his partner's body. An interesting hypothetical question emerges here: Since Kelp's potion is unstable, why not have Julius become stuck within Buddy Love's rhythmically coordinated persona, a Buddy that is perhaps humanized by Julius's kind and gentle demeanor? What is Lewis doing by seducing us with Love's "black magic" but then returning to the unsexy Kelp? A sadistic positioning (the "prick" Buddy) is relinquished for a masochistic one. Julius is still subordinated to a woman who "calls the shots" and treats him in a maternal way, but instead of a threatening phallic mother he now has a benevolent one. He has gone from a controlling woman (his mother) to one who is in control (Stella).

Stella's possession of the potion and her wink into the camera at the end, then, epitomize the contradiction raised by her choice of the professor as love interest: it's all fine and dandy to pay lip service to intelligence as a "talent" and to disown Love's looks and personality, but we all really know better. Insofar as we are "in" on the joke and are complicit with Stella, we place ourselves in the exact same position she earlier articulated: we can't, as it were, for the life of ourselves figure out why, in order to be sexually exciting, a potion must liberate the Buddy Love within a Julius Kelp rather than the Julius Kelp within a Buddy Love. Why is it that we as a culture believe that a body guy such as Buddy Love is a good lover in a way that a mind guy such as a professor can never really be? And it is here that Bukatman's overlooked question emerges. Why is it that this film can never for a moment imagine a professor as successful lover, or to put it in narrative terms, why can't the film imagine Love transforming himself into Kelp? Bukatman's psychoanalytic account totally bypasses this by simply positing Love as Kelp's alter ego. And that's true as far as it goes. But why can't an intelligent professor be an alter ego to a stumbling, bumbling body guy? In psychoanalytic terms there is no answer. That in cultural terms we accept the answer as obvious speaks volumes.

Working hard freeing one's mind from mundane issues. Herbert H. Heebert (Jerry Lewis) awakening in *The Ladies Man* (Jerry Lewis, Paramount, 1961). Frame enlargement.

# 14

# Working Hard Hardly Working

## Labor and Leisure in the Films of Jerry Lewis

Dana Polan

CURIOUSLY PERHAPS, Jerry Lewis's cinema seems obsessed by labor. Indeed, several films refer to the world of work through titles that emphasize the jobs that people have: *The Bellboy* (1960), *The Errand Boy* (1961), *The Nutty Professor* (1963). There is a clear sense in these films that to be a notable character means to have a work-related identity. Thus, in *The Family Jewels* (1965), each of the six uncles is most directly associated with his profession (ferryboat captain, circus clown, fashion photographer, airline pilot, private detective, and gangster), whereas in *The Ladies Man* (1961),[1] much of Herbert H. Heebert's problem is that he has no job and must endlessly search for one. (He gains worth when he finally succeeds.) And a number of the films chronicle patterns of training or instruction in which characters learn to take up roles that others have designed and designated for them: in *The Patsy* (1964), for instance, the protagonist is trained in the art of entertainment, and in *Which Way to the Front?* (1970) a team of men have to learn how to be soldiers.

At first glance the films would appear to suggest that professions are emphatically activities of alienated labor: characters only rarely work for themselves and are in thrall to a power and authority that lord over them (although the boat-captain narrative in *The Family Jewels* evinces a nostalgia for a situation in which workers might labor for their own benefit and according to their own desires). In other words, these seem initially to be films of vocation and not avocation. (Again, an exception might be the aptly titled *Hardly Working* [1980], where there is also a nostalgia for a vanishing way of life—the clown as folk performer.) Overall films display a recurrent emphasis on bosses, managers, directors—figures who try to discipline the worker into place and extract benefits from him (often in directly exploitative ways, as *The Patsy* chronicles). Laborers find themselves ordered about, checked up on, ruled, and regulated.

This emphasis on the work world in Lewis's films—portrayed moreover as a site of alienation in which one submits to the demands of others—might seem to contradict the status of these films as comedies. After all, isn't comedy supposed to be one of the ways in which we imaginatively escape from worldly responsibility, such as the need to labor? Indeed, isn't there nothing less funny than the alienated world of work?

This chapter addresses this question in a number of ways. First of all, there may be a need to challenge the very premise of the question of funniness in relation specifically to the cinema of Jerry Lewis. That is, it may be that the assumption that Lewis's cinema is one geared primarily to comic effect, to fun and laughter, is itself incomplete. As the reactions of both detractors and fans of Lewis's films demonstrate, whatever its comic effects his cinema is also an exercise in abjection, an often excruciating displeasure. For instance, central to Lewis's cinema, as many writers have noted, is the "slow burn"—that overextended minimalist reaction by a character to an indignity he or she has suffered—and this technique incites both comic emotion and suffering. Likewise, we might note the omnipresence of repetitions and stutterings of language, and gags that seem to go on too long, way beyond any comic efficacy, turning instead into protracted deflations of gag effect. Temporality often becomes palpable in Lewis films, to the point of turning them into veritable experiments with the experience of duration. And, as is suggested by the attraction of this rigorous deconstruction of comedy for many admirers of Lewis's work, it is not necessarily the case that the subversion of easy comic effect represents a failing on the part of Lewis's films. What for the detractors is failed comedy is for the fans a successful attempt to do something other than just comedy. For instance, this undoing of comedy by means of comic techniques that become excessive and turn comedy against itself was a central aspect of the appreciation for Lewis's work in the French criticism of the 1950s and especially the 1960s, in such journals as *Cahiers du Cinéma* and *Positif*. In *Cahiers* especially, Lewis's cinema was treated less as a perfected art of hilarity than as a formalism in which the emphasis was on an experiment with elongation and duration (the overbearing nature of the slow burn), with a permutation of effects, and with a rigorous calculus of technique intended to empty the films of comic affect and turn them instead into games played with cinematic plasticity. In other words, there is a sense in which the films strategically make fun of fun.

But even if we were to accept that comic effect is sometimes the function of Lewis's films, we could find there explanations for the presence of the grubby, oppressive world of work. On the one hand is what we might call the *comedy of failure*: an almost painful glee at seeing people make mistakes in the world of work, what the Germans refer to as *Schadenfreude*—pleasure in others' misfortunes. For example, in *The Ladies Man*, Herbert's cleaning of a painting makes it smear (all of this registered with slow panic on Lewis/Herbert's face); his incompetence (and his reaction to that incompetence) is a source of glee for us. Likewise, with director Frank Tashlin in such films as *Who's Minding the Store?* (1963) and *The Disorderly Orderly* (1964)—another film whose title is about work, but also in this case about the disruption of work—Lewis engages energetically with a comic tradition based on figures who mess up, who ruin things, who sow chaos wherever they turn.

The comedy of laborious failure can involve derision of the disastrous efforts of the worker and achieve its comic effect at the worker's expense, but it can also rebound on the ruling class that puts the worker to work. Comedy here would be one of the ways in which the dominance of that world is defied. In particular, there is in many of the films a subversion of the force of authority figures, bosses, and managers. In many is an unintentional challenge to the sway of figures of power: for example, the destructiveness that Stanley sows in *The Patsy* comes from his well-intentioned desire to follow orders coupled with his inability to follow through on that desire. But there also may be an intended defiance of power: for example, in *The Nutty Professor* one long (slow-burn) sequence has to do with Buddy Love's mocking of the college dean's pretensions to the world of theater. Here the figure of rule—the figure we had seen bossing Professor Kelp around—has the tables turned on him, and his authority to lead and direct others is assailed. There can be a comic pleasure in seeing resistance to the established system of power, in seeing power's own foibles displayed in all their ridiculousness.

On the other hand, there is also, we might suggest, a *comedy of success in work*. This is a comedy that comes from a job well done or, as is often the case, done beyond the expectations of the system of rule. A minor immediate example would be the speed at which the bellboy (in the film of that name) is able to set up thousands of folding chairs in an immense banquet room of the hotel. This image of a job done better than expected runs through many of the Lewis films. Think, for instance, of the unexpected success of Stanley in *The Patsy*: while the managers' attempt to mold him into one performative identity leads to an overbearing comedy of failure, they eventually discover that Stanley can best be a success just by being himself, by discovering the inner core of talent he has within him. (This notion of inherent personal skill is a recurrent theme in Lewis.) He becomes a bigger hit than they ever intended or expected. If the comedy of failure finds triumph either in the defeat of the worker or in the defeat of the manager, the comedy of success imagines outcomes that accrue to both. First, the employer benefits financially from the results of work. Even more, just as the employee's excessive completion of the task reveals unexpected additional benefits—often the benefits of moral self-amelioration—so the boss or manager learns that there are things more important and valuable than financial gain. In other words, in Lewis's films there is often not only an amelioristic discovery of the worker's own skill and worth but also a discovery on the part of managers and bosses that their lives can be improved morally when those who work for them receive benefit. Obviously, this utopian image of workers who give back something deep and important to their bosses has a strong ideological component to it and serves as a particularly pointed reference to the ostensibly uplifting nature of labor.

Lewis's films constantly emphasize the moral benefits of labor, a sense of work as a process of fulfillment of character—work, then, not really imagined as alienation after all. As I have already noted, some of this more affirmative valorization of work derives from a nostalgia for cottage-industry practices in which lone figures labor for their own account (for example, the boat captain in *Family Jewels*). But even as the range of films that deal with labor often present it as fully caught up in patterns of control and managerial surveillance, they manage to find a joyfulness in the activity of work.

Here Lewis's cinema in the 1960s seems to come out of a sociological legacy of the 1950s, one that sets out to make work seem joyful, beneficial, playful. The 1950s witnessed a new ideological presentation of the beneficent values of work: with challenges to working-class militancy in the wake of the Red Scare (see *On the Waterfront* [1954]), with a fear that suburbia and the life of the man in the gray flannel suit were situations of alienation, with the growing tendency of the "feminine mystique" both to push women back into a domestic realm (a realm of work not acknowledged as such by dominant ideology) and to valorize men as the real laborers and their activities as the real labor, there was an ideological need to make work palatable, a positive good. As H. F. Moorhouse suggests in a valuable essay on hot-rod culture in the 1950s, one form of this ideological effort came in a 1950s valorization of skilled technique, of a virtually scientific application of engineering procedures to the activities of everyday life (Moorhouse 1999). In Moorhouse's analysis, hot-rod culture was not just a hobby but a form of labor—an unpaid, capitalistically unprofitable one—in which there was a strong predilection for rationalism and planning, for expertise, for gadgetry and technological control. The culture of the 1950s justified work by imagining it as one more activity subtended by the cheerful injunction to "do it yourself," an exhortation that shows up also in the decade's fascination with practices of tinkering and personal yet calculated creation: for example, amateur radio, paint by numbers, home carpentry, and so on. In these practices, the goal is to efficiently bring some scientific marvel into being.

Pride in work becomes then a pride in rationalized, engineered construction, and the ultimate goal, the ultimate source of pride, is the well-crafted object. From the personal realm up through the abstract reaches of corporate production, there is a valorization of marvels of science and engineering.

Much of the lesson of Frank Tashlin for Lewis manifests itself as a pride in creation. For there to be such pride, the activity that goes into creation has to be evident, visible. In other words, the created object has explicitly—and often in an ostentatious manner—to bear the marks of the process of production: these have to be dramatic and even flamboyant. Tashlin's and Lewis's campy, kitschy cinematic vision—which is also the vision of much of the American 1950s and early 1960s—is a propitious and inspirational fount of such techniques for making manifest the palpability of created form. First of all, there is the sheer self-reflexiveness of the films: moments that speak directly of the process of production of cinema. Secondly, there is the splashy showing off of cinematic form even in moments that aren't directly self-reflexive. Thirdly, there is a fascination for the imaging of processes of engineering through recurrent motifs of machines and gadgets—especially ones that are visually dynamic (vehicles out of control and racing around, technologies that produce excessive and even explosive effects, as in *Who's Minding the Store?* or in the grocery market finale of *The Disorderly Orderly*). Tashlin's and Lewis's cinema eminently enacts a machinic universe, a Rube Goldberg fantasmagoria dominated by technical linkages and short circuits, flows of energy, complex technologies with complex outcomes.

Further, the films demonstrate a concern to substitute for an ostensible natural world (i.e., a world without artifice, a world that would appear unmediated and owing its existence to no creator, a world that simply appears and is as it is) a fully artificial, manifestly constructed one. Hence, the emphasis on sets that appear as such (taken to an extreme in Lewis's *The Patsy*, with its self-reflexive end reflection on the fabrications and falsities of studio filmmaking); the generation of improbable situations that exceed the limits of realism; the use of actors whose very bodies seem live-action versions of cartoons (Jayne Mansfield and her big bosom in such Tashlin films as *The Girl Can't Help It* [1956], Lewis and his facial contortions); the frequent recourse to shooting in locales that are themselves unnatural or anti-natural (for example, the use of a sea-world park in *The Big Mouth* [1967]); and the omnipresent use of lurid color that is not so much unnatural as aggressively anti-natural.

The question of color, in fact, crystallizes much of the influence of Tashlin and of a vibrant image of 1950s America on Lewis's cinema. (We might note that the next stage in the history of influences has Lewis's artificial colors strongly impacting on New Wave filmmaker Jean-Luc Godard, whose "It's not blood, it's red" is a self-reflexive ode to cinema's artifice.) Color in this case is not something that objects in the world naturally possess; rather, it is a look pasted onto the image of the world by cinematic technology, and in this way it speaks again of filmmaking as a feat of applied engineering.

Cinematically, color for the 1950s is at once the subdued tones of Eastmancolor and the radiant, dazzlingly loud, often strident tones of Technicolor. Technicolor, we might note, is not a process that reproduces the colors of the world; rather, by a use of dyes, it constructs colors, offering the possibility for an intensification of effects. By a complicated irony, color comes to be the mark of anti-realism, and the absence of color through black-and-white cinematography becomes the guarantee of realism. (To be sure, the Technicolor process is supposed to lead to an approximation of real-world colors, but that is not a scientific necessity of the process, and some of the science of Technicolor even mitigates against realism: for example, dyes tend to spread out and saturate the area they're coloring so that Technicolor tends to have fewer gradients of color and more bright solid blocks.)

But the example of film color reveals a seemingly paradoxical aspect of 1950s life: the artificiality of cinematic color processes comes ultimately to seem not so much an addition of luxurious colors to a subdued world as a recognition of the radiantly tacky and colorful nature of that world itself. In other words, in 1950s America everyday reality itself is presented as already artificial, already a paint-by-numbers world on which colors are applied extravagantly. For instance, one kitschy yet omnipresent and quotidian symbol of the 1950s is Jell-O, and I suggest that, more than just a food, it is a visual phenomenon that sums up the age. Through its vivid artificial colors it replays the period's fascination with the brightly colorful (it is a kind of Technicolor food, with exaggerated and excessive brightness and artificiality). In its partial translucence it invokes the period's fascination with an openness of sight, with a transparency of vision that we also see in the design of suburbia (all those low-slung houses with big bay windows and sliding doors out to the patio and barbecue); and it calls up, too, a concurrent fascination with the lambent inner space of the postwar home as a site of circulation and unfettered flow. In its vibratory qualities it suggests the energy of the period, witnessed also in such visual practices as the hula hoop and the dances of rock 'n' roll. In its lightness it suggests the superficiality of the age, a historical moment given over to impermanence and often to a lack of seriousness (Jell-O has as little substantiality as many of the disposable films of the period). Such phenomena are described usefully by Karal Ann Marling in her volume on visuality in the 1950s (Marling 1994).

In this respect the films of Tashlin and Lewis are "Jell-O movies" that speak of the technical marvels that brought them into being. The films revel in bright kitsch and in a world dominated by the insubstantial ephemera of popular culture. Certainly, a number of films Lewis starred in in the 1950s are in black and white (notably the modest comedies he does with Norman Taurog), and the Martin and Lewis TV efforts are bereft of color. But with Tashlin, Lewis engages with a master colorist (remember that Tashlin was a cartoonist and animator before turning to live action) whose cinematic vision is a veritable anticipation of 1960s Pop Art, in the popular-cultural subject matter it draws on (both *Artists and Models* [1955] and Roy Lichtenstein's paintings are about the world of comic books) and in its vibrant, radiantly colored reconstruction of the narrative world.

But if it is easy to assimilate Tashlin and Lewis to the Pop Art movement of the period, another 1950s visualist to whom they can be compared is Jackson Pollock, a figure whose gloppy action-paintings are also about the artificial application of colors. Now, this linking of the Abstract Expressionist and the cinematic purveyors of tacky popular culture may seem inappropriate. After all, didn't Pollock defender Clement Greenberg notoriously posit kitsch as the enemy and veritable polar opposite of serious avant-garde endeavor (1986)? Yet, as the French were perhaps the first to note, there is in Lewis's cinema, and Tashlin's before it, a frequent use of popular subject matter as a springboard for taking off into visually abstract experiments with tone, contrast, brightness, and so on. Several aspects of Pollock's work are pertinent to this physiognomy of 1950s culture and its legacy for Lewis's films in the 1960s. First is the fact that, as Greenberg notes, Abstract Expressionism works as an autotelic self-reflexive work, the dripping of paint on the surface of canvas creating a physical reality that is interesting in itself and without referent. Likewise, the constructed look of the Tashlin and Lewis films transfers attention from narrative to the process of fabrication. Also, Abstract Expressionist painting not only speaks of the made object but bears traces of the act of making. That is, it refers as much to the explicit activities of the artist as to the works that result from those activities. This is why it is an art of "expressionism": the streaks of paint serve as traces of the action the painter engaged in. In comparable fashion, both Lewis's films and Tashlin's come to the spectator as clearly authored works, as artificial environments with an explicit artificer behind them. This focusing of attention onto the artist behind the work is probably even more strongly the case with Lewis than with Tashlin, insofar as Lewis's films were promoted as originating with him—that is, as works of a known public personality—and involved frequent blurring of the onscreen actor and the offscreen director, a blurring explicitly recognized by French distributors, who always retitled Lewis films to include the name "Jerry" in the title as in *Dr. Jerry et Monsieur Love* (*The Nutty Professor*).

Most important, abstract expressionist artists offer up a visuality that seems to be applied to surfaces, a realistically unmotivated spreading of colors over the painting frame rather than an in-depth rendering of a naturally colored everyday world. Likewise, in both Tashlin and Lewis, colors seem painted onto the world, smears of radiance that are plopped down onto the image and seem to float above it—cinematic visuality as a veritable dripping of color onto the world of the film. For example, the city street on which Herbert Heebert sits toward the beginning of *The Ladies Man* is filled with colors that seem to be pasted over the image or recently painted onto its objects. Even more pointedly, in *The Nutty Professor* the transformation sequence includes a moment where Kelp is seized by pain, thrashes around on a floor covered with brightly colored chemicals, and becomes a veritable model of 1960s body painting. The interlude has no narrative function and exists only to foreground the splashy look of smeared colors. Interestingly, this motif of blurs of color for their own sake continues in the next scene, in the famous first-person shot of Buddy Love gliding through the city streets. Here we see the city at night represented as a panoply of colors—oil slicks on the roadways, a multiplicity of tonalities in the people who stop to stare at the camera, a variety of decor. And the next scene—in the aptly named Purple Pit—is also invested in a bacchanalia of color in the blend of lurid lighting and overly bright costuming.

Among Lewis's films, *The Ladies Man* is a veritable condensation of many of the themes around labor that I have been tracing. From its very first scene, depicting a mechanistic causality in which everyday life is figured as a linkage of moments of chaos and catastrophe, *The Ladies Man* signals its status as a calculated and rationally built object. Quickly, this depiction of the constructed nature of the narrative universe becomes a full-fledged self-reflexivity in the famous shot where, to a musical fanfare, the camera pulls back and reveals the ladies' boardinghouse as a large-scale cutaway. The set manifests itself explicitly as a set: lateral to the camera, the rooms of the boardinghouse are sliced open so that we can see into each and every one of them at the same time. This set, legendary in its status in film history, speaks of the act of creation in several ways. First, obviously, its artificiality and unreality signal the constructed nature of this narrative universe: this is decidedly, emphatically, a set. Secondly, the resemblance of the set to a dollhouse resonates with the thematics of the latter: the dollhouse is a form of creativity in which its owner manipulates reality as a godly figure lording over a controlled universe. The dollhouse set of *The Ladies Man* speaks not only of the creation of its narrative world but of the omnipresence and even omnipotence of its creator, the auteur who generated this fictional universe.

In keeping with these larger functions of the cutaway set, the division of the boardinghouse into a series of individual rooms allows for a self-reflexive commentary on the nature of narrative. As Herbert enters each room, a new story, a new sketch, can begin and signal the constructed nature of all such scenes, the way they are called into being by a narratorial agent. (The set here bears obvious comparison to one used by another famous director whose films are often also about the director as a veritable authoring god: the courtyard of Hitchcock's *Rear Window* [1954], where what Jeffries peers into is the world of narrativity itself, each window that is facing him a mini-story of life, love, or death.) Additionally, the multiplicity of rooms goes beyond narratological function to enable formal experimentation: each room has its own look, its own design, and its own coloration arranged according to unique and irreducible palettes. At the same time, it is important to note that each of the bedrooms reveals not any-story-whatsoever but stories or scenes specifically connected to a world of spectacle and showmanship, thereby signaling self-reflexively the film's emphasis on a world of performance: for example, in one room a woman auditions for the theater, while in the strangest of rooms, Herbert dances with a batlike woman while a band plays hip music, all of this in a decor that is highly stylized, offering hyperaware commentary on its own constructedness. When, toward the end of the film, a TV crew comes to the boardinghouse to film a documentary, the self-reflexive function of the set comes full circle and we participate in a film filming a filming (with Herbert Heebert then mimicking Jerry Lewis when he looks through the viewfinder and plays with the sound-recording technology).

Thus far I've been conjoining Tashlin and Lewis as avatars of 1950s visual culture. But it seems to me that through the course of the 1960s the careers draw apart, as Lewis comes to participate in a new mutation in the image of work. The title of a late Lewis film could serve as the culmination of this new tendency—*Hardly Working*. If the 1950s imagine creative work as a way to obscure the alienating core of labor, the 1960s add to this a unique inflection: creative work is imagined to come not from concerted effort (for example, all those postwar GI Bill students who studied hard to make a go of it) but from casualness, a carefree insouciance, an unflagging low-key cool. Creation is valorized when it comes from no major expenditure of energy but seems instead to appear naturally, easily, smoothly. The early 1960s, for instance, are the moment of John F. Kennedy alternating politics with games of football on the White House lawn, and doing so with unflappable boyish charm; of *Playboy*'s full entrance into the middle-class bachelor scene; of James Bond and a mod British cool; and of the Rat Pack, to which, as Shawn Levy's *Rat Pack Confidential* bears out, Lewis had an off-and-on relationship (Levy 1998). In all these cases, men do work in a way that turns it into a lark, a game, a veritable pastime that demands no real expenditure or commitment. (I pointedly say "men" here since the ideology of carefree creativity is associated primarily with men, although there is the complementary phenomenon of the "swinging single" woman, as defined by Helen Gurley Brown.)

In the case of Lewis, labor becomes a divided activity: on the one hand, a process of rigorous calculation and careful invention (all the preplanning and fascination with technology encapsulated in the idea of "the total filmmaker") and, on the other, a carefree nonchalance that seems content to let things unfold without much direction. Here again we see the value of the cutaway doll's house in *The Ladies Man*. As noted before, the architecture of this set serves a self-reflexive function to reiterate Lewis's craft as total filmmaker. But it also participates in a dialectic between this sort of heavily calculated and conscientiously applied craft and a carefree insouciance. The rooms of the boardinghouse become so many sites where narratives seem to unfold naturally, easily, and effortlessly (even as they seem highly stylized). When the camera moves back from the set and views it at a distance, there is the impression of a nonchalant, passive glance at this narrative universe rather than an active intervention in it. Even in closer shots there is relatively little editing, with instead a general emphasis on long takes that allow sketches and routines to unfold themselves in meandering, insouciant, often lackadaisical fashion.

Of course, the sheer magnitude of the set—one of the biggest interior sets in the history of cinema—reminds us that nothing is really effortless here. To choreograph actions on such a set, to light them in appropriate ways, to orchestrate the multiple narratives such a complex architecture enables obviously requires great will, foresight, control, and a sharp sense of the relationship between planning and the generation of desired artistic effects. Even as Lewis, here and elsewhere, may to a certain degree encourage us to imagine that he builds success by "hardly working," it is clear that rigorous forms of work are intrinsic to the effects and impressions (including the impression of effortlessness) he produces.

Part of the complexity of the experience of Lewis films comes from their blend of audacious and evidently hyperplanned experiments (for instance, the tracking shot to introduce Buddy Love in *The Nutty Professor*) and a leisurely, even lazy slackness. There are stunning moments in Lewis films, but there are also moments that come off as painful in their sloppiness, their seeming lack of effort and refusal to worry about results. (I would argue that this is the case for much of *The Family Jewels* and *Which Way to the Front?*) And complicating this distinction are moments that seem slack but turn out to have deliberative functions behind them, so that one realizes that the initial impression of laziness is something the films are toying with even as they luxuriate in it. As much as Lewis and the Rat Pack together disdain the rise of the hippie movement, their early 1960s ethos of casual masculinity anticipates some of the late 1960s concerns around leisure, slacking off, tuning out, detaching oneself from quotidian responsibility, and freeing one's mind from mundane issues.

It is common in discussions of *The Nutty Professor* to see Buddy Love as Lewis's commentary on Dean Martin, perhaps the ultimate incarnation of the worker as slacker/the slacker as worker. But it is necessary that in changing into Buddy Love, Professor Kelp actually physically become more like Jerry Lewis himself. He begins physically to resemble the person of Lewis, and as Shawn Levy's biography asserts, he approximates many of Lewis's attitudes and emotions—for example, haughty superiority and nastiness toward the little people, narcissism and arrogance, and especially a honed sense of casual cool in which effort comes to seem effortless (Levy 1996). As Levy's biography shows, Lewis as much as the members of the Rat Pack saw himself as a playboy figure of facile seductiveness, of carefree insouciance, of a graceful aplomb. Not for nothing is one of his key films titled *The Ladies Man*: if, as I've noted, so many of the Lewis film titles and narratives speak of the centrality of vocation in defining personality, *The Ladies Man* blurs vocation and avocation and signals a quite 1960s sense of man's "work" as highly sexualized and apparently not laborious. A Ladies Man, as the possessive overtone of the title indicates, is an object of women but he is also someone who specializes in possessing women through his seductive charm (just as Herbert wins over the hearts of the women in the boardinghouse). But it is important to the 1960s image of the determined bachelor (which Herbert is, in his own way) that seductiveness seem unplanned, a natural radiance from the person rather than a calculated effect (just as the *Playboy* ethic is to train oneself to seem a spontaneous, untrained casual force of seductiveness). Herbert charms in a guileless manner: it is even central to Lewis characters that they become sexy even as they're geeky. The ending of *The Nutty Professor*—where Kelp combines features of both of his personalities (professor and playboy)—encapsulates this desire to capture 1960s masculine identity as a blend of cool suaveness and carefree spontaneity.

This sexualization of a breezy, light, fun-loving masculinity is central to a 1960s ethos of the enjoyability of man's work. For all their (perhaps deliberate) image of a painfulness in the realm of labor, Jerry Lewis's films work to overcome the pressures of the everyday work world and imagine an avoidance of its negative effects through skill and pride in work as well as insouciant and sexy cool. It is in this respect that the films belong to the genre of comedy: not just as works that elicit laughter (in fact, they frequently don't) but as activities of transcendence, exhilarating and fully ideological challenges to the centrality of alienation in everyday life.

## NOTE

1. In much of the current critical literature about this film, the title is given as *The Ladies' Man*. Indeed, some of the contemporary reviews of the film do likewise, for instance, that in the *Hollywood Reporter*. For their part, Paramount Pictures did the same: in the April 19, 1961, submission to the Academy of Motion Picture Arts and Sciences (by Curtis Kenyon) of the official Data for Bulletin of Screen Achievement Records, the title is given with an apostrophe. However, the motion picture itself has no apostrophe in the title crawl; York Pictures filed the film with the Library of Congress Catalog of Copyright without an apostrophe; the majority of contemporary publications about the film had no apostrophe (*Box Office* and the *Motion Picture Herald* among others); and there is no titular apostrophe in the inventory of the Paramount Script Collection at the Margaret Herrick Library, Beverly Hills. Given the many interesting ways in which the title is opened to new meaning without the possessive implied in the apostrophe, I use the original screen-titling version in this chapter.

"I'll face the unknown, I'll build a world of my own," sings Sydney Pythias (Jerry Lewis) in *The Delicate Delinquent* (Don McGuire, Paramount, 1957). Frame enlargement.

# 15

# Hello Deli!

## Shtick Meets Teenpic in *The Delicate Delinquent*

Barry Keith Grant

*THE DELICATE DELINQUENT* (1957) is, I would argue, an important, although hitherto largely neglected, film in the Jerry Lewis canon. Despite its historical significance within the trajectory of Lewis's career, few scholars or critics discuss it at any length or even mention it at all. But *The Delicate Delinquent* may be seen as an essential Lewis text to the extent that it expresses the contradictions that inform the cultural icon known as Jerry Lewis. Already in *The Delicate Delinquent* the fundamental clashes, both ideological and aesthetic, that characterize the mature Jerry Lewis (if one may speak thus) find full expression at every level. *The Delicate Delinquent* is neither a good nor even a particularly enjoyable Jerry Lewis movie—"an agreeable blend of sentiment and slapstick" is the kindest description one might offer (Maltin 1999, 338)—yet an appreciation of it does speak directly to what Gerald Mast calls "The Problem of Jerry Lewis": that is, "whether he should be taken seriously at all" (Mast 1973, 298).

The very place of *The Delicate Delinquent* in Lewis's career is a pivotal one, for it sits on the cusp of the Great Divide, Lewis's breakup with Dean Martin. The film thus occupies a crucial transitional position for Lewis, marking a step forward in independence and assertion of creative control. Lewis produced the film, his first without Martin, but did not direct it. (He would wait until *The Bellboy* in 1960, three years and eight films later, before stepping behind the camera.) For *The Delicate Delinquent*, Lewis hired an old friend, Don McGuire, a writer and director who had just completed his first film as director, *Johnny Concho* (1956), an undistinguished Western with Frank Sinatra.

McGuire, with a few routine pictures to his credit, merits no entries in any of the standard reference books or encyclopedias on American filmmakers. He is unacknowledged, for example, in Andrew Sarris's comprehensive *The American Cinema* (1968), and indeed, in Sarris's entry for Lewis, *The Delicate Delinquent* is neither mentioned nor even italicized as important in the filmography. Familiar to Lewis as one of the group involved in making his amateur film parodies, McGuire is described by Lewis biographer Shawn Levy as "a former yes-man, someone he [Lewis] could control without argument" (Levy 1996, 215). Lacking the stylistic influence of a strong director like Frank Tashlin or even a very competent one like Norman Taurog, *The Delicate Delinquent* inevitably reveals much of its aspiring auteur, Jerry Lewis, newly liberated from Martin.

The screenplay, written by McGuire, was based on the story of Damon and Pythias, the Greek legend about two friends who switch places in prison, willing to die for each other. According to Levy, Lewis regarded the legend as a metaphor in some way of his relationship with Dean Martin (207), so the story was personally important to the comedian. Levy sums up the plot of *The Delicate Delinquent* perfectly: "It's another schnook-makes-good story: A nebbishy apprentice janitor (Jerry) is mistaken for a young hoodlum by the cops, and a do-good patrolman (Darren McGavin) decides to take him under his wing and reform him. Jerry resists McGavin's help at first, but pretty soon he wants not only to reform but to join the police force . . . and, incredibly, he makes it (though not, of course, without the usual complications)" (226). Just as in the legend the tyrant Dionysius was so impressed by the pair's unwavering friendship and loyalty that he pardoned both of them, so in the film Pythias (Sydney L. Pythias) is rehabilitated by Damon (Mike Damon, the cop), and, in turn, Pythias's success at becoming a policeman redeems the comfortable liberalism of Damon. The slim plot serves as a pretext for a moral sermon, an argument for the redemptive value of niceness that would constitute an essential aspect of the Lewisian vision in later films.

The legend of two such intimate friends is an ideal narrative context for the Lewis persona, given its essentially split nature. As Dana Polan has noted, "There are two Jerry Lewises—the Id (short for Idiot but also suggesting the roots of comic idiocy in a primal unreason) and

Jerry Lewis the Serious Man (with capital letters, *si'l vous plaît*)" (Polan 1984, 42–43). Lewis's own conception of The Idiot is defined by a split: when Lewis acts as his own director, as he has flatly said, "The Idiot is another person" (Lewis 1973, 82). Indeed, in his book *The Total Film-Maker*, Lewis sounds almost schizophrenic about his dual role as director and actor: "There is no easy way to shake that schmuck you sleep with at night. No matter how you toss and turn, he's always there," he writes (36). One of the reasons Lewis's films have not been well received in North America is because The Idiot is simultaneously silly and sentimental—although, for the French, Lewis's life and films "appear to combine the contradictory sides of America, the United States as a clash of attitudes and styles" (Polan 1984, 45). Damon and Pythias are individuals yet ideal soulmates; for each to be the other assumes a defined self either to become or to abandon. Their story assumes the kind of stability of identity that the Lewis persona is forever seeking.

Lewis's characteristic split between stupidity and seriousness is central to *The Delicate Delinquent*. The title of the film already suggests that this particular Idiot is an *oxy*moron. Sydney Pythias is both a good boy who embraces bourgeois values and a bad boy ready to rebel at whatever you've got. Sydney has a kind of Jekyll-Hyde personality split that anticipates Lewis's most important film, *The Nutty Professor* (1963), in which he plays both the endearing nebbish Professor Kelp and the obnoxious lounge lizard Buddy Love. But where Lewis's personality split is given a narrative motivation in *The Nutty Professor* through the metaphor of a chemical potion, in *The Delicate Delinquent* the two types simply coexist in the same unbelievable character. Sydney's encounter with the theramin, improbably housed in the apartment of a mad scientist who lives in the building where Sydney works as a janitor, perfectly illustrates Lewis's split character in the film. According to Levy, "The idea of a gifted physical comic interacting with a musical device that is activated by the movement of human bodies in front of it is truly inspired"; but while Levy thinks that the scene is "primally satisfying, like watching a chimpanzee figure out a mirror" (1996, 227), this bit of comic business is disappointingly brief and stands out as an anomaly in a film that is primarily preachy (compare, for instance, Lewis's more sustained physical comedy with the Buddy Rich band in the beatnik café in *Visit to a Small Planet* [1960]).

At the same time as Lewis's Sydney is The Idiot, he is also an idiot savant, the wisest character in the film. Even as Sydney is silly enough to become involved in the scientist's crackpot plan to evacuate all of Earth's frogs in tiny spaceships with little toilets, he frequently drops pearls of moral wisdom, like a Shakespearean fool. For example, despite his tongue-tied embarrassment in the presence of Patricia (Mary Webster), Sydney's obligatory love interest in whom the film is wholly uninterested as a character, he articulately explains his shyness to her by observing, "You got to find out what you are before you can know what you want to be." When Damon and Martha Henshaw (Martha Hyer), the prim, naive representative of the city council, argue over Sydney as a sociological "case" in his presence, Sydney has the sense to get up and leave. He protests, "You two think I'm a freak or something, or a guinea pig," and his indignation seems to us eminently sane and entirely justified. While Sydney's conceptual capacity limits him to forcing round pegs into square holes (as we see with one of the standard intelligence tests he has to take to become a policeman), it is also the case that, as Damon says in defense of him as a police candidate to the captain (Horace McMahon), "He's honest, he's got guts, and he's a decent human being."

Raymond Durgnat has described Lewis's "idiocy" as his ability to unleash "frenetic cadenzas" of emotional signifiers that do not "so much emote, as disintegrate into an emotional gamut" (1970, 234). Lewis's performance in *The Delicate Delinquent* is a prime example. As Sydney walks out in anger on Damon and Henshaw, he says, "If you'll be good enough to excuse me, I'm going home"—Lewis's voice, with the last three words, suddenly and inexplicably changing in tone from The Idiot to The Serious Man. The radically altered "grain of the voice" (Barthes 1977) gives these words a more emphatic symbolic connotation (home as one's proper place) but is impossibly inconsistent in terms of conventional realist character construction.

At times in the film, Lewis's spastic physical humor, a barrage of emotional signifiers, suggests that Sydney is torn between the delicate and the delinquent. Initially deporting himself as a distrustful youth when approached by Damon, as soon as the policeman asks him about his school experience Sydney's body language changes and the sweet, vulnerable kid emerges; Lewis enfolds himself in his legs, his defensive caution melting away and the unselfconscious child blossoming before our eyes. Sydney's split character is literalized when Damon and Henshaw argue over him, standing on either side of him as he sits in a chair, like the proverbial angel and devil at his shoulders. When Martha describes Sydney as "a confused, unbalanced young man with only one thought in mind—self-destruction," Damon responds by asking Sydney if he would like to help him with the salad. Sydney, who had entered the scene wielding a switchblade knife with comic exaggeration, promptly switches both blades and modes, enthusiastically offering to lend a hand.

Lewis's particular inflection of The Idiot in *The Delicate Delinquent* cleverly mobilizes aspects of contemporary youth culture that parallel the Lewis character's own bifurcated construction between delicate and delinquent. As a delinquent, however delicate he may be, Sydney reflects the period's concerns over the development of postwar youth culture, the invention of the teenager, and the new phenomenon of juvenile delinquency. According to Thomas Doherty, the 1950s witnessed the first generation of bona fide teenagers (1988, 44–46), and throughout the decade the media exploited fears over rebellious youth, stereotypically fixing on "the image of the urban juvenile as a switchblade-brandishing menace" (51). Only four years before the release of *The Delicate Delinquent* a well-publicized Senate Judiciary Subcommittee led by Estes Kefauver was investigating juvenile delinquency and its causes. The year before the film's release, Frankie Lymon and the Teenagers sang "I'm Not a Juvenile Delinquent" in the rock 'n' roll musical *Rock Rock Rock* (1956).

Sociological and anthropological discourses were commonly invoked at the time to explain youth as a "subculture" (e.g., Cohen 1955), and these discourses are referenced in a number of ways in *The Delicate Delinquent*. Most obviously, they inform the conflict between Damon and Henshaw over Sydney. Martha Henshaw, who spouts traditional social determinist theory (as she says, she has come "to investigate the deplorable situations in neighborhoods that are a breeding ground for crime"), is well intentioned but naive (she mistakes Sydney for "a perfect example of what juvenile delinquency represents") compared to Mike Damon, who, we discover, has experience in the field since he used to run with the pack himself. Ultimately, Martha is a caricature of the well-meaning but ineffective liberal do-gooder, an upper-class interloper, as signified by her clean white gloves. (Damon describes her as "an emissary for would-be reformers who think that juvenile delinquency can be curtailed if we treat these hoodlums with kid gloves.") Also, Sydney's dilemma of being caught between the world of the delinquents on the streets around him and his desire to find a better life for himself invokes David Riesman's contemporary and influential distinction between other-directed and inner-directed man in *The Lonely Crowd* (Riesman 1950). And Sydney's conception of this better life ("There's an awful lot of nice people in the world, Monk, and I just wanna be one of them," he tells the leader of the gang when they corner him in the alley) marks him as the type of *homo americanus* that William H. Whyte Jr., just the year before *The Delicate Delinquent*, had defined as "the organization man" (Whyte 1956).

Durgnat cites two main themes in Lewis's films, both of which are fully apparent in *The Delicate Delinquent*: "Jerry's desperate attempts to live up to his own ideals of 'benevolent toughness,' and his equally desperate search to find, be worthy of, and be accepted by a loving world" (1970, 235). As a comedy, *The Delicate Delinquent* seeks narrative closure, with Sydney successfully integrated into just such a "loving world" and his values valorized. The opening scene, to which I return shortly, shows the explosive presence of The Idiot when he suddenly bursts into view through a door, garbage flying out of his hands; but by the end of the film The Idiot all but disappears within The Serious Man (garbage, some have implied, replaced with rubbish).

The last scene shows Sydney in his new police uniform, embracing a suddenly proud Patricia, who describes him as "tall and handsome" and "respectable." Sydney then moves on to talk to Monk (Robert Ivers) and Artie (Richard Bakalyan), two of the neighborhood delinquents, as well as one younger boy flanking him. Thus, at the end of *The Delicate Delinquent*, Sydney becomes the normative heterosexual lover and the father figure to some dead-end kids who ultimately are merely wayward, errant boys reclaimed by Sir Jerry, the knight-errant. In his police uniform and occupying a commanding position in the center of the final images, Sydney is now the embodiment of the Law of the Father rather than the butt of its humor, as he was early on when he was reduced to a sniveling crybaby after mistakenly being rounded up in a rumble bust and put into the police lineup. Tellingly, the last shot of the film is a close-up of Sydney touching his badge with reverence.

His transformation in the narrative is a perfect example of the frequent oedipal scenario operating in Lewis's films (Bukatman 1991, 196), as suggested in the apparently irrelevant comic business about the threatening male voice asking for Zelda on Sydney's telephone, a voice that refuses to be stifled even when Jerry cuts and strangles the cord. Mr. Herman (Milton Frome), the bullying tenant whose aggressive masculinity is signified by his T-shirt, calls Sydney a "nothing," and when Sydney tries to stand up to the bullying Monk, who challenges him by asking what he is going to do about it, Sydney meekly backs down, saying, "Nothin', not now," his own voice muted. Sydney is nothing because he hasn't yet acceded to his place within patriarchy: as he tells Patricia in their first meeting, "When I was a boy, I was jerky. And now, now I'm a man. And I'm empty. I'm nothing—but I would sure like to be something." In other words, Sydney is grown physically but not psychically.

And as the film moves toward its climax, Sydney becomes "something," now capable of standing up to Monk: when he and the other cops scuffle with the boys in the alley, Sydney is shown exchanging punches blow for blow, holding his own. A close-up at the end of the fight shows a dribble of blood at the side of Sydney's mouth, his red badge of masculine courage. Sydney's growth into manhood is metaphorically suggested when, a rookie on his first patrol, he has to help a pregnant woman deliver her baby. The film cuts from a shot of Sydney in panic when he realizes the situation to another of Sydney calmly and proudly holding the baby as the ambulance arrives. Contemplating Sydney's achievements in the penultimate scene, Damon asks of him admiringly, "Is that a boy? Is that a boy?"—an acknowledgment of Sydney's maturation as well as a reference to the earlier *That's My Boy* (1951), in which The Idiot similarly must grow up and take his place in the masculine order.

Sydney's transformation from awkward and alienated youth to full male member of the symbolic order recalls the Charles Atlas bodybuilding ads familiar to all youth in the 1950s, which Lewis explicitly invokes as Clayton Poole in *Rock-a-Bye Baby*, made in 1958. The ads appeared with ritual regularity in comic books of the decade, elevating them to the level of teen myth. The ads tell a story, in comic-book panels, of the ninety-pound weakling who, bullied on the beach by a seemingly cool muscle-bound guy, loses his girl and is humiliated in public; but with the aid of Atlas's Dynamic Tension program, he gains both confidence and physical strength, returns to the scene of the trauma, defeats the bully, and wins back his girl. In the variant of the myth in *The Delicate Delinquent*, the nerd doesn't triumph by physical might but rather by bringing the delinquent boys who bully him around to his own values: for just when things look darkest for Sydney, accused of shooting one of the young hoodlums involved in the fight with police and therefore about to be suspended from the force, Monk appears and confesses that it was really an accident for which Sydney was being framed by one of Monk's buddies.

With a narrative built around Sydney's rite of passage, *The Delicate Delinquent* employs the central plot structure of the teen film. According to Doherty, in the 1950s "the teen years became a unique transitional phase between childhood and adulthood, in some sense an autonomous and in most cases a privileged period in an individual's life" (Doherty 1988, 44). Teens, in other words, developed a distinct subculture, here taken literally, with Sydney's apartment located in the basement. Sydney says at one point that he "doesn't know what he wants to be when he grows up," and so the basement also represents his transitional status. On first entering Sydney's apartment (which requires a giant step from the doorway to the floor, emphasizing the initial gap between Sydney and "respectable" integration into society), Damon looks around and declares, "You're alone," to which Sydney replies, "You ain't kiddin'." (Even the milkman and streetcleaner avoid Sydney, obviously dubious beneficiaries of his "help" in the past.) But as Sydney emerges into adulthood, the movie also fulfills the central ideological task of youth films: "the restoration of the adult culture informed rather than radicalized by youth" (Jon Lewis 1992, 3).

*The Delicate Delinquent* overlays the generic codes of the newly emergent teenpic genre in postwar American cinema on the similarly emerging auteur Jerry Lewis. Riding the wave of teen exploitation movies that began with *Rock Around the Clock* in 1956, the film incorporates the teen film's tendency to represent teens as two opposing hyperbolic stereotypes: wild or mild. Richard Staehling describes these images as "the fantasy sociology of the 1950s":

> The wild-youth-kid stereotype was of a bum who rode around in his hot rod, half-crazed from drugs and liquor, looking for a chick to lay, a store to rob, or another car to drag; discourteous, greasy, irresponsible, and mean. . . . His mild youth counterpart was everybody's baby: clean, honest, moral and bright; everything a parent could hope for, incarnate. He was a little mixed up about love, and did silly things like playing the record player too loud and tying up the telephone, but he was all-American nonetheless, another clean-living member of the silent majority. (1975, 230–231)

Perhaps these two versions of youth in the 1950s, the delicate and the delinquent, represent the Lewis and Martin sides of Jerry Lewis, which Scott Bukatman sees as the juvenile and virile sides of Lewis's personality, respectively (Bukatman 1991, 191).

Staehling sees both mild and wild youth as defining distinct genres within the wider category of the youth exploitation film, but *The Delicate Delinquent* oscillates between both, tantalizing viewers with the latter's sensationalist possibilities but ultimately opting for the former's bland platitudes. Monk's expression of alienation in his debate with Sydney, wherein he cites Sydney's $60-a-week janitor's salary as class exploitation, hints at a potential social critique—always lurking as a possibility in crime films—that is never developed. (Sydney responds simply that Monk looks at the world "sideways.") Although the film elsewhere offers hints of such a critique—for example, in the caricatured depiction of Henshaw ("There's a beer in the icebox. I don't think you'll like it, though, it's domestic," says Damon insultingly) and in the references to inner-city ghettos—ultimately, *The Delicate Delinquent* may be one of the films Staehling had in mind "that masquerade as 'juve' movies but are really nothing more than mainstream Hollywood wearing leather jackets and saddle shoes" (Staehling 1975, 226). When the press's interest in juvenile delinquency waned in 1958, the year after *The Delicate Delinquent*, the image of wild youth evolved into the tamer existentialist surfers of beach movies such as *Gidget* (1959) and *Where the Boys Are* (1960) (Staehling 1975, 236). *The Delicate Delinquent* is at once a parody of wild youth movies and, infused with Lewis's characteristic tendresse, a harbinger of the mild youth cycle to come.

Within the larger generic landscape, the film occupies a contradictory position. On the one hand, *The Delicate Delinquent* is a movie in the venerable tradition of the postwar social problem film—movies such as *Gentleman's Agreement* (1947) and *Pinky* (1949) as filtered through *Blackboard Jungle* and *Rebel Without a Cause* (both 1955), films that present juvenile delinquency as a social problem. On the other hand, it is a comedy, and one, moreover, that often goes for cheap laughs. Treating serious issues with humor is always a difficult aesthetic balancing act, so given its confusing mixture of tones it is no surprise that contemporary reviews of *The Delicate Delinquent* described the film as confusing, "neither fish nor fowl" (Levy 1996, 226).

The film is Lewis's attempt at making socially conscious comedy in the tradition of Charles Chaplin. Indeed, several moments in *The Delicate Delinquent* seem deliberate references to Chaplin. Sydney's comic business with the Murphy bed in his apartment inevitably recalls Chaplin's short *One A.M.* (1916), in which, writes Gerald Mast, "the bed is one of the few inanimate objects in film history that could have been nominated as best supporting actor" (1973, 79). Sydney's being mistaken for one of the boys involved in the rumble and trundled off with them in the police wagon brings to mind the scene in *Modern Times* (1936) where poor Charlie is carted away as the leader of a Communist protest rally when he has innocently picked up a red flag that has fallen off a passing truck. Attempting a Chaplinesque combination of pathos and comedy, Sydney's lovelorn look through the banister bars in the hallway stairs at Patricia's apartment door, showing him a prisoner of his own emotions, evokes such images as the rebuffed Charlie looking in on the dancing Georgia in *The Gold Rush* (1925) or gazing upon the blind flower girl in *City Lights* (1931).

The film's motif of garbage as a physical emblem of human refuse and waste seems a particularly Chaplinesque attempt at pathos. When we first meet Sydney, he bursts into the alley in the middle of a gang fight, stumbling and spilling the garbage he's collected from the tenants in the building. Hauled away with the other boys by the police, Sydney protests, "I was only taking out the garbage." When he meets Patricia at her apartment door and they are both too embarrassed and shy to speak, she gives him her garbage. At the conclusion of his musical number "By Myself," Sydney moves two garbage cans from one side of the door to the other, a visual metaphor for the burden of his woes in the world. And when Monk confesses the truth about Artie's gunshot wound in the climax, he explains that there "ain't no reason for Sydney not to climb out of the garbage."

From scene to scene, *The Delicate Delinquent* veers clumsily between slapstick and social significance, just as Lewis lurches from stupid to smart. Where one scene is funny, the next is serious. The film's very tone and style pull in two different directions, mirroring the tension within Sydney, and are foregrounded immediately in the opening precredit scene. Beginning with shots of a city street complete with expressionist shadows and pools of water on the pavement, the film starts as film noir. (Or this could be from a wild youth exploitation movie produced by AIP or Sam Katzman.) Along with these images, jazzy percussion

rises in volume on the soundtrack, the staccato rhythms connoting bo-
hemianism, urban culture, and decadence (Gorbman 1997, 86). But
when the delinquents begin to appear, their actions are expressionistic,
stylized, like the gangster choreography of "The Girl Hunt Ballet" in
*The Band Wagon* (1953). When three of the youths confront three others
in the alley, they take out their weapons sequentially—first chain, then
knife, then brass knuckles—with dramatic flair and in perfect time with
nondiegetic musical accents. And when the cops arrive and surround
the hapless Sydney, the images invoke at once the stark determinism of
Fritz Lang's compositions and the surreal absurdity of Buster Keaton's.

Later in the film, when Damon and Pythias are riding in the prowl
car and receive a call about the disturbance in the alley, we see two exterior location shots of a police car driving through the streets of New
York that might well have come from *The Naked City* (1948), a Mark
Hellinger–produced thriller recognized for its pioneering location pho-
tography. These are followed by studio shots of the two policemen inside the car, then a shot of the vehicle arriving at the alley, which is
clearly a studio set. The fight that follows is clearly choreographed and
not merely unconvincing realism. So in this single sequence we have
abrupt joining of studio fabrication to realistic location shots, bleak noir
sensibility to choreographic, almost musical, artificiality. I wouldn't
agree that *The Delicate Delinquent* is "a minor work of American neore-
alism, a forgotten cousin of *On the Waterfront* (1954) or *Marty* (1955)"
(Levy 1996, 226); but while the film is generally a studio-bound fantasy,
there are moments in which reality suddenly and noticeably intrudes.

Shawn Levy criticizes the inconsistencies of *The Delicate Delinquent*
as "sloppy" and dismisses the film because Lewis cannot stay in character. "And," he adds, "he's wearing the inevitable wedding band and
pinky ring" (227). But the film is riven with inconsistencies at every
level, and they are, in fact, part of what makes it so interesting. Lewis's
unconvincing character challenges the typical representation of masculinity—here, delinquent adolescent masculinity—in Hollywood cinema, suggesting it is less monolithic than performative. As Bukatman
notes, Lewis's presence in his films "demolishes any prospect of a coherent masculine subjectivity" because "the multiplicity of identities in
the world of Jerry Lewis belies the existence of identity as anything
other than a necessary but unworkable fiction" (Bukatman 1991, 188,
201). This is certainly true of *The Delicate Delinquent*, in which Lewis's
presentation of himself is marked as performance consistently within

the film. When Martha, looking for a "typical" delinquent to bring to Damon's apartment, walks past Sydney in the alley, she sees him gesturing with the switchblade Monk had given him, exactly embodying "the urban juvenile as switchblade-brandishing menace"—and so mistakes him for the perfect example of juvenile delinquency. Sydney also imagines himself a policeman, addressing his own reflection in the mirror ("Good morning, Officer") like a mild Travis Bickle, and elsewhere imitates a sumo warrior for an audience of appreciative cadets during his police training. Lewis's performance of "By Myself" in the film is also emphasized as a performance when spotlighting from a nondiegetic source above him in the alley illuminates him as he reaches his emotional climax.

Just as Sydney—as he himself tells Patricia—is a torn man, a nobody who wants to be a somebody, so Lewis is torn between the comic and the social critic in *The Delicate Delinquent*. The film is on one level about Lewis—without the anchor of straight-man Martin—looking for himself. Seeking to define himself as a solo performer after the departure of Dino, by film's end Lewis plays both partners of *Pardners* (1956), The Idiot and The Serious Man rolled into one New Man. It is no coincidence that the one song Lewis sings in the film is "By Myself," the Howard Dietz–Arthur Schwartz tune that Fred Astaire sang several years earlier in *The Band Wagon*. Lewis's allusion here is apt and very precise, for in Minnelli's musical Astaire's character, Tony Hunter, is a self-reflexive meditation on the evolving, maturing image of the star who is playing him, Astaire himself, just as the character of Sydney Pythias is for Jerry Lewis. Moreover, Astaire played Hunter, a performer whose career is at a turning point, at a turning point in his own career, just as *The Delicate Delinquent* inevitably constituted a turning point for Lewis. In Lewis's version the song begins and ends as a voiceover of Sydney thinking to himself, literalizing the idea of Lewis talking to himself ("I'll face the unknown, I'll build a world of my own," he sings).

Gerald Mast argues that the problem with Lewis is that he "simply does shtick. He contrives gags—many of them good ones. But the gags do not flow from any human or personal center" (1973, 298). But such a criticism is true only if we measure Lewis's characters by realist criteria. Lewis's films might more accurately be called "incoherent texts" in Robin Wood's sense. For Wood, in certain fragmented films the fragmentation "becomes a structuring principle, resulting in works that reveal themselves as perfectly coherent once one has mastered their rules" (1986, 46). Lewis's films, with all their inconsistencies of narrative, mise-en-scène, and style, speak to the difficulties of maintaining the kind of masculine ego ideal typically constructed by Hollywood movies and reveal it *as* constructed, rather than natural. Thus it might be said that they remain of interest to the degree that they fail to fulfill the kind of seamless illusionism of classic cinema.

Andrew Sarris refuses to consider Lewis as an auteur because, he argues, there is a gap between Lewis's sentimentality and his sensibility. Unlike John Ford, to whom he compares Lewis, there is no "essential unity" to his personality (1968, 244). But as *The Delicate Delinquent* demonstrates, it is precisely this lack of unity that is fundamental to Lewis's vision—indeed, the disunity is perhaps its most consistent, that is to say, unifying aspect. At war with itself—like adolescents in much of the discourse of the time—*The Delicate Delinquent* is fully representative of Lewis's cinema, built as it is on a number of tensions between auteur and genre, between style and content. It is these tensions that reveal the ongoing attempt by "Jerry Lewis" to negotiate his place in "the world," the Symbolic Order. Because of and not despite these tensions, *The Delicate Delinquent* emerges as an essential Jerry Lewis film.

A musical mind. Morty S. Tashman (Jerry Lewis) conducting in the "Chairman of the Board" sequence from *The Errand Boy* (Jerry Lewis, Paramount, 1961). Frame enlargement.

# 16

# The Errant Boy

## Morty S. Tashman and the Powers of the Tongue

Murray Pomerance

MORTY S. TASHMAN, the persona and foil of Jerry Lewis in *The Errand Boy* (1961), is a nerdish sign poster co-opted by the head of Paramutual Pictures to act as corporate spy in order to discover why the company is ceaselessly losing money. The film is a series of escapades with Morty awkwardly stumbling through the studio, relentlessly disintegrating every vestige of moviemaking with which he comes in contact. I here look at this film, Lewis's fourth directorial effort and a work I consider to be a minor masterpiece, as a study in the social structure of language and linguistic power.[1] I believe *The Errand Boy* makes it possible to see something of the structure of studio filmmaking by highlighting Morty's "lack" as a predominant feature of his involvement in situations. As we shall see, although in being a boy who cannot quite become a man Morty invokes consideration of gender, his is not the sort of "lack" many psychoanalytically based gender theorists talk about. It concerns power, not genitalia; and in this film, power is language.

Language and gender are not unrelated. Throughout her academic and popular analyses of gender and language, Deborah Tannen (1993, 1994, 1998, 2001) points to a reflection, in the social organization of language and speaking, of tenacious cultural gender distinctions that scholars have been querying with increasing frequency.[2] One pernicious, long-standing cultural arrangement that originates in gender distinction, what psychoanalytic criticism calls phallocentrism, surfaces in Tannen and is addressed by Mulvey in her comment that woman "first symbolizes the castration threat by her real absence of a penis and second thereby raises her child into the symbolic. Once this has been achieved, her meaning in the process is at an end, it does not last into the world of law and language except as a memory" (Mulvey 1990, 29). Tannen reflects this argument, claiming that in talk males dominate, being directive and competitive rather than descriptive, achievement-oriented rather than emotional, and knowledgeably powerful and controlling rather than impressionistic, tentative, experientially focused, fastidious, or vague. In western society linguistic gender bifurcation typically tends to play up a particular distinction related to precision of expression: for females, pointed language is to be seen as facilitating clarity of experience and efficacy of movement, while for males it is— like other concentrations of attention and condensations of capital—an avenue to accomplishment, status, and success. I hope to show, however, in relation to *The Errand Boy,* that rather than male talk's being controlling in itself, controlling talk flows from social power, not maleness. What we call *masculinity* is an attribution of power.

As has been suggested in different ways by Michel Chion (1982) and Martin Jay (1994), we linger in the world as hearers before the world is an object of vision; plenitude precedes lack. The sound we hear, at first in the womb diffuse and embracing,[3] a world-ocean's voice, becomes subsequently more localized in situations with boundaries and then increasingly articulate and discriminable as we gain facility with language and are opened to the sharply sounded alienation of tongues not our own. The polarity between music and verdict nicely exemplifies the extremities of this range of acoustic development; verdict is the cultural domain most proximate to Mulveyan patriarchy.[4] To this characteristic of language, its tendency to be enveloping or punctual, we may add a consideration of various forms of ambiguity, the ratio of sound to silence. What is not said can be—or can fail to be—meaningful; and part of our growing up to linguistic competence is our learning how we can contract, elide, avoid, or hyperextend expression to make our melody or our point.[5] Hearing and speaking correctly, then, become at last a matter of extreme complexity and delicacy, and the ability to seem grown up can depend signally on one's repertory of *langue* and *parole*—call it "tongue" and "tonguing" or "vocabulary" and "lexicon."

But the psychoanalytic model may be inadequate to the challenge presented by this film's offer of a portrait of masculinity firmly grounded in capitalistic production. If, as Basil Bernstein (1972) notes, gender identity is fundamentally linguistic, it depends upon a form of capital, owned language, a resource that is denied to Morty S. Tashman in an important way. As linguistic competence marks successful social- ization, a male with linguistic impairment, such as Morty, is an errant boy. Finding himself in a foreign situation without language, he is a child who cannot seem to be an adult, which is to say, one managerially and proactively competent to engage with others in the politics and chi- canery of everyday competition. Morty's predicament at Paramutual Studios, as staged by Lewis, is that his feelingful vocalization is verbally challenged, since he has not had the opportunity to learn how properly to make speech to talk his way into history. As Dell Hymes puts it, each kind of act and genre of speech

> has a history, and a set of conditions for its origin, maintenance, change, and loss. . . . we can see the need for an "existential" or "expe- riential" explanatory adequacy, a kind of explanation that will link speaking with human history and praxis. (1974, 65)

If, generally in our loquacious urban social world, linguistic cor- rectness and facility constitute the dominant path toward adult status, how much more precarious must linguistic learning be in that notably expressive subworld the movie studio. Here the person who has spec- tacularly failed to move forward toward accomplishment is not only immature but also wayward, deviant, off the company line—since in the movie studio, talk is essential. It is hardly some predilection of the actor Lewis for wailing, imitating infants, or manipulating language to the point of irritation that is the root of the mouthplay we observe in *The Errand Boy*, then, but the director Lewis's artful staging. That at the same time Lewis's character Morty stumbles incompetently through the linguistic jungle of Paramutual Pictures Lewis himself demon- strates extreme expressive competency in his use of the Paramount lot to show all this is something of a grand irony. Language does not come naturally, this film reminds us, and is absent or deficient in persons— like Morty—whose situations have not privileged them to learn it.

Although the extremity of his performance may waylay us from noting this, Jerry Lewis occupies a dual status in *The Errand Boy*, pres- ent for us not only as an onscreen bumbler and stutterer but also, and ontologically a priori, as an offscreen choreographer and singer.[6] The Jerry Lewis who creates the errant boy is no errant boy himself, contrary to a large volume of received opinion about him and even to his own off-camera linguistic turn as the outspoken but not always informative author of *The Total Film-Maker* (1973)—a book, by the way, in which he oddly neglects this film. Our most direct access to Lewis's double status is by noting the gap between the precise, economically spare, optical framing of the picture (by him, with W. Wallace Kelley operating the camera)—in short, the crystalline view—and the ostensible fact that Morty S. Tashman is functionally blind. One need hardly elaborate all the demonstrations of Morty's inability to make visual sense of the world (for instance, Morty trapped on the billboard with the preglued poster tumbling around him), or his tendency to be optically stunned (Morty entering the dauntingly daffy Paramutual boardroom for the first time), or his inadroitly positioning himself so as not to be able to get a good view (Morty cluttering up a director's rushes of a cocktail party), or his having been forced into contact with potentially aggressive agents who are hiding their weapons (Morty on the elevator between the man with the protruding toothpick and the man with the overactive cigar), or his navigational impairments (Morty caught in the Western shoot-em-up, attacked by GIs while trying to eat his lunch at Café Monique, or going amok at the wheel of a little prop train at Stage Four). It's worth noting that the skills and capacities referenced by all these awkwardnesses—(1) visually organizing a scene, (2) having a clear focus, (3) getting a good point of view, (4) avoiding danger, and (5) seeing past what is immediately present to what is forthcoming—are necessary technical requirements of filmmaking and also technically impossible for any of us when we are brought into cultural or geographic situations in which we have not yet learned to demonstrate easy familiarity and control.[7] Morty's errance is therefore not only incompetent but also somewhat unsurprising in this complicated territory in which he has never had any power; and it also demonstrates how he is not yet—at least, not before the finale of the picture—the denizen Jerry Lewis is. Therefore we can identify with him and feel the pain of his exclusion, experiencing the properties of that exclusion ourselves. Lewis's *Total Film-Maker*, if it is less a directive to young film students than an autobiographical spiel, does make it perfectly clear that for him, at least, learning filmmaking was a question of meeting a lot of people, asking a lot of questions, and slowly turning the awkward ignorance of alienness into a fluid and substantial comfort with sound stages, lenses, dollies, catwalks, electricians, and so on—the exact material constitution of Morty S. Tashman's jungle environment.

Notwithstanding Georg Simmel's interesting observation that in city environments the organization of the eye takes precedence over the organization of the ear (1924), hearing correctly is a necessary precondition of linguistic facility, most notably so in the case of learning foreign languages. When, as in a movie studio, social organization is complex and highly ramified, based on arcane technical considerations not widely applicable elsewhere, and facilitating a status hierarchy and supporting a class system that make considerable reference to local history and technical ability, the organizational talk one hears is foreign indeed—removed from the everyday. At Paramutual Studios we find ourselves in a delightful but precarious dream state in which English as we knew it outside the theater is not spoken. (Everyone we see seems to share Jerry Lewis's fabled penchant for fractured speech as a matter of course.) Further, a logical ground of sorts is provided for Morty's infantilistic vocal stylings when we recall that he is an infant in the studio community as the film begins. His dysfunctions correlate with his difficulties in speech and hearing.

Cultures can be language barriers. The movie studio scene of the 1950s and 1960s was culturally specific, even if the product turned out there was intended for the universal—thus most lucrative—audience. Technicians were usually L.A. locals; extras, whose voices were not heard, tended to be immigrants in an ocean of hopefuls marching to Hollywood from everywhere. But studio executives were typically immigrants to California from either the urbane East Coast or the Midwest. Often in their social world, and certainly in the one inhabited by Joseph Levitch, the immigrant from Newark, one heard a pithy language of coastal sophistication, both political and economic; nor was it rare to hear gilding inflections from Eastern Europe. The linguistic torture Morty is soon to suffer at Paramutual is foreshadowed for the viewing audience when the bored but omnipotent male—and distinctly, by its pronunciation, goyisch—Californian voiceover guiding us (with our dominating gaze) above the rooftops of Los Angeles and Beverly Hills swoops in on Paramutual Pictures with a class-obliterating reference to "the tzars and tzaresses, and their *tzourises*." This pure New York—certainly pure East Coast—Yiddishism prepares us for the arcane post-European Brooklynese babble of Miss Giles (Renée Taylor) on the telephone in the Personnel Department and the voice of Morty (and Jerry under him), and it echoes the controlling coterie (Barney Balaban et al.)[8] that ran Paramount in 1960. The offscreen narrative voice of the film, however, like the Paramutual family (Brian Donlevy, Isabel Elsom, et al.) who own the diegetic studio, rings Californian and constitutes for Morty an alien linguistic space throughout.

Obviously, the weirder the pronunciatory challenge, the more mileage Jerry Lewis the comedian can get out of the situation, using his abstracting routines of syllabic inversion and artful incompletion. But what makes *The Errand Boy* both fascinating and important is that the linguistic abstraction is here rendered germane to both the diegesis (because of the particular setting of the film) and the analysis (because of the narrative mode through which we enter and reside in that setting). Linguistically and operationally, we are no more at home at Paramutual (Paramount) than Morty (Jerry) is; and as Erving Goffman says of effortful participation (describing, I think, both Morty and the viewer of the film), "routines that allow the individual unthinking, competent performance [are] attained through an acquisition process whose early stages were negotiated in a cold sweat" (1971, 248). In the Hollywood studio, those far from the top are continually sweating.

For example, even Morty's sympathetic ear for Miss Giles's language cannot ready him for the bizarre and special names she will soon call upon him to learn and repeat as her protégé and a bona fide initiate of the studio production scene. Names and nominatives are, after all, vital interactional resources in bureaucracies; resources, further, not equally shared among all workers. Getting people's names right can affect one's future. The first obstacle is "Mr. Babewosentall": Taylor's enunciation is unassailable—"Babe . . . woes . . . ent . . . [oo]all." Mr. Babewosentall: Is he a man named Wosentall, whose first name has been modified by local consent and sensitivity into the nickname "Babe"? Yet why would a department head at a studio be introduced to a new errand boy by his first name? Perhaps he's just a Mr. whose name is Babewosentall. Or is he a man named Rosentall, not Wosentall, incorrectly adduced by Miss Giles because in general she has trouble with R's, being afflicted with a speech impairment to match her Brooklynese? But the Brooklyn accent is no affliction—it's a way of speaking English. So our own alienation from Brooklyn culture as non-Brooklynites (many New Yorkers are non-Brooklynites but all Californians are) is called up by this challenge to our reading. Until one knows language well, this scenic moment may be telling us, one cannot grasp the difference between a way of talking and a talking problem. Perhaps we are hearing the more common German Jewish name Rosenthal (Valley of Roses)? Is Morty attempting to pronounce it "Wosental" in respectful imitation of hapless Miss Giles? In any case, he fails utterly, gargling hopelessly and self-deprecatingly, and with no serious attempt at a verbal skill he has no reason—having been a sign poster—to believe he can master, "Benvedbenten." Then, with real optimism, he tries, "Ben-pay-bobo-pay-b'pay."

Soon enough, the hapless initiate meets someone else, Mr. Wabenlottnee (Benny Rubin), and this time must take a face-to-face pronunciation test that he explicitly fails. "Wa—ben—-lott—-nee . . . Wabenlottnee!" says the man, beaming self-congratulatorily at having succeeded in saying his own name (a joke in itself). The audience, uninitiated like Morty, is equally incapable of swiftly and accurately getting a tongue around such a bizarre syllabic assemblage and is in this way brought into sympathetic alignment with Morty's point of view as he helplessly tries on, "Hobbinoppin." One is reminded of William Empson's dictum that "a passage as a whole may have a meaning, while its component words are practically meaningless" (1967, 319). Here, prefiguring Jerome Littlefield in *The Disorderly Orderly* (1964), Morty is infected by his confounding environment, and his symptom reveals his world. At Paramutual—as presumably at countless other complex bureaucracies—the capitalization of craft production has led to more people bound by fewer relationships, more limited and precisely defined jobs, fewer responsibilities per person, more limited and controllable interaction, economic rationalization, alienation of creative people from their labor, and panoptical measurement and control. Paramutual, then, signifies a certain kind of economic arrangement: a way of organizing labor and experience. Babbling Morty, infected by these surroundings, both reflects and critiques the condition of the modern worker through his exteriorization of experience.

Language and linguistic competence are interactional, not mental, and this distinctly anti-psychological bias is faithfully reflected in Lewis's analysis and construction in *The Errand Boy*. Morty is errant because he cannot manage quickly enough to apprehend the subtleties of a new system of interaction (for every word and every phrase correctly uttered in social space is systematic), but not because he cannot in fact hear or because he cannot imagine the world acoustically. His troubles originate in his class relation to the studio in which he is trapped. That Morty's deafness is purely social; that he is in his own imagination of himself an utterly articulate, acoustically sensitive, optically focused, and artfully commanding being; and that therefore his social failures at Paramutual are indications of an inability to make capital on this deeply buried resource are the open themes of a sequence that is signal not only in the work of Jerry Lewis but also in modern film: the jazzy "Chairman of the Board" pantomime, in which at once (1) Morty is voluminously and fulsomely expressive in gesture and simulated vocalization, waving a cigar, while an invisible but diegetic band fancifully accompanies his movements point by point and phrase by phrase; and (2) Morty-speaking-his-mind-within-his-mind reveals the mind-within-a-mind to have the elaborate, variegated, and integrated structure and character of a jazz band; to be capable of precision, harmony, phrasing, modulating tonality—all the qualities of both music and sophisticated language. Morty can talk, but the studio scene is dumbing him.[9]

Morty's continual disempowerment, foiled in situation after situation by the overweening and capricious power of either studio executives (who have "made" him by the end of the film) or co-opted employees working the system to further their own security, serves a function here beyond setting the comedian up for contexted pratfalls. It illuminates the brutal and exigent character of the studio system, where a production apparatus touts itself as glamorous while constituting a pervasive and unyielding field of pressure for profit on every scale, and where, as Karl Marx said of such organizations, "we have demonstrated that the worker is degraded to the most miserable sort of commodity; that the misery of the worker is in inverse proportion to the power and size of his production" (1971, 133). Only toward profitability can the goal of efficiency be framed as a value. So Morty, humble and hopeful, is operating out of his own class-bound need in trying to find a life for himself at the studio and being embedded in the executives' machinations to evaluate production efficiency, itself the inner mechanism of class differentiation in this place. The powerful are those who demand efficiency of others and who are in a position to measure them, in somewhat the same way as that for John Berger (1972, 45–64), Sol Worth and John Adair (1975, 244–248), and Mulvey, the powerful are those who demand that others be visible and who are in a position to benefit from seeing them. The studio as bureaucracy is a complex mechanism for regulating daily production activity through constant observation, measurement, and calculation. The top brass want a secret spy, an estimator who is camouflaged; but in the end, what ruins production after production on this lot, far from the wastrel nature of the denizens of Hollywood who work here, is the studio's own secret spy. Morty causes more disruption of film shooting than any other character we see. So our final view of Paramutual shows a place where the senior executives themselves unknowingly sabotage their own operation by trying too relentlessly and too dishonestly to count the pennies being expended on it. But this critical view has been fashioned by Lewis—indeed, it is Lewis's view.

In making this beautifully articulated film about being cut off from honest and serious participation in the social scene (what Paul Goodman called "community" [1972]), Lewis comments on exclusion and alienation in relation to social value. Morty is locked out of genuine participation in the world he is observing for his superiors and thus stands as a figuration of the bureaucratic personality. *The Errand Boy* can be seen as a statement about exclusion, its inherent comedy—that is, the persistent cues to which we may respond by laughing—an index of our presumed superiority to Morty and safety from the powerlessness with which he must repeatedly contend. Exclusion was, at the time this film was made, a central concern of Jerry Lewis's. Indeed, it is difficult to read his later recollections of his gradual alienation from and final split with Dean Martin, or for that matter the quality and narrative content of his solo films, without sensing that the "nuttiness" of his stage persona was gradually shifting from the nominal weirdness of an eccentric neurotic coupled with (shackled to) Dean Martin's conventionality to an entirely different kind of isolation, an existential singularity and essential unrelatedness, a man enisled. The disassociated person, while he can conceive of the social and recognize the importance of social bonds in which he does not participate, is linguistically separated too— apparently monomaniacal in speech, like Morty. If the name games described above hint at Morty's alienation by suggesting the importance of correct articulation and how it can spectacularly go wrong, scenes written to invoke other linguistic competencies provide us with even more evidence. Let us begin with silence.

Any social organization reveals both sacred and profane nodes, arrangements that are taken as commonplace and vulgar and others in which the highest values of the group and activity are materially embodied, represented, and made vulnerable. From a purely linguistic point of view, we may examine situations in which respectful silence is called for, since in these it is frequently true both that speech or noise may disrupt engagements and that engagements so disrupted are considered to be central resources. Morty's "loudness" and verbal "explosiveness" in the typing pool is a good example and reveals as well Lewis's ability at precise staging of dramatically relevant action. Entering the studio typing pool to make a delivery of script additions, Morty is confronted by some twenty secretaries, each at her own desk, and all working mum against the echoing crackle of their machines. What Morty learns (and we along with him) as he moves from desk to desk, interrupting one secretary after another, is something of the structure of the scripting process in a major Hollywood studio: (1) that scripts for numerous films are typed simultaneously, this revealing something of the economic logic of producing many motion pictures at the same time in the same physical space and thus using the real estate to its fullest efficiency. But (2) the script is also a property exploited intensively.[10] Differently colored pages are used by the typists for different drafts of the scenes being typed, so that it is possible in reading a shooting script to have a visual record (through the coding of page colors) of the number of drafts various scenes have undergone—this being a strategy for keeping records of the labor of writers hired onto a picture and so a panoptical exercise in its own right, though Morty is unaware of it. (3) The various scripts and various draft stages are managed through an intense division of labor in the typing pool, different typists handling different projects and also different colored pages—another example of the extreme complexity of the production process evident by the late 1950s, which yielded efficiency at the cost of the alienation of labor. From the worker's point of view, no one person has typed a single movie script. Finally (4), the work of all the typists must be coordinated and integrated, so that the work of one does not pollute the work of another. It is precisely this system that Morty manages to explode, by causing the pages from all the secretaries to become intercalated with one another in an entropic mess. Here, then, the inability to recognize an appropriate moment for delicate silence reveals Morty's disconnection from—ignorance of—a vital aspect of studio integration and threatens that integration in a practical way. In the diegetic studio Morty has just compromised, it will be days before the various scripts can be reassembled correctly. In 1960, a day of studio production time on even one film was worth a small fortune.

In the dubbing-room scene, Morty reveals ignorance of the capital basis of film language itself. The "problem" here, diegetically, is that he destroys the synch sound overdub for a musical number during a lunch break when he finds himself alone at a mixing board in the dubbing studio. While the comedic effect of this scene—drawn to its climax only in the adjacent "rushes" scene, where the director and producer are watching the edited clips—depends on our grasping that a "creative" input from Morty has been inept and misplaced, in short that his voice isn't up to snuff for dubbing, Lewis carefully structures the scene to demonstrate normal studio procedure with respect to expensive capital equipment, in this case the mixing board. The problem for Paramutual is hardly only that Morty has a strange voice when he sings the dub track and that a few clips will therefore need to be redubbed but that a stranger with no technical expertise has gained access to the technology of voicing, to a restricted area in which elaborate equipment—part of the capital structure of the studio—is housed under the supervision of highly skilled experts. In a purely technical sense, the studio is an agglomeration of physical and technical resources. The sound dubbers who can stitch together disparate pieces of film through a proper mix[11] are workers and also assets themselves, part of the capital of the studio, their knowledge wedded to the equipment by means of which they bring it into play. The equipment, indeed, is theirs to play with, through a rigid scheme of assignation, but now it has been appropriated. Morty has taken to himself—but without know-how—the organizational voice.

Morty's ignorant aggression here also consists of a vigorous destabilization of the contrived unity between the exchange and use value of an actor's labor. The studio effects that unity as an address to—and negation of—contradictions inherent in the production relation, whereby actors who dub and actors who are dubbed have both a recognizable (often celebrated) face in a particular marketplace and at the same time a set of capabilities the studio managers can avidly (and unceremoniously) milk, and whereby each actor is consigned to be, in Barry King's term, the "bearer of effects that he or she does not or cannot originate" (quoted in Clark 1995, 22). Here the dubbable soundstage performance and the dub that will cover it, taken as separate constructive elements, are laid on and overlayered systematically—not arbitrarily, by the employees' goodwill—utilizing what Goffman might have called the "animative" capacities of the performer (1981): the use value.

The apparently homogeneous characterization ultimately assembled is a coherent (exchange) value for the audience, a nugget of entertainment. By tampering with the dub, Morty opens the screen characterization (tested for us and for the production personnel in the showing of the dailies) to fragmentation and dissolution. The entertainment or exchange value dissipates, and the use value of the actors is debased. When he finishes, not only are the actors not precisely in touch with their own performances, but the studio personnel responsible for producing those performances through use of those actor-resources have lost control too. Because labor in a Hollywood studio like Paramutual is strictly unionized and sound mixing boards are manned by sound engineers only, union agreements are also violated, to the studio's legal peril. Through his agent Morty, Jerry Lewis has constructed onscreen what Stuart Hall has termed "one of those moments when the equilibrium of consent is disturbed . . . when the whole basis of political leadership and cultural authority becomes exposed and contested" (quoted in Clark 1995, 38).

The swimming-pool scene is a handy exemplification of Morty's overall detachment from studio life in the face of an intense physical involvement there, his alienation, as it were, from the labor process in which he is a committed participant. It is also a profoundly comic moment, unique, as far as I can tell, in that it seems unrelated to any of the six categories of visual gag that Noël Carroll presents (1991, 28–38) and also in that its punch line has the merit of seeming, at the moment of its delivery, entirely self-evident in both the conclusion of the gag and the gag's pretext in the scene. Morty approaches a swimming pool, rigged on one side with a wooden dolly track extended along a plank over the water, and he sees a scuba diver jumping in. He steps onto the track to try to see the diver (pretending to be a camera), "dollying" closer and closer to the water. We are certain that because he is looking at the water and not the plank rapidly disappearing under his feet, he will fall in. Suddenly we are underwater, where the diver is placidly preparing some equipment at the bottom of the pool. Morty casually enters the shot, swimming calmly toward the diver, then around him, then back and forth across the screen. He approaches the diver, who stares at him and writes on a huge underwater pad, "HOW COME I NEED ALL THIS UNDERWATER STUFF, TO STAY DOWN HERE, AND YOU DON'T NEED ANY?" Morty takes the pad, rubs off the diver's question with his sleeve, and patiently writes, "I'M <u>DROWNING!</u> HELP!"

This scene contains both a joke and a twist. The joke is Morty's ineffable ability to maintain a relaxed bodily attitude, patiently waiting through the diver's plodding inscription of his question then patiently reading it and erasing it before composing an answer that will reveal him in mortal distress. Here Lewis has constructed a violation of what Kenneth Burke calls the act:purpose ratio (1969), which would conventionally call for a desperate message of this sort to be sent by means of an articulation that was itself desperate, urgent, even fanatical in its strain. The calmness prepares us for any sort of answer but the one we receive, and the surprise of it is interpretable as funny. The twist in the scene is that the diver, a regular operative of the studio and thus a familiar to the territory, takes Morty at face value as a hero who must possess special survival qualities, not a fool pathetically lacking them who is "drowning" in his airless environment. How could Morty be anything *but* desperate? Implicit in the diver's question is high regard for anyone who can swim around without oxygen like a prodigy, *and this is precisely the regard the studio assists the performer in rousing in the willing public.* It is a view Tashman is generally undermining by dismantling the studio operation from within, and one Jerry Lewis is systematically calling into question by choreographing Tashman. In fact, the exchange value for the audience of the performer as glamorous presence is constructed at the price of a use value of the performer to the studio, one that submerges him and makes his struggle to express his condition a desperate one.

I want to take a second look at Morty as lacking in order to say something about how this film can be seen as an address to the claim, put forward by radical feminist psychoanalytical critics, about plenitude being a projection of anxious males and about female "lack" being a primary unconscious structure of patriarchy. Such a critique would purport Morty to be *feminized* in his weak vocality and suggest that at the end of the film, as he achieves stardom and finally cruises through the studio in his own limousine, he has finally become—"learned to swim as"—a man. But feminization as victimization is a cipher that can be found without regard to the features of a particular film, as though the culture blind-stamps all cultural artifacts in the same way. Mulvey herself claims the problem is everywhere in Hollywood culture (1990).

But I argue such a view ultimately reveals a blind spot. More is to be learned by looking at how films vary. How does *The Errand Boy* differ substantially, as a tale of "lack" redeemed, from the other films Lewis made around the same time?

In all his solo films since 1957, Jerry's character is deficient—he lacks skill, cultural knowledge, grace, dignity, tactical acumen; even, in *The Bellboy* (1960), words themselves. In nine films made between the breakup with Dean Martin in July 1956 and 1961, Lewis's characters show the same verbal eccentricities as does Morty S. Tashman, threatening through their manner of making or twisting words to disintegrate the narrative world in a persistent, "comic" way. Partly as a result of these films, indeed, Lewis's audience had stylistic expectations of him: that he would initiate but fail to complete sentences, that his syllables would intermingle, that his vocal tone would modulate out of control from register to register, that his vocabulary would become both inventive and unrecognizable in antics Scott Bukatman has referred to as "pirouettes around tropes of broken syntax, shifting tonalities and free-association" (1991, 193) and Dana Polan has called "derailing" (1984, 46). If the ability to articulate is analogous in any way to the empowering gaze, Jerry Lewis's characters would be without power because linguistically maimed.

*The Errand Boy* is distinctive, however, precisely in its self-reflexivity. The film is set outside the precincts of everyday society, within the confines of a tightly organized production facility, a world where language is far from simply the medium of expression by means of which characters make their positions, feelings, alignments, and plans known to one another to some degree. In the film studio, language is the preeminent stuff of production, both the *materiel* of the shooting script around which production is organized and a resource controlled and exploited by the ownership through marshaling and measurement of the workers. Ultimately, in virtually all the disintegrations comically produced in this film, some lack or fracture of a purely linguistic kind structures the filmic scene and indexes the aspect of studio production that makes such a scene possible.

Setting *The Errand Boy* in a studio when an errand boy/spy could have figured in dozens of settings, much as Lewis's other characters had, brings to the surface a suggestion that Morty Tashman's lack has nothing to do with gender and everything to do with the mechanics of social production and social class. He is not a feminized weakling who gains independence and masculinity when he becomes a star, because in a film studio, where language is preeminent, deficiencies of the tongue invoke class—not gender—distinction. Speaking wrong threatens the system and leads to the measuring—not the ogling—gaze of the boss. The central variation in the film is not sexual but material, so that the characters are differentiated one from another on the basis of their access to the resources and means of production. Morty's "lack" is therefore quite a different one, with different consequences, than the lack Mulvey generalizes as central to the unconscious of our culture.

Richard Dyer suggests that stars (such as Jerry Lewis and, one might add, Morty Tashman by the end of this film) "serve to mask people's awareness of themselves as class members" and are "ideologically significant in the most general sense of cutting audiences off from politics, rendering them passive" (1999, 27). However, the defusing of political meaning produced by stars is obviated in this film by means of the specific self-referentiality conjured through the setting of the action. Lewis here offers one of the most complex readings of the social world to be found in his work (or in any studio narratives of the time) and a signally complex reading of his own persona as filmmaker as well. The counterhegemonic authorial stance that leads him to frame the story of a linguistic bumbler in—of all places—a film studio opens for us the possibility to see that studio in full exploitative swing as a site of capitalism. In that context, the boy who runs errands is, more than merely a male, a person who is powerless (nor need one lack a penis to experience this condition). Whether or not female "lack" is a fundamental organizational principle in our society, capitalism surely is, and the lack of power is all around us. While some critics would suggest with Mulvey that masculinity is a force that structures culture and power a reflection of masculinity, *The Errand Boy* suggests the reverse: that "masculinity" is an attribution of power and that our use of the label "male" is a production itself, not the natural outcome of an intrinsic force. Hortense Powdermaker noted, for instance, that "in a major studio a handsome star is colloquially referred to as 'the penis'" (1950, 207), that epigram being applied by and through the studio process rather than emerging spontaneously from some "essential" masculinity inherent in the actor so named. In *Errand Boy*, Morty's "failure in masculinity" is a reflection of his travails and troubles in the studio working environment and no statement about who he "deeply" is. How perfect, therefore, that Morty should be a screen character, with no "depth."

That the studio environment—a model of capitalist society—is far from a utopia, *The Errand Boy* reminds us persistently, as we listen to Morty not fitting in as any proper employee should. The Jerry Lewis who constructed him arranged carefully for that bad fit and used his prodigious talents to cultivate it, with some real awareness of the damage hierarchical social arrangements could do in the prevailing economic conditions of the time. In the face of the kind of disenfranchisement shown so clearly in *The Errand Boy*, indeed, the idea of society as a sanctuary is only a dream. Jerry Lewis said as much himself, speaking to *Cahiers du Cinéma* in 1966 (Madsen 1966, 31; my translation): "One can talk about society, but in fact absolutely everyone is excluded."

## NOTES

1. I am deeply grateful to Kathleen Kellett-Betsos *pour l'assistance linguale* and to David Desser, C. T. Gillin, Barbara Klinger, and Nellie Perret for responding to various drafts of the manuscript.

2. See, for example, Guattari 1981; Mulvey 1990; Lehman 1993; and Kaplan 1997.

3. The voice described by Chion is dismissed by Kaja Silverman as a "symptom of male paranoia and castration" (1988, 73).

4. What I am calling music and verdict are analogous to Kracauer's "anonymous" and "recognizable" noises:

> Sounds—this term meaning exclusively noises here—can be arranged along a continuum which extends from unidentifiable to recognizable noises. As for the former, think of certain noises in the night: they are, so to speak, anonymous; you have no idea where they come from. At the opposite pole are sounds whose source is known to us, whether we see it or not. In everyday life, when we hear barking, we immediately realize that a dog must be around; and as a rule we do not go wrong in associating church bells with the sound of chimes.

See Siegfried Kracauer, "Dialogue and Sound," in Belton and Weis 1985.

5. This theme was elaborated by Harold Garfinkel in "Studies in the Routine Grounds of Everyday Activities" (1967).

6. For further elaboration of Lewis's vocalization, see Peter Lehman and Susan Hunt, "'The Inner Man': Mind, Body, and Transformations of Masculinity in *The Nutty Professor*," chapter 13 in this book.

7. For a considerably more elaborate analysis of the unfamiliar and uncontrolled situation, see Goffman 1971, especially 248–256.

8. One of Lewis's closest contacts was with Y. Frank Freeman, who hailed from Georgia but who was still a member of the East Coast cultural elite.

9. Lewis explained in a seminar in Toronto in May 2001 that the origin of this scene was a mime piece he was working on for an orchestration with a symphony for his ABC television show; he got the idea to speak the instruments verbally in pantomime. I am grateful to Chuck Hsuen for the account of this seminar.

10. For an elaborate analysis of the role of the shooting script in organizing studio production, see Janet Staiger, "The Central Producer System after 1914," in Bordwell, Staiger, and Thompson 1985, 137–139.

11. John Belton writes,

Contrary to André Bazin's idealist notions of the history of technology and of cinematic forms, their evolution is not natural but "cultural," responding to the pressures of ideology. These pressures suppress signs of technique and technology. For Jean-Louis Baudry, the technological apparatus of the cinema, i.e., the camera, transforms what is set before it but conceals the work of that transformation by effacing all traces of it. Thus the basic apparatus reflects the actions of bourgeois ideology in general, which seeks to mask its operations and to present as "natural" that which is a product of ideology.

Recent studies of film sound by Rick Altman and Mary Ann Doane extend this argument to the study of the evolution of sound technology, viewing it as an ideologically determined progression toward self-effacement. For Altman, technological innovations "derive from a felt need to reduce all traces of the sound-work from the sound track."

(Belton and Weis 1985, 63).

# Works Cited

Altman, Rick. 1989. *The American Film Musical*. Bloomington: Indiana University Press.

Anonymous. 1965. "The Disorderly Orderly" (review). *Times* (London), January 7, 17.

Ansen, David. 1981. Review of *Hardly Working*. *Newsweek*, April 27, 90.

Aumont, Jacques, Jean-Louis Comolli, André S. Labarthe, Jean Narboni, and Sylvie Pierre. 1973. "A Concise Lexicon of Lewisian Terms." In Claire Johnson and Paul Willemen, eds., *Frank Tashlin*, 89–115. Edinburgh: Edinburgh Film Festival.

Barclay, Brian James. 1999. Viewer's review. International Movie Data Base page on *Arizona Dream*, January 5. Available at http://www.us.imdb.com /search.html.

Barol, Bill. 1987. "I Stayed Up with Jerry." *Newsweek*, September 21, 66–68.

Barthes, Roland. 1977. "The Grain of the Voice." In Stephen Heath, ed. and trans., *Image/Music/Text*, 179–189. New York: Hill and Wang.

Belton, John, and Elisabeth Weis, eds. 1985. *Film Sound: Theory and Practice*. New York: Columbia University Press.

Benayoun, Robert. 1972. *Bonjour Monsieur Lewis*. Paris: Eric Losfeld.

Bennetts, Leslie. 1993. "Jerry vs. the Kids." *Vanity Fair*, September, 26–37.

Berger, John. 1972. *Ways of Seeing*. London: BBC.

Bernstein, Basil. 1972. "A Sociolinguistic Approach to Socialization; with Some Reference to Educability." In John J. Gumperz and Dell Hymes, eds., *Directions in Sociolinguistics: The Ethnography of Communication*, 465–497. New York: Holt, Rinehart and Winston.

Bérubé, Allan. 1990. *Coming Out under Fire: The History of Gay Men and Women in World War Two*. New York: Free Press/Macmillan.

Bogdanovich, Peter. 1973. "Frank Tashlin: An Interview and an Appreciation." In Claire Johnston and Paul Willemen, eds., *Frank Tashlin*, 55–61, 63–88. Edinburgh: Edinburgh Film Festival.

———. 2002. "And for Best Idea by a Star: Jerry Lewis." *New York Times*, March 10, sec. 2, 3.

Bordwell, David, Janet Staiger, and Kristin Thompson. 1985. *The Classical Holly-wood Cinema: Film Style and Mode of Production to 1960.* New York: Columbia University Press.

Boyarin, Daniel. 1997. *Unheroic Conduct: The Rise of Heterosexuality and the Invention of the Jewish Man.* Berkeley: University of California Press.

Brecht, Stefan. 1997. "The Sheer Beauty of Junk." In Edward Leffingwell, Carole Kismaric, and Marvin Heiferman, eds., *Flaming Creature: Jack Smith: His Amazing Life and Times*, 43. New York: The Institute for Contemporary Art, P.S. 1 Museum and Serpents Tail.

Bukatman, Scott. 1991. "Paralysis in Motion: Jerry Lewis's Life as a Man." In Andrew S. Horton, ed., *Comedy/Cinema/Theory*, 188–205. Berkeley: University of California Press.

———. 1993. *Terminal Identity: The Virtual Subject in Postmodern Science Fiction.* Durham, NC: Duke University Press.

Burke, Ken. 2000. "Martin and Lewis on the Colgate Comedy Hour." *Roctober Magazine* 29. Available at http://roctober.com/roctober/greatness/martinlewis.html.

Burke, Kenneth. 1969. *A Grammar of Motives.* Berkeley: University of California Press.

Capp, Al. 1961. Review of *The Ladies Man. Los Angeles Times,* June 12, 34.

Carringer, Robert L., ed. 1979. *The Jazz Singer.* Wisconsin/Warner Bros. Screenplay Series. Madison: University of Wisconsin Press.

Carroll, Noël. 1991. "Notes on the Sight Gag." In Andrew Horton, ed., *Comedy/Cinema/Theory*, 25–42. Berkeley: University of California Press.

———. 1998. "Buster Keaton, the General, and Visible Intelligibility." In *Interpreting the Moving Image*, 64–79. Cambridge: Cambridge University Press.

Cavell, Stanley. 1988. *Themes Out of School: Effects and Causes.* Chicago: University of Chicago Press.

Chervet, Bernard. 1996. "Cycle de la latence, clivage du moi et conversion mystique." *Revue Française de la Psychanalyse* 60: 1585–1596.

Chion, Michel. 1982. *La voix au cinéma.* Paris: Éditions de L'Étoile.

Clark, Danae. 1995. *Negotiating Hollywood: The Cultural Politics of Actors' Labor.* Minneapolis: University of Minnesota Press.

Cohan, Steve. 1999. "Queering the Deal: On the Road with Hope and Crosby." In Ellis Hanson, ed., *Out Takes: Essays on Queer Theory and Film*, 23–45. Durham, NC: Duke University Press.

Cohen, Albert K. 1955. *Delinquent Boys: The Culture of the Gang.* Glencoe, IL: Free Press.

Cooley, Mason. 1986. *City Aphorisms.* 3d selection. New York. Cited in *Bartlett's Familiar Quotations*, online at http://Bartleby.com.

Coursodon, Jean-Pierre. 1975. "Jerry Lewis's Films: No Laughing Matter?" *Film Comment* 11, 4 (July–August): 9–15.

Crafton, Donald. 1999. *The Talkies: American Cinema's Transition to Sound 1926–1931*. Berkeley: University of California Press.

Cremonini, Giorgio. 1980. *Jerry Lewis: Il castoro cinema in nuovo Italia*. Città di Castello: Delta Grafica.

Crowther, Bosley. 1953. Review of *The Stooge*. *New York Times*, November 13, 40.

———. 1954. "Money from Home" (review). *New York Times*, February 27, 11.

———. 1964. "Screen: A Lewis Farce." *New York Times*, August 13, 24.

Davidson, Bill. 1951. "Anything for a Laugh," *Colliers*, February 10, 30–31, 65.

Debord, Guy. 1983, originally published in 1964. *Society of the Spectacle*. Detroit: Black & Red.

Deleuze, Gilles. 1986. *Cinema 1: The Movement-Image*. Translated by Hugh Tomlinson and Barbara Habberjam. Minneapolis: University of Minnesota Press.

———. *Cinema 2: The Time-Image*. Translated by Hugh Tomlinson and Robert Galeta. Minneapolis: University of Minnesota Press.

Doherty, Thomas. 1988. *Teenagers and Teenpics: The Juvenilization of American Movies in the 1950s*. Boston: Unwin Hyman.

Durgnat, Raymond. 1963. "The Nutty Professor," *Films and Filming* 10, 1 (October).

———. 1970. *The Crazy Mirror: Hollywood Comedy and the American Image*. New York: Dell.

Dyer, Richard. 1982. "Don't Look Now: The Male Pin-Up." *Screen* 23, 3–4: 61–73.

———. 1999. *Stars*. New ed. London: British Film Institute.

Elsaesser, Thomas. 1996. *Fassbinder's Germany: History, Identity, Subject*. Amsterdam: Amsterdam University Press.

Empson, William. 1967. *The Structure of Complex Words*. Ann Arbor: University of Michigan Press.

Eyman, Scott. 1997. *The Speed of Sound: Hollywood and the Talkie Revolution, 1926–1930*. Baltimore: Johns Hopkins University Press.

Farson, Daniel. 1952. "They Made Me a Myth: Funny Men Dean Martin and Jerry Lewis." *Sight and Sound* 22, 1 (July–September): 30–31.

Foucault, Michel. 1998 (1965). *Madness and Civilization*. Translated by Richard Howard. New York: Vintage.

Freud, Sigmund. 1930. *Civilization and Its Discontents* Translated by Jean Riviere. New York: J. Caret & H. Smith.

———. 1960 (1928). *Jokes and Their Relation to the Unconscious*. Translated by James Strachey. London: Routledge & Kegan Paul.

Fuller, Graham. 1993. "Thank You Jerry Much." *Interview* (April): 92–93, 115.

Gabbard, Krin. 1996. *Jammin' at the Margins: Jazz and the American Cinema*. Chicago: University of Chicago Press.

Gansera, Rainer. 1974. "Jerry Lewis: Films for Fun," *Filmkritik* xviii, 4: 145–185.

Garfinkel, Harold. 1967. "Studies in the Routine Grounds of Everyday Activities." In *Studies in Ethnomethodology*, 35–75. Englewood Cliffs, NJ: Prentice-Hall.

Gehman, Richard. 1964. *That Kid: The Story of Jerry Lewis*. New York: Avon.

Goffman, Erving. 1971. *Relations in Public*. New York: Harper and Row.

———. 1979. *Gender Advertisements*. New York: Harper and Row.

———. 1981. *Forms of Talk*. Philadelphia: University of Pennsylvania Press.

Goodman, Paul. 1972. *Speaking and Language: Defence of Poetry*. New York: Random House.

Gorbman, Claudia. 1997. *Unheard Melodies: Narrative Film Music*. Bloomington: Indiana University Press.

Gordon, Rae Beth. 2001a. *Why the French Love Jerry Lewis*. Palo Alto: Stanford University Press.

———. 2001b. "From Charcot to Charlot: Unconscious Imitation and Spectatorship in French Cabaret and Early Cinema." *Critical Inquiry* 27 (Spring): 514–549.

Greenberg, Clement. 1986. "Avant-Garde and Kitsch" (1939). In John O'Brian, ed., *Clement Greenberg, the Collected Essays and Criticism*, vol. 1: *Perceptions and Judgments, 1939–1944*, 5–22. Chicago: University of Chicago Press.

Guattari, Félix. 1981. "Becoming-Woman." *Semiotext(e)* 4, 1: 86–88.

Haller, Beth. 1994. "The Misfit and Muscular Dystrophy." *Journal of Popular Film and Television* 21, 4: 142–150.

Hoberman, J. 1991. "The Show Biz Messiah." In *Vulgar Modernism: Writing on Movies and Other Media*, 64–68. Philadelphia: Temple University Press.

Horton, Andrew. 1988. "Oedipus Unresolved: Covert and Overt Narrative Discourse in Emir Kusturica's *When Father Was Away on Business*." *Cinema Journal* 27, 4 (Summer): 64–81.

———. 1998. "Cinematic Makeovers and Cultural Border Crossings: Kusturica's *Time of the Gypsies* and Coppola's *Godfather* and *Godfather II*." In Andrew Horton and Stuart Y. McDougal, eds., *Play It Again, Sam: Retakes on Remakes*, 172–190. Berkeley: University of California Press.

———. 1999. "But to Have Dreamed It All: The Balkan's Healing Irony." *Chronicle of Higher Education*, July 2, B-11.

———. 2000. *Laughing Out Loud: Writing the Comedy Centered Screenplay*. Berkeley: University of California Press.

———, ed. 1991. *Comedy/Cinema/Theory*. Berkeley: University of California Press.

Horton, Andrew, and Michael Brashinsky. 1992. *The Zero Hour: Glasnost and Soviet Cinema in Transition*. Princeton: Princeton University Press.

Hugo, Victor. 1889. *The Man Who Laughs*, Illustrated Cabinet Edition. Vol. 1. Boston: Dana Estes & Co.

Hymes, Dell. 1974. *Foundations in Sociolinguistics: An Ethnographic Approach.* Philadelphia: University of Pennsylvania Press.

Iordanova, Dina. 2001. *Cinema of Flames: Balkan Film, Culture and the Media.* London: BFI.

JAS Productions Inc. 1992a. *Martin and Lewis: Their Golden Age of Comedy.* Part 1: "The Birth of the Team." First broadcast on the Disney Channel.

———. 1992b. *Martin and Lewis: Their Golden Age of Comedy.* Part 2: "The Kings of Comedy." First broadcast on the Disney Channel.

Jay, Martin. 1994. *Downcast Eyes: The Denigration of Vision in Twentieth-Century French Thought.* Berkeley: University of California Press.

Johnson, Mary. 1992. "Jerry's Kids." *The Nation* 255, 7, September 14, 232–234.

Kakutani, Michiko. 1999. "Scorsese's Past Colors His New Film." In Peter Brunette, ed., *Martin Scorsese: Interviews,* 100–105. Jackson: University Press of Mississippi.

Kaplan, E. Ann. 1997. *Looking for the Other: Feminism, Film, and the Imperial Gaze.* New York: Routledge.

Kaplan, James. 2000. "The Laughing Game." *New Yorker,* February 7, 52–63.

Kass, Robert. 1953. "Jerry Lewis Analyzed." *Films in Review* 4, 3: 119–123.

Kelly, Kevin. 1977. Review of *Hellzapoppin'. Boston Globe,* January 16, 68.

Kelly, Mary Pat. 1991. *Martin Scorsese: A Journey.* New York: Thunder's Mouth Press.

Koestenbaum, Wayne. 1993. *The Queen's Throat: Opera, Homosexuality, and the Mystery of Desire.* New York: Poseidon.

Kozarski, Richard. 1977. *Hollywood Directors, 1941–1976.* New York: Oxford University Press.

Krutnik, Frank. 1994. "Jerry Lewis: The Deformation of the Comic." *Film Quarterly* 48, 1 (Fall): 12–26.

———. 1995. "The Handsome Man and His Monkey: The Comic Bondage of Dean Martin and Jerry Lewis." *Journal of Popular Film and Television* 23, 1 (Spring): 6–26.

———. 2000. *Inventing Jerry Lewis.* Washington, DC: Smithsonian Institution Press.

Krutnik, Frank, and Steve Neale. 1990. *Popular Film and Television Comedy.* London: Routledge.

Leffingwell, Edward, Carole Kismaric, and Marvin Heiferman, eds. 1977. *Flaming Creature: Jack Smith: His Amazing Life and Times.* New York: The Institute for Contemporary Art, P.S. 1 Museum and Serpents Tail.

Legman, Gershon. 1982. *No Laughing Matter: Rationale of the Dirty Joke.* 2d series. New York: Breaking Point. Reprint, London: Hart-Davis McGibbon, 1978; Bloomington: Indiana University Press, 1982.

Lehman, Peter. 1993. *Running Scared: Masculinity and the Representation of the Male Body.* Philadelphia: Temple University Press.

Lehman, Peter, and Susan Hunt. 1999. "'Something and Someone Else': The Mind, the Body, and Sexuality in *Titanic*." In Kevin S. Sandler and Gaylyn Studlar, eds., *Titanic: Anatomy of a Blockbuster*, 89–108. New Brunswick: Rutgers University Press.

Levine, Joseph. 1961. "Regression in Primitive Clowning." *Psychoanalytic Quarterly* 30: 72–83.

Levy, Shawn. 1996. *King of Comedy: The Life and Art of Jerry Lewis*. New York: St. Martin's Press.

———. 1998. *Rat Pack Confidential: Frank, Dean, Sammy, Peter, and the Last Great Showbiz Party*. New York: Doubleday.

Lewis, Jerry. 1973. *The Total Film-Maker*. New York: Warners Paperback Library.

Lewis, Jerry, with Herb Gluck. 1982. *Jerry Lewis in Person*. New York: Atheneum.

Lewis, Jon. 1992. *The Road to Romance and Ruin: Teen Films and Youth Culture*. New York: Routledge.

Liebman, Robert Leslie. 1984. "Rabbis or Rakes, Schlemiels or Supermen? Jewish Identity in Charles Chaplin, Jerry Lewis and Woody Allen." *Literature/Film Quarterly* 12, 3 (July): 195–201.

Lloyd, Ann, ed. 1982. *Movies of the Fifties*. London: Orbis.

Lott, Eric. 1993. *Love and Theft: Blackface Minstrelsy and the American Working Class*. New York: Oxford University Press.

Luhr, William. 1978. "Victorian Novels on Film." Unpublished Ph.D. diss., New York University.

Luhr, William, and Peter Lehman. 1977. *Authorship and Narrative in the Cinema: Issues in Contemporary Aesthetics and Criticism*. New York: G. P. Putnam's Sons.

MacDonald, Scott. 1998. "Ken and Flo Jacobs." In *A Critical Cinema 3: Interviews with Independent Filmmakers*. Berkeley: University of California Press.

Madsen, Axel. 1966. "L'oncle d'Amérique: Entretien avec Jerry Lewis." *Cahiers du Cinéma* 175 (February): 30–34.

Maltin, Leonard. 1999. *Movie and Video Guide 2000*. New York: Signet.

———. 2000. *Leonard Maltin's 2001 Movie and Video Guide*. New York: Signet.

Marchesini, Mauro. 1983. *Un comico a perdire*. Verona: Mazziana.

Marchetti, Gina. 1993. *Romance and the "Yellow Peril": Race, Sex and Discourse Strategies in Hollywood Fiction*. Berkeley: University of California Press.

Marling, Karal Ann. 1994. *As Seen on TV: The Visual Culture of Everyday Life in the 1950s*. Cambridge, Mass.: Harvard University Press.

Marx, Arthur. 1974. *Everybody Loves Somebody Sometime (Especially Himself): The Story of Dean Martin and Jerry Lewis*. London: W. H. Allen.

Marx, Karl. 1971. *The Early Texts*. Edited by David McLellan. New York: Oxford University Press.

Mast, Gerald. 1973. *The Comic Mind: Comedy and the Movies*. Indianapolis: Bobbs-Merrill. Reprinted 1979, Chicago: University of Chicago Press.

McConnell, Frank. 1975. *The Spoken Seen: Film and the Romantic Imagination*. Baltimore: Johns Hopkins University Press.

McLuhan, Marshall. 1964. *Understanding Media: The Extensions of Man*. New York: New American Library.

McLuhan, Marshall, and Quentin Fiore. 1967. *The Medium Is the Massage*. New York: Random House.

———. 1968. *War and Peace in the Global Village: An Inventory of Some of the Current Spastic Situations That Could Be Eliminated by More Feedforward*. New York: McGraw-Hill.

Miller, Mark Crispin. 1988. *Boxed In: The Culture of TV*. Evanston: Northwestern University Press.

Moorhouse, H. F. 1999. "The 'Work' Ethic and 'Leisure' Activity: The Hot Rod in Post-War America." In Lawrence B. Glickman, ed., *Consumer Society in American History: A Reader*, 277–297. Ithaca: Cornell University Press.

More, Ellen Singer, and Maureen A. Milligan, eds. 1994. *The Empathetic Practitioner: Empathy, Gender and Medicine*. New Brunswick, NJ: Rutgers University Press.

Mulvey, Laura. 1990. "Visual Pleasure and Narrative Cinema." In Patricia Erens, ed., *Issues in Feminist Film Criticism*, 28–40. Bloomington: Indiana University Press.

Neibaur, James L., and Ted Okuda. 1995. *The Jerry Lewis Films: An Analytical Filmography of the Innovative Comic*. Jefferson, NC: McFarland.

Passport Video. 1990. *Young Jerry Lewis*.

Polan, Dana. 1984. "Being and Nuttiness: Jerry Lewis and the French." *Journal of Popular Film and Television* 12, 1: 42–46.

Posner, Michael. 2000. "The Day the Clown Bombed." *Globe and Mail*, February 19, R1ff.

Powdermaker, Hortense. 1950. *Hollywood the Dream Factory: An Anthropologist Looks at the Movie-Makers*. Boston: Little, Brown.

Prince, Stephen. 1999. *A New Pot of Gold: Hollywood under the Electronic Rainbow, 1980–89*. New York: Scribner's.

Ray, Robert B. 1985. *A Certain Tendency of the Hollywood Cinema, 1930–1980*. Princeton: Princeton University Press.

Recasens, Gérard. 1970. *Jerry Lewis, Cinéma d'aujourdhui*. Paris: Seghers.

Reynaud, Bérénice. 1989. "Qui a peur de Jerry Lewis? Pas nous, pas nous." *Cahiers du Cinéma* 416 (February): viii.

Riesman, David. 1950. *The Lonely Crowd*. New Haven: Yale University Press.

Rogin, Michael. 1996. *Blackface, White Noise: Jewish Immigrants in the Hollywood Melting Pot*. Berkeley: University of California Press.

Rosenblatt, Samuel. 1954. *Yoselle Rosenblatt: The Story of His Life as Told by His Son*. New York: Farrar, Straus and Young.

Sarris, Andrew. 1968. *The American Cinema: Directors and Directions 1929–1968*. New York: E. P. Dutton.

Schickel, Richard. 1981. Review of *Hardly Working*. *Time*, May 25, 80–81.

Schindler, Merrill. 1980. "Jerry's Revenge." *Los Angeles Magazine*, August, 25–29.

Seesslen, Georg. 1996. "Cinderfella and Big Mouth: Jerry Lewis and Dean Martin," *EPD Film* 13, 4 (April): 23–33.

Shaviro, Steven. 1993. *The Cinematic Body*. Minneapolis and London: University of Minnesota Press.

Sikov, Ed. 1994. *Laughing Hysterically: American Screen Comedy of the 1950s*. New York: Columbia University Press.

Silverman, Kaja. 1988. *The Acoustic Mirror: The Female Voice in Psychoanalysis and Cinema*. Bloomington: Indiana University Press.

Simmel, Georg. 1924. "On Visual Interaction." In Robert E. Park and Ernest W. Burgess, eds., *Introduction to the Science of Sociology*, 356–361. Chicago: University of Chicago Press.

Smith, Jack. 1997. *Wait for Me at the Bottom of the Pool: The Writings of Jack Smith*. Edited by J. Hoberman and Edward Leffingwell. New York: High Risk Books, Serpents Tail and P.S. 1.

Soapbox Productions Inc. 1996. "Jerry Lewis—the Last American Clown." Broadcast in the *Biography* series on the U.S. Arts & Entertainment network.

Sobchack, Vivian. 2001. "Thinking Through Jim Carrey." In Murray Pomerance and John Sakeris, eds., *Closely Watched Brains*, 199–213. Boston: Pearson Education.

Soulé, M. 1980. Oedipe au cirque devant le numéro de l'Auguste et du Clown blanc." *Revue Française de la Psychanalyse* 44, 1: 99–126.

Staehling, Richard. 1975. "From *Rock Around the Clock* to *The Trip*: The Truth about Teen Movies." In Todd McCarthy and Charles Flynn, eds. *Kings of the Bs: Working within the Hollywood System*, 220–251. New York: Dutton.

Tannen, Deborah. 1993. *Gender and Conversational Interaction*. New York: Oxford University Press.

———. 1994. *Gender and Discourse*. New York: Oxford University Press.

———. 1998. *The Argument Culture: Moving from Debate to Dialogue*. New York: Random House.

———. 2001. *I Only Say This because I Love You: How the Way We Talk Can Make or Break Family Relationships throughout Our Lives*. New York: Random House.

Tesson, Charles. 2001. "Jerry Lewis, cuisine et chorégraphie." *Cahiers du Cinéma* 563 (December): 37.

Thompson, David, and Ian Christie, eds. 1989. *Scorsese on Scorsese*. London: Faber & Faber.

Thompson, Howard. 1961. "*Ladies Man* Heads New Double Bill." *New York Times*, July 13, 26.

———. 1964. "New Jerry Lewis Film." *New York Times*, December 24, 8.

Thorson, James, and F. C. Powell. 1991. "Measurement of Sense of Humor." *Psychological Reports* 69: 700.

Tiger Television/BBC. 1992. *Funny Business*. Part 3: "Let There Be Love." First broadcast on BBC2, December 6.

Tosches, Nick. 1992. *Dino: Living High in the Dirty Business of Dreams*. New York: Doubleday.

Tye, Larry. 2001. "The Changing Face of Mental Illness." *Boston Globe*, April 19, 45–47.

*Variety*. 1983–1997. *Variety Film Reviews, 1907–1996*. 24 volumes. New Providence, NJ: R. R. Bowker.

Virilio, Paul. 1991. *The Lost Dimension*. Translated by Daniel Moshenberg. New York: Semiotext(e).

Weis, Elizabeth, and John Belton, eds. 1985. *Film Sound: Theory and Practice*. New York: Columbia University Press.

Wertheim, Arthur. 1992. *Radio Comedy*. New York and Oxford: Oxford University Press.

Whyte, William H. Jr. 1956. *The Organization Man*. New York: Simon and Schuster.

Wilde, Larry. 2001. *Jerry Lewis on Comedy*. CD. Laugh.com Comedy Recording Series LGH1045.

Williams, Linda. 2001. *Playing the Race Card: Melodramas of Black and White from Uncle Tom to O.J. Simpson*. Princeton: Princeton University Press.

Wolff, Craig. 2001. "Love, Loneliness and Jerry Lewis." *New York Times*, March 18, sec. 2, 1ff.

Wood, Robin. 1986. *Hollywood from Vietnam to Reagan*. New York: Columbia University Press.

Worth, Sol, and John Adair. 1975. *Through Navajo Eyes: An Exploration in Film Communication and Anthropology*. Bloomington: Indiana University Press.

# Contributors

Mikita Brottman is professor of liberal arts at the Maryland Institute College of Art. Her work deals with various kinds of cultural pathologies. She is the author of three books on the horror film, the editor of *Car Crash Culture*, and writes regularly for both academic and alternative publications.

Scott Bukatman is assistant professor of Media Studies in the Department of Art and Art History at Stanford University. He is the author of *Terminal Identity: The Virtual Subject of Postmodern Science Fiction* and *Blade Runner*, as well as of *Matters of Gravity: Special Effects and Supermen in the Twentieth Century* (forthcoming). In 1988 he curated a major retrospective of the film and television work of Jerry Lewis at the American Museum of the Moving Image in New York.

David Desser is head of the Cinema Studies Unit at the University of Illinois, Urbana-Champaign, and visiting scholar at Hong Kong Baptist University. A former editor of *Cinema Journal*, he is the author, coauthor, editor, or coeditor of numerous books, including *The Samurai Films of Akira Kurosawa, Eros Plus Massacre: An Introduction to the Japanese New Wave Cinema, American Jewish Filmmakers: Traditions and Trends, Ozu's Tokyo Story, The Cinema of Hong Kong: History, Arts, Identity*, and *Hollywood Goes Shopping*.

Leslie A. Fiedler is the Distinguished Samuel Clemens Professor of English at the State University of New York at Buffalo and an associate fellow of Calhoun College at Yale University. A recipient of the National Institute of Arts and Letters Award, he has been a Fulbright scholar, a Guggenheim fellow, and a judge for the National Book Awards. He is the author of more than twenty-five volumes, including *Love and Death in the American Novel, Waiting for the End, The Return of the Vanishing American, An End to Innocence, No! In Thunder, Freaks, What Was Literature?*, and *Fiedler on the Roof.*

Craig Fischer is an assistant professor in the English Department of Appalachian State University. He is a past member of the Executive Committee of the Society for Cinema Studies and a previous assistant editor of *Cinema Journal*. He has published articles in the *Velvet Light Trap* and *Spectator* and currently maintains the "This Week in Avant-Garde Cinema" list on Scott Stark's Flicker Web site (http://www.hi-beam.net).

Lucy Fischer is a professor of Film Studies and English at the University of Pittsburgh, where she serves as director of the Film Studies Program. She is the author of *Jacques Tati, Shot/Countershot: Film Tradition and Women's Cinema, Imitation of Life, Cinematernity: Film, Motherhood, Genre* and *Sunrise*. Her latest book, titled *Designing Women: Art Deco, Cinema and the Female Form*, is forthcoming.

Krin Gabbard is professor of Comparative Literature at the State University of New York at Stony Brook. He is the author of *Jammin' at the Margins: Jazz and the American Cinema* and the editor of *Jazz Among the Discourses* and *Representing Jazz*. With Glen O. Gabbard he has written *Psychiatry and the Cinema*, now in a second edition from American Psychiatric Press. He is currently finishing a book tentatively titled *Magical Negritude: White Hollywood and African American Culture*.

Barry Keith Grant is professor of Film Studies and Popular Culture and director of the Interdisciplinary M.A. Program in Popular Culture at Brock University in St. Catharines, Ontario. He is the author of *Voyages of Discovery: The Cinema of Frederick Wiseman*, coauthor of *The Film Studies Dictionary*, and editor of numerous volumes, including *The Dread of Difference, Documenting the Documentary* and, most recently, *John Ford's Stagecoach*. His *Film Genre Reader III* is forthcoming.

Andrew Horton is the Jeanne Hoffman Smith Professor of Film and Video Studies at the University of Oklahoma. The author of seventeen well-received books, including *Writing the Character Centered Screenplay* and *Laughing Out Loud: Writing the Comedy Centered Screenplay*, he is also an award-winning screenwriter who wrote Brad Pitt's first feature film (*The Dark Side of the Sun*).

Susan Hunt is an associate lecturer at Santa Monica College. She has coauthored with Peter Lehman various essays on the representation of sexuality and the mind/body split in movies, and they are currently writing a book on that subject. Susan regularly wrote film commentary for the daily *Phoenix Gazette* and is currently involved in the national movement to include media education in grades K–12.

Frank Krutnik is a professor in Film Studies at Sheffield Hallam University. He is the author of *In a Lonely Street: Film Noir, Genre, Masculinity, Inventing Jerry Lewis*, and, with Steve Neale, *Popular Film and Television Comedy*. He has contributed numerous articles to leading international film journals, including *Screen*, *Framework*, and *Film Quarterly*, and is currently working on a new book on film noir titled *Losing Face*.

Marcia Landy is Distinguished Service Professor of English/Film Studies at the University of Pittsburgh. Her publications include *British Genres, Cinema and Society, 1930–1960, Imitations of Life: A Reader on Film and Television Melodrama, Film, Politics, and Gramsci, Cinematic Uses of the Past, The Folklore of Consensus: Theatricality in the Italian Cinema, 1930–1943, Italian Film, The Historical Film*, and, with Amy Villarejo, *Queen Christina*. Her essays have appeared in major periodicals and in anthologies.

Peter Lehman is a professor in the Interdisciplinary Humanities Program and the Hispanic Research Center at Arizona State University. He is the author of *Running Scared: Masculinity and the Representation of the Male Body* and the editor of *Masculinity: Movies, Bodies, Culture*. He is also editor of *Defining Cinema* and coauthor, with William Luhr, of *Thinking about Movies: Watching, Questioning, Enjoying*.

Shawn Levy is the author of *King of Comedy: The Life and Art of Jerry Lewis, Rat Pack Confidential: Frank, Dean, Sammy, Peter and Joey and the Last Great Show Biz Party*, and *Ready, Steady, Go! The Smashing Rise and Giddy Fall of Swinging London*. He is film critic for *The Oregonian* and writes regularly for *Sight and Sound*, *Movieline*, and *Pulse!*

Dana Polan teaches in the division of Critical Studies in the School of Cinema-TV at the University of Southern California. He is the author of several books, including *Power and Paranoia: History, Narrative, and the American Cinema, 1940–1950, Pulp Fiction* and *Jane Campion*. He is currently at work on a book on academic culture and the mass media representation of academia.

Murray Pomerance is professor and chair in the Department of Sociology at Ryerson University. His short fiction has appeared in the *Paris Review*, the *Kenyon Review*, and *New Directions*, and he is the author of *Magia d'Amore* as well as editor or coeditor of *Sugar, Spice, and Everything Nice: Cinemas of Girlhood, Ladies and Gentlemen, Boys and Girls: Gender in Film at the End of the Twentieth Century, Closely Watched Brains*, and *Bang Bang, Shoot Shoot! Essays on Guns and Popular Culture*.

J. P. Telotte, a professor in the School of Literature, Communication, and Culture at Georgia Tech, teaches courses in Film and Technology, Film Genres, and Media Studies. His work includes books on Val Lewton, film noir, the cult film, science fiction, and the Machine Age. His *The Science Fiction Film* has recently been published, and he is currently at work on a study of Disney television.

# Index

(Italicized pages bear photographs)